WILLIAM JAMES
PRAGMATISM
in focus

Edited by
Doris Olin

London and New York

First published 1992
by Routledge
11 New Fetter Lane, London EC4P 4EE

Simultaneously published in the USA and Canada
by Routledge
a division of Routledge, Chapman and Hall, Inc.
29 West 35th Street, New York, NY 10001

Typeset by Florencetype Ltd, Kewstoke, Avon
Printed in Great Britain by TJPress Ltd, Padstow, Cornwall

British Library Cataloguing in Publication Data
James, William, *1842–1910*
William James: *Pragmatism* in focus.
I. Title   II. Olin, Doris,
191

Library of Congress Cataloging in Publication Data
William James: *Pragmatism*, in focus / edited by Doris Olin.
p.   cm.
Contents: Pragmatism / William James –
Meaning and metaphysics in James / Robert Meyers –
Truth and its verification / James Bissett Pratt –
Professor James' Pragmatism / G.E. Moore –
William James' conception of truth / Bertrand Russell –
Notes on the pragmatic theory of truth / Moreland Perkins –
Was William James telling the truth after all? / D.C. Phillips.
1. James, William, 1842–1910. Pragmatism.   2. Pragmatism.
I. James, William, 1842–1910. Pragmatism. 1992.   II. Olin, Doris.
III. Title: Pragmatism, in focus.
B945.J23P7339   1992
144'.3 — dc20   91–35744

ISBN 0-415-04056-6
ISBN 0-415-04057-4 pbk

WILLIAM JAMES
PRAGMATISM
in focus

ROUTLEDGE PHILOSOPHERS
IN FOCUS SERIES
Series editor: Stanley Tweyman
York University, Toronto

GODEL'S *THEOREM* IN FOCUS
Edited by S.G. Shanker

DAVID HUME: *DIALOGUES CONCERNING
NATURAL RELIGION* IN FOCUS
Edited by Stanley Tweyman

CIVIL DISOBEDIENCE IN FOCUS
Edited by Hugo Adam Bedau

JOHN LOCKE: *LETTER CONCERNING
TOLERATION* IN FOCUS
*Edited by John Horton and
Susan Mendus*

J.S. MILL: *ON LIBERTY* IN FOCUS
Edited by John Gray and G.W. Smith

CONTENTS

PREFACE

Doris Olin

The resurgence of interest in the great figures of the classical period
of American philosophy makes this opportunity to present James's
Pragmatism, together with critical commentary, most welcome.
The volume has been constructed with the hope that it will be both
accessible to those just beginning their study of James, and of use to
those with an ongoing interest.

The introduction and the critical discussion both focus on the
theories of meaning and truth central to Pragmatism. In choosing
articles for the discussion section, a mix of classic and more recent
papers was considered desirable. The essays selected include three
whose first appearance was roughly contemporaneous with the
publication of *Pragmatism* (Pratt, Moore and Russell); the other
three have appeared in the last four decades.

I am grateful to the publishers and individuals who have granted
permission to reprint copyrighted material. I also wish to thank the
editor of the Philosophers in Focus series, Stanley Tweyman, for
his expert advice as I was preparing this volume, and Bernard Katz,
for his helpful suggestions.

ACKNOWLEDGEMENTS

Author and publisher gratefully acknowledge permission to reproduce the following:

Robert G. Meyers, 'Meaning and metaphysics in James', from *Philosophy and Phenomenological Research* 31 (1971), 369–80. Reproduced by permission of the publisher and the author.
James Bissett Pratt, 'Truth and its verification', from *The Journal of Philosophy* 4 (1907), 320–4. Reprinted by permission of the publisher. Every effort was made to contact the Pratt estate for permission; unfortunately these efforts were not successful.
G.E. Moore, 'Professor James's "Pragmatism"', from *Proceedings of the Aristotelian Society* 8 (1907–8), 33–77. Copyright The Aristotelian Society 1907–8, reprinted by courtesy of the editor.
Bertrand Russell, 'William James's conception of truth', from *Philosophical Essays* by Bertrand Russell, London, Allen & Unwin (1966), 112–30. Reproduced by permission of Unwin Hyman Ltd.
Moreland Perkins, 'Notes on the pragmatic theory of truth', from *The Journal of Philosophy* 49 (1952), 573–87. Reprinted by permission of the publisher and the author.
D.C. Phillips, 'Was William James telling the truth after all?' from *The Monist* 68 (1984), 419–34. Reprinted by permission of the publisher.

INTRODUCTION
Doris Olin

William James is one of the most noted philosophers of the American classical period – the late nineteenth and early twentieth centuries. The philosophy which he expounded, Pragmatism, was the dominant philosophical movement of the time, and it continues to exert an influence on American philosophy today.

James lived from 1842 to 1910. He was the son of Henry James, Sr, an eccentric theologian and writer, and the older brother of Henry James, Jr, the well-known American novelist. James's early education took place largely in the home, where there was a lively and intellectually open atmosphere. The children of the family travelled to Europe, and attended, on an irregular basis, schools in England, France, Germany and Switzerland.

In 1861, James entered the Lawrence Scientific School, Harvard. Three years later, he began medical studies at Harvard although he had no intention of practising medicine. Despite major interruptions in his studies while he pursued other interests, he received the medical degree from Harvard in 1869.

From the mid–1860s to the early 1870s there were frequent bouts of ill health and interrupted work in James's life. He had difficulties with his eyes, his back, and with serious depression. In the 1870s, however, James began to come out of this troubled period. He started teaching at Harvard in 1872, first anatomy and physiology, then psychology in 1876. He married Alice Howe Gibbons in 1878, which was also the time of a noticeable improvement in his health.

In 1840, James published *The Principles of Psychology*, a two-volume work which surveys experimental findings in psychology and which remains a classic today. Thereafter, James turned increasingly to philosophy. It is striking that his period of most intense philosophical activity seems to have occurred in roughly the

1

last fifteen years of his life. 'The Will to Believe' was published in 1896. In 1907, his major work, *Pragmatism*, was published. The year 1909 saw two other books, *A Pluralistic Universe* (a reprint of lectures) and *The Meaning of Truth* (a collection of essays). *Essays in Radical Empiricism* and *Some Problems in Philosophy* were both published posthumously.

The work reprinted here, *Pragmatism*, is characteristic of James's philosophical style. It is in many ways a pleasure to read – vivid, forceful, breezy, filled with imagery and humour. All this is an invitation to the reader. But it is coupled with a lack of concern for technical niceties, a glossing over of possibly helpful distinctions, and seemingly little effort to provide exact statements of crucial theses. In short, the precision and rigour we might reasonably expect are notably absent. The explanation for this lies at least partly in the fact that James's intended audience is not the professional philosopher, but the educated, literate American. (Indeed, *Pragmatism* is a reprint of a series of public lectures given in Boston in 1906.) The philosophical concerns which James shares with the wider audience have to do with the impact of science, notably Darwinian evolutionary theory, on our understanding of human life and its significance. For James and his audience, the developments of science threaten a religious view of the universe, and a conception of persons as free agents. It is these larger concerns which fuel James's philosophical endeavours on questions of meaning and truth; his eye is always on the big picture and the general audience. Seen in this light, James's impatience with detail and technical subtleties may be somewhat more comprehensible and less provoking.

Pragmatism is an exciting work in part because is so ambitious. James begins by noting that 'the history of philosophy is to a great extent that of a certain clash of human temperaments' (*Pragmatism*, 22).[1] The temperaments he has in mind are dubbed 'tender-minded' and 'tough-minded'. Roughly, the distinction coincides with the rationalist – empiricist dichotomy. The tender-minded temperament looks for abstractions and eternal principles; it is drawn to, or accepting of, religion and metaphysics; it is optimistic and affirms freedom of the will; it looks for certainty. The tough-minded temperament emphasizes facts and experience; it is materialistic and, generally, reductionistic; it is pessimistic and fatalistic; it finds little certainty and is content with probability. James's aim in this work is to find a system which can mediate between these two styles of philosophy – a system which can combine scientific awareness of facts with religion, optimism and the significance of the human being. The philosophy of Pragmatism, he believes, can satisfy both kinds of demands and serve as a 'mediating way of thinking' (37).

In showing how the central doctrines of Pragmatism can play this mediating role and help us deal with long-standing philosophical disputes, James covers an enormous amount of philosophical territory. The topics of substance; materialism versus spiritualism; free will and determinism; monism versus pluralism; and religion are all treated. In this introduction, however, the focus will be on the foundations of the whole system, the core of Pragmatism. That consists in two closely related doctrines – a theory of meaning and a theory of truth.

James begins with the pragmatic method, from which his theory of meaning is derived. 'To attain perfect clearness in our thoughts of an object, then, we need only consider what conceivable effects of a practical kind the object may involve – what sensations we are to expect from it, and what reactions we must prepare. Our conception of these effects, whether immediate or remote, is then for us the whole of our conception of the object, so far as that conception has positive significance at all' (39). Thus, the first tenet of Pragmatism gives us not only a method for achieving clarity in our ideas but, as well, an account of what their meaning is – it consists entirely in the practical effects of the object. From the latter, a *criterion* of meaning is easily derived: an idea (or proposition) has meaning if and only if it has practical consequences. It is this conception of the criterion and nature of meaning which James applies to a variety of philosophical disputes in an attempt to achieve resolution or clarification.

Although the general character of the pragmatic theory of meaning is clear enough, several problems of interpretation lurk immediately below the surface. First, there is considerable vagueness about what is to count as 'a practical consequence'. Given the insistence that a meaningful hypothesis must make 'a difference to our experience', one might reasonably expect that a meaningful proposition would be one which has some consequences for experience. (Not that this notion is itself so easy to unpack.) However, in lecture IV, discussing possible meanings of the monistic hypothesis, James takes, as consequences of monism, that the world is one subject of discourse; that there is a single,

3

final purpose served by all things; that there is one Knower which knows all. These are taken as constituting (part of) the pragmatic meaning of the hypothesis that the world is One. But whether these statements have any consequences for experience is moot. It is simply unclear in what sense, if any, they count as practical consequences.

Another puzzle concerning James's theory of meaning has to do with its use in the broader context of Pragmatism. The criterion, in its standard interpretation, is certainly suggestive of modern positivist theory. Yet James professedly wishes to *reconcile* or *mediate* between the positivist (tough-minded) and the metaphysical (tender-minded) approaches. How can this criterion serve a mediating function?

First, one must recognize that there is not precisely one way in which James applies his pragmatic criterion. In his treatment of substance, for example, he is entirely negative. He endorses Berkeley's treatment of material substance, and expresses approval of Hume's handling of spiritual substance. The notion of a bearer of attributes which cannot itself be apprehended by us has no 'cash-value' and therefore no meaning. So far, this is entirely tough-minded. The discussions of materialism versus spiritualism, and of design, however, take a different course. James does not simply reject these as empty metaphysical disputes. Rather, he finds *some* meaning in each. The dispute between materialism and spiritualism has meaning because materialism (in particular, evolutionary science) implies that mankind will cease to exist and consequently the moral order is not eternal. With regard to design, a 'vague confidence in the future is the sole pragmatic meaning at present discernible in the terms design and designer' (66).

James's use of the criterion in the context of spiritualism and of design is perhaps most characteristic. He is not rejecting the metaphysical propositions in question as utterly meaningless. He is assigning a meaning to them; but their meaning is severely reduced. An ardent metaphysician would claim a great deal *more* meaningful content in, for example, the thesis that there is a God who designed the world. In this sense, then, James typically offers a *reductionistic* account of metaphysical statements. Positive metaphysical hypotheses are not rejected as meaningless; but their meaning is reduced to some statement of optimism about the course of world events. It is when metaphysical propositions are handled in this reductionistic manner that we can readily see the

4

pragmatic philosophy as a mediator between the positivist and the metaphysician.

A final problem of interpretation is pointed out by A.O. Lovejoy.[2] He suggests that James's theory of meaning is ambiguous in that what James takes as crucial for meaning may be either: (a) that the statement itself have experiential consequences; or (b) that belief in the statement have an effect on future experience. There seems no doubt that James took (a) as sufficient. What is less clear is his view of (b). This issue is taken up in the article by Robert G. Meyers; and we shall encounter a version of it again in discussing the theory of truth.

In *Pragmatism*, the very first application of the pragmatic theory of meaning is to the notion of truth. What results is James's distinctive version of the pragmatic theory of truth. Of all his philosophical contributions, it is the account of truth which has drawn the largest share of critical attention, and is generally regarded as James's most original and substantive contribution to philosophy. It is also, apart from the monism–pluralism debate, the topic to which he devotes the greatest attention in *Pragmatism*.

Before examining James's theory of truth of detail, it will be helpful to set the stage with some contemporary background material. There is currently a general consensus that any adequate theory of truth must satisfy the following constraint:

(T) The proposition that p is true if and only if p.

More specifically, an adequate theory must, at the very least, be consistent with truth of (T) for any legitimate substitution instance of 'p'. Although formulations differ, this requirement is standardly credited to Alfred Tarski, and schemata such as (T) are referred to as 'Tarskian'.[3]

The issue which animates much of contemporary discussion of truth is the debate between realism and anti-realism. Realism concerning truth is, minimally, the view that the truth of a proposition does not depend on inquiry, experience, or belief – that it exists independently of the proposition's being believed, verified, and so on. Given that truth is thus independent, it is a corollary that every proposition is either true or false, even though the actual truth-value may never be discovered. This corollary, the thesis of bivalence, is considered an essential ingredient of a realistic theory. A stronger version of realism has it that truth is a genuine *property* of propositions, on a par with redness and triangularity; and that property is neither epistemic nor can it be cashed in terms of the Tarskian equivalence.[4] A correspondence theory of truth, according to which a proposition p is true if and only if p corresponds to reality, would be an instance of strong realism if it held that correspondence is an orthodox non-epistemic property and that the statement of correspondence says something more than does the Tarskian schema. James often refers to what we would call the realist position as the 'intellectualist' or 'rationalist' view. Sometimes he has in mind the weak version, sometimes the strong.

Let us look now at James's theory. On one level, the question of how truth is to be defined is perfectly straightforward for James. An idea is true if it agrees with reality, and false if it disagrees with reality (99). According to James, the realist (intellectualist) and anti-realist may *both* accept this definition. (Notice that James Bissett Pratt, in his article, seems to identify this equivalence with the realist position.) Where they begin to quarrel, says James, is over the meaning of 'agree'. The realist might understand 'agree' in terms of 'copy' (or, more recently, 'correspond'). Not so for the pragmatist.

For James, the only way to achieve an understanding of truth deeper than that given by this equivalence is to apply the pragmatic method to the concept of truth. 'Grant an idea or belief to be true . . . what concrete difference will its being true make in anyone's actual life? . . . What experiences will be different from those which would obtain if the belief were false?' The answer immediately given is: '*True ideas are those that we can assimilate, validate, corroborate and verify. False ideas are those which we cannot*' (100).

Thus, for James, truth is a matter of agreement with reality and truth is also to be identified with verifiability. He concludes that agreement with reality can be identified with verifiability. To attain greater clarity, we must inquire into the meaning of 'verify' and 'verifiability'.

Verification, as James understands it, does not involve conclusive proof. Rather, it is identified with corroboration or confirmation – a notion which admits of degrees. How does it work? In simplest terms, a proposition is verified when it has an implication for experience which is realized. Often, the implication for experience will be of conditional form: If I do act *A* (move my hand to the left), the result will be *B* (I will feel something smooth). This is what leads James to speak of verification as an 'agreeable leading' (101). Verified or corroborated ideas fulfil our expectations and thereby contribute to the success of actions based on them. (Clearly, an idea which is thus corroborated on one occasion may not be so on another.)

Consider now the notion that a proposition p is verifiable. Clearly, this is a dispositional concept and one might, as a first attempt, explicate it as: 'If one were to test p, p would be verified (that is, positive evidence would be forthcoming).' Unfortunately, this formula might well be true of a false proposition; as well, it might fail to hold of a true proposition (the evidence might be misleading). James seems aware of the inadequacy of this definition; he suggests elsewhere that truth must be expedient 'in the long run and on the whole' (109). That is, the evidence forthcoming on a particular occasion need not favour the truth. But if a proposition p is true, at some point in time the total evidence must support p and must continue to do so thereafter. A more sympathetic reading, in the light of these remarks, would be as follows:

> 'p is verifiable' means 'If one were to test p carefully over a sufficiently long period, then there would be some time after which the total accumulated evidence would always favour p'.

Supposing that James's notion of verifiability is to be understood in roughly this fashion, let us consider some consequences of his general view. A definition of truth in terms of verifiability will undoubtedly be an anti-realist theory of truth (in both the strong and the weak sense). What is less clear is how the pragmatic theory will fare with regard to bivalence. Is there a factual proposition such that neither it nor its negation is verifiable in the relevant sense? G.E. Moore, in the article reprinted in this volume, suggests that certain propositions about the past pose a problem for the pragmatic theory in that they are unverifiable. His example is the proposition that I used certain words in a letter which is in fact now destroyed. Moore's point, which has also been argued by other critics of verifiability, is that there need not be any discernible effects of the past fact in the present. There can, I think, be no denying this. But perhaps what it shows is that it is a mistake to assume, in thinking about verifiability, that the appropriate process of testing must start now – that it must take place in the present. Perhaps the notion of verifiability should be understood as requiring only that there be *some* time period during which the appropriate evidence would be forthcoming. That is, we should construe an assertion of the verifiability of p as claiming that there is *some* period of time such that if one were to test p carefully over that period, then there would be a point after which the total accumulated evidence would always favour p. This rendering of verifiability would appear to handle Moore's problem concerning the past.

However, the verifiability definition also poses a threat to bivalence in at least one other way. In this case, the threat arises from negative existential propositions. Consider a proposition such as the following:

(n) There will never be a pink, brown and green striped Louis XIV chair at exactly location X.

The significant feature of (n) here is that if true, it would, presumably, be accidentally true. There are no laws of nature which necessitate its truth. Now even if no such chair were to be observed at location X for some (lengthy) period of time, would this provide good evidence for (n)? Many would argue that because there are no law-like connections here, a proposition such as (n) can *never* be confirmed, can never be made probable – in which case a verifiability definition of truth must be in conflict with the thesis of bivalence.

Another important issue which should be addressed in appraising the pragmatic theory of truth is the question whether there are any significant logical disparities between the predicates 'true' and 'verifiable'. James's definition says that

(i) p is true ≡ p is verifiable.

Given the Tarskian formula introduced earlier, we should be able to replace an occurrence of 'p' by 'p is true' and thus obtain

(ii) p is true ≡ [(p is true) is verifiable].

But now, making use of (i), we can infer from (ii)

(iii) p is true ≡ [(p is verifiable) is verifiable].

In general, if (i) is correct, we should be able to go on indefinitely replacing 'p' by 'p is verifiable'. However, the plausibility of the resultant formula seems to diminish dramatically. The predicate 'is true' clearly can be iterated without change of meaning. Given the inferences which lead from (i) to (iii), we can see that the *definiens* in a definition of truth must also be capable of iteration. Unfortunately, this does not appear to hold of the predicate 'is verifiable'. The right-hand side of (iii) is a meta-statement which does not seem to be equivalent to 'p is verifiable'. Whether there is any response here for the pragmatic theory of truth is an issue which certainly merits further exploration and study.

Thus far, the pivotal notion in James's theory of truth appears to be verifiability. *'True ideas are those that we can assimilate, validate, corroborate and verify'* (100). Considering the example of our taking something to be a clock, even though its inner workings have not been seen by us, he says: 'We let our notion pass for true without attempting to verify. . . . ought we then to call such unverified truths as this abortive? No. . . . Verif*ability* of wheels and weights and pendulum is as good as verification' (102–3). Although this seems to have been James's considered view, there can be no doubt that at times he also advanced a definition in terms of actual verification. 'The truth of an idea is not a stagnant property inherent in it. Truth *happens* to an idea. It *becomes* true, is *made* true by events. Its verity *is* in fact an event, a process: the process namely of its verifying itself, its veri-*fication*' (100). This account of truth of course meshes perfectly with James's assertions that truth is mutable and that truth is man-made – two views which have been ready targets for the critics. (See, for example, the article by G.E. Moore.) James Bissett Pratt argues, in his article, that verification is the notion which a pragmatic theory of truth *must* use if it is to be truly pragmatic. Moreland Perkins, in his paper, wrestles with the perplexing question of how James could have produced these two incompatible theories.

Perhaps the most memorable expression of the pragmatic theory is the following: ' *"The true"*, *to put it very briefly, is only the expedient in the way of our thinking, just as "the right" is only the expedient in the way of our behaving'* (109). James's apparent equation of the true with what it is expedient or useful to believe has also been the subject of considerable critical fire. (The papers by G.E. Moore and by Bertrand Russell both take up this apparently provocative notion.) What so offends the critics is the idea that it is sufficient, for a proposition to be true, that believing that proposition should produce some good effect. Before attributing this radical view to James, however, it must be noted that there is a more modest interpretation of what it is for a belief to work. An idea which works, James says, is an 'idea that will carry us prosperously from any one part of our experience to any other part, linking things satisfactorily' (44). He also says: 'You can say of it then either that "it is useful because it is true" or that "it is true because it is useful". Both these phrases mean exactly the same thing, namely that here is an idea that gets fulfilled and can be verified' (101–2). In these passages, James gives the clear impression that a belief's working is a matter of its guiding us successfully, enabling us to predict the course of experience. Working, in this sense, amounts to nothing more than verifiability.

So a more modest interpretation is available. In fact, James explicitly considers the broader reading which has been imputed to him and rejects it as 'impudent slander' (114). It seems fair to say that in factual, empirical contexts James thinks of a belief's utility in terms of 'satisfactory leading'. Nevertheless, there can be no doubt that in contexts of a metaphysical nature, he does venture into the more radical position. Speaking of the Absolute, for example, he says that it yields 'religious comfort to a class of minds. . . . As a good pragmatist, I myself ought to call the Absolute true "in so far forth", then . . . an idea is "true" so long as to believe it is profitable to our lives' (50–1). Of course, it is easy to understand why this broader interpretation would tempt James, given his desire to accommodate the views of the tender-minded.

For James, the pragmatic theory stands in sharp contrast to what we would now call a 'realist' theory of truth. 'This pragmatist talk about truths in the plural, about their utility and satisfactoriness, about the success with which they "work", etc., suggests to the typical intellectualist mind a sort of coarse lame second-rate make-shift article of truth. . . . As against this, objective truth must be something non-utilitarian, haughty, refined, remote, august, exalted. It must be an absolute correspondence of our thoughts with an equally absolute reality' (48). James grants, as we saw earlier, that an idea is true only if it agrees with reality. What is at issue is what is to be understood by 'agree'. The intellectualist (realist) position is that 'agree' means 'copy'. This is plausible enough, says James, if we restrict our attention to sensible things. But how can we understand 'copying' when we talk of elasticity or the time-keeping function of a clock? (100) And if the agreement cannot be understood as copying, nor with the pragmatists, as a leading or some other pragmatically definable process, then the notion is unintelligible; it is a 'meaningless abstraction' (115).

James considers the standard realist charge against his position. 'Truth is not made . . . it absolutely obtains, being a unique relation that does not wait upon any process, but shoots straight over the head of experience, and hits its reality every time. Our belief that yon thing on the wall is a clock is true already, altho no one in the whole history of the world should verify it. The bare quality of standing in that transcendent relation is what makes any thought true that possesses it' (107–8). James admits there is some plausibility to this charge; there is truth independent of actual verification. But 'the quality of truth, obtaining *ante rem*, pragmatically means, then, the fact that in such a world innumerable ideas work better by their indirect or possible than by their direct and actual verification. Truth *ante rem* means only verifiability' (108). For James, whatever is plausible in realism can be accommodated by his pragmatic, anti–realist theory; the advantage is that we avoid being saddled with meaningless metaphysical notions.

The pragmatic theory of truth has been presented here as an account of the nature of truth – that is, as a definition of truth. It must be pointed out, however, that James's pronouncements are often couched in terms of how one comes to accept new beliefs or to accept a proposition as true. This has led some commentators to conclude that James's concern is not to define truth, but to express the conditions under which we do and should take a proposition to be true. (See the paper in this volume by D.C. Phillips.) In other words, the suggestion is that James's central theory is really an exercise in epistemology.

While this interpretation might make some of James's assertions more plausible (for example, those concerning truth's mutability), it is difficult to square with the text. There are many explicit statements about *what truth is*. Furthermore, it is unlikely that James would accept a serious criterion/definition dichotomy with regard to truth. He says: 'The reason why we call things true is the reason why they *are* true, for "to be true" *means* only to perform this marriage-function' (47). And he describes pragmatism as 'first, a method; and second, a genetic theory of what is meant by truth' (47). Indeed what might be argued, with considerable plausibility, is that the key fallacy in the Jamesian position is the *conflation* of a criterion and a definition of truth. James's account of the origin of belief, of how we come to accept a proposition as true, is frequently illuminating. But it would seem illegitimate simply to transfer such an account to an attempt to say what truth is.

The general outline of James's theory of truth is fairly clear. We have seen, however, that there are a number of perplexing questions which can be raised, and which indicate the need for further study and discussion. The intrinsic worth of James's philosophy, as well as its historical importance, surely suffice to justify this continued attention. As well, there is, on the contemporary philosophical scene, a resurgence of interest in truth and the anti-realist approach. This cannot help but give an added dimension of relevance to James's anti-realist theory. Those with an interest in contemporary treatments of truth may well find illumination in James's contribution to the debate.

NOTES

1 All references to *Pragmatism* are to the pagination in this volume.
2 A.O. Lovejoy, 'The thirteen pragmatisms', *The Journal of Philosophy* 5 (1908), 5–12 and 29–39.
3 Alfred Tarski, 'The concept of truth in formalised language', in J. Woodger (ed.), *Logic, Semantics and Metamathematics* (Oxford, Clarendon Press, 1956).
4 This formulation is taken from Paul Horwich, 'Three forms of realism', *Synthese* 51 (1982), 182. Horwich calls this view 'metaphysical realism'.

PRAGMATISM

A NEW NAME FOR SOME OLD
WAYS OF THINKING

William James

To the memory of John Stuart Mill
from whom I first learned the
pragmatic openness of mind
and whom my fancy like to picture as
our leader
were he alive to-day

PREFACE

The lectures that follow were delivered at the Lowell Institute in Boston in November and December, 1906, and in January, 1907, at Columbia University, in New York. They are printed as delivered, without developments or notes. The pragmatic movement, so-called – I do not like the name, but apparently it is too late to change it – seems to have rather suddenly precipitated itself out of the air. A number of tendencies that have always existed in philosophy have all at once become conscious of themselves collectively, and of their combined mission; and this has occurred in so many countries, and from so many different points of view, that much unconcerted statement has resulted. I have sought to unify the picture as it presents itself to my own eyes, dealing in broad strokes, and avoiding minute controversy. Much futile controversy might have been avoided, I believe, if our critics had been willing to wait until we got our message fairly out.

If my lectures interest any reader in the general subject, he will doubtless wish to read farther. I therefore give him a few references.

In America, John Dewey's 'Studies in Logical Theory' are the foundation. Read also by Dewey the articles in the *Philosophical Review*, vol. xv, pp. 113 and 465, in *Mind*, vol. xv, p. 293, and in the *Journal of Philosophy*, vol. iv, p. 197.

Probably the best statements to begin with however, are F.C.S. Schiller's in his *Studies in Humanism*, especially the essays numbered i, v, vi, vii, xviii and xix. His previous essays and in general the polemic literature of the subject are fully referred to in his footnotes.

Furthermore, see J. Milhaud: *Le Rationnel*, 1898, and the fine articles by Le Roy in the *Revue de Métaphysique*, vols 7, 8 and 9. Also articles by Blondel and de Sailly in the *Annales de Philosophie Chrétienne*, 4me Série, vols 2 and 3. Papini announces a book on Pragmatism, in the French language, to be published very soon.

To avoid one misunderstanding at least, let me say that there is no logical connection between pragmatism, as I understand it, and a doctrine which I have recently set forth as 'radical empiricism'. The latter stands on its own feet. One may entirely reject it and still be a pragmatist.

Harvard University, April, 1907

CONTENTS

17

CONTENTS

LECTURE I
THE PRESENT DILEMMA IN PHILOSOPHY

In the preface to that admirable collection of essays of his called 'Heretics', Mr. Chesterton writes these words. "There are some people – and I am one of them – who think that the most practical and important thing about a man is still his view of the universe. We think that for a landlady considering a lodger it is important to know his income, but still more important to know his philosophy. We think that for a general about to fight an enemy it is important to know the enemy's numbers, but still more important to know the enemy's philosophy. We think the question is not whether the theory of the cosmos affects matters, but whether in the long run anything else affects them."

I think with Mr. Chesterton in this matter. I know that you, ladies and gentlemen, have a philosophy, each and all of you, and that the most interesting and important thing about you is the way in which it determines the perspective in your several worlds. You know the same of me. And yet I confess to a certain tremor at the audacity of the enterprise which I am about to begin. For the philosophy which is so important in each of us is not a technical matter; it is our more or less dumb sense of what life honestly and deeply means. It is only partly got from books; it is our individual way of just seeing and feeling the total push and pressure of the cosmos. I have no right to assume that many of you are students of the cosmos in the classroom sense, yet here I stand desirous of interesting you in a philosophy which to no small extent has to be technically treated. I wish to fill you with sympathy with a contemporaneous tendency in which I profoundly believe, and yet I have to talk like a professor to you who are not students. Whatever universe a professor believes in must at any rate be a universe that lends itself to lengthy discourse. A universe definable in two sentences is something for which the professorial intellect has no use. No faith in anything of that cheap kind! I have heard friends and colleagues try to popularize philosophy in this very hall, but they soon grew dry, and then technical, and the results were only partially encouraging. So my enterprise is a bold one. The founder of pragmatism himself recently gave a course of lectures at the Lowell Institute with that very word in its title – flashes of brilliant light relieved against Cimmerian darkness! None of us, I fancy, understood *all* that he said – yet here I stand, making a very similar venture.

I risk it because the very lectures I speak of *drew* – they brought good audiences. There is, it must be confessed, a curious fascination in hearing deep things talked about, even though neither we nor the disputants understand them. We get the problematic thrill, we feel the presence of the vastness. Let a controversy begin in a smoking-room anywhere, about free-will or God's omniscience, or good and evil, and see how every one in the place pricks up his ears. Philosophy's results concern us all most vitally, and philosophy's queerest arguments tickle agreeably our sense of subtlety and ingenuity.

Believing in philosophy myself devoutly, and believing also that a kind of new dawn is breaking upon us philosophers, I feel impelled, *per fas aut nefas*, to try to impart to you some news of the situation.

Philosophy is at once the most sublime and the most trivial of human pursuits. It works in the minutest crannies and it opens out the widest vistas. It 'bakes no bread,' as has been said, but it can inspire our souls with courage; and repugnant as its manners, its doubting and challenging, its quibbling and dialectics, often are to common people, no one of us can get along without the far-flashing beams of light it sends over the world's perspectives. These illuminations at least, and the contrast-effects of darkness and mystery that accompany them, give to what it says an interest that is much more than professional.

The history of philosophy is to a great extent that of a certain clash of human temperaments. Undignified as such a treatment may seem to some of my colleagues, I shall have to take account of this clash and explain a good many of the divergencies of philosophers by it. Of whatever temperament a professional philosopher is, he tries, when philosophizing, to sink the fact of his temperament. Temperament is no conventionally recognized reason, so he urges impersonal reasons only for his conclusions. Yet his temperament really gives him a stronger bias than any of his more strictly objective premises. It loads the evidence for him one way or the other, making for a more sentimental or a more hard-hearted view of the universe, just as this fact or that principle would. He *trusts* his temperament. Wanting a universe that suits it, he believes in any representation of the universe that does suit it. He feels men of opposite temper to be out of key with the world's character, and in his heart considers them incompetent and 'not in it,' in the philosophic business, even though they may far excel him in dialectical ability.

Yet in the forum he can make no claim, on the bare ground of his temperament, to superior discernment or authority. There arises thus a certain insincerity in our philosophic discussions: the potentest of all our premises is never mentioned. I am sure it would contribute to clearness if in these lectures we should break this rule and mention it, and I accordingly feel free to do so.

Of course I am talking here of very positively marked men, men of radical idiosyncracy, who have set their stamp and likeness on philosophy and figure in its history. Plato, Locke, Hegel, Spencer, are such temperamental thinkers. Most of us have, of course, no very definite intellectual temperament, we are a mixture of opposite ingredients, each one present very moderately. We hardly know our own preferences in abstract matters; some of us are easily talked out of them, and end by following the fashion or taking up with the beliefs of the most impressive philosopher in our neighborhood, whoever he may be. But the one thing that has *counted* so far in philosophy is that a man should *see* things, see them straight in his own peculiar way, and be dissatisfied with any opposite way of seeing them. There is no reason to suppose that this strong temperamental vision is from now onward to count no longer in the history of man's beliefs.

Now the particular difference of temperament that I have in mind in making these remarks is one that has counted in literature, art, government, and manners as well as in philosophy. In manners we find formalists and free-and-easy persons. In government, authoritarians and anarchists. In literature, purists or academicals, and realists. In art, classics and romantics. You recognize these contrasts as familiar; well, in philosophy we have a very similar contrast expressed in the pair of terms 'rationalist' and 'empiricist,' 'empiricist' meaning your lover of facts in all their crude variety, 'rationalist' meaning your devotee to abstract and eternal principles. No one can live an hour without both facts and principles, so it is a difference rather of emphasis; yet it breeds antipathies of the most pungent character between those who lay the emphasis differently; and we shall find it extraordinarily convenient to express a certain contrast in men's ways of taking their universe, by talking of the 'empiricist' and of the 'rationalist' temper. These terms make the contrast simple and massive.

More simple and massive than are usually the men of whom the terms are predicated. For every sort of permutation and combination is possible in human nature; and if I now proceed to define more fully what I have in mind when I speak of rationalists and empiricists, by adding to each of those titles some secondary qualifying characteristics, I beg you to regard my conduct as to a certain extent arbitrary. I select types of combination that nature offers very frequently, but by no means uniformly, and I select them solely for their convenience in helping me to my ulterior purpose of characterizing pragmatism. Historically we find the terms 'intellectualism' and 'sensationalism' used as synonyms of 'rationalism' and 'empiricism.' Well, nature seems to combine most frequently with intellectualism an idealistic and optimistic tendency. Empiricists on the other hand are not uncommonly materialistic, and their optimism is apt to be decidedly conditional and tremulous. Rationalism is always monistic. It starts from wholes and universals, and makes much of the unity of things. Empiricism starts from the parts, and makes of the whole a collection – is not averse therefore to calling itself pluralistic. Rationalism usually considers itself more religious than empiricism, but there is much to say about this claim, so I merely mention it. It is a true claim when the individual rationalist is what is called a man of feeling, and when the individual empiricist prides himself on being hard-headed. In that case the rationalist will usually also be in favor of what is called free-will, and the empiricist will be a fatalist – I use the terms most popularly current. The rationalist finally will be of dogmatic temper in his affirmations, while the empiricist may be more sceptical and open to discussion.

I will write these traits down in two columns. I think you will practically recognize the two types of mental make-up that I mean if I head the columns by the titles 'tender-minded' and 'tough-minded' respectively.

THE TENDER-MINDED	THE TOUGH-MINDED
Rationalistic (going by 'principles'),	Empiricist (going by 'facts'),
Intellectualistic,	Sensationalistic,
Idealistic,	Materialistic,
Optimistic,	Pessimistic,
Religious,	Irreligious,

24

Free-willist,	Fatalistic,
Monistic,	Pluralistic,
Dogmatical.	Sceptical.

Pray postpone for a moment the question whether the two contrasted mixtures which I have written down are each inwardly coherent and self-consistent or not – I shall very soon have a good deal to say on that point. It suffices for our immediate purpose that tender-minded and tough-minded people, characterized as I have written them down, do both exist. Each of you probably knows some well-marked example of each type, and you know what each example thinks of the example on the other side of the line. They have a low opinion of each other. Their antagonism, whenever as individuals their temperaments have been intense, has formed in all ages a part of the philosophic atmosphere of the time. It forms a part of the philosophic atmosphere to-day. The tough think of the tender as sentimentalists and soft-heads. The tender feel the tough to be unrefined, callous, or brutal. Their mutual reaction is very much like that that takes place when Bostonian tourists mingle with a population like that of Cripple Creek. Each type believes the other to be inferior to itself; but disdain in the one case is mingled with amusement, in the other it has a dash of fear.

Now, as I have already insisted, few of us are tender-foot Bostonians pure and simple, and few are typical Rocky Mountain toughs, in philosophy. Most of us have a hankering for the good things on both sides of the line. Facts are good, of course – give us lots of facts. Principles are good – give us plenty of principles. The world is indubitably one if you look at it in one way, but as indubitably is it many, if you look at it in another. It is both one and many – let us adopt a sort of pluralistic monism. Everything of course is necessarily determined, and yet of course our wills are free: a sort of free-will determinism is the true philosophy. The evil of the parts is undeniable, but the whole can't be evil: so practical pessimism may be combined with metaphysical optimism. And so forth – your ordinary philosophic layman never being a radical, never straightening out his system, but living vaguely in one plausible compartment of it or another to suit the temptations of successive hours.

But some of us are more than mere laymen in philosophy. We are worthy of the name of amateur athletes, and are vexed by too much inconsistency and vacillation in our creed. We cannot preserve a good intellectual conscience so long as we keep mixing incompatibles from opposite sides of the line.

And now I come to the first positively important point which I wish to make. Never were as many men of a decidedly empiricist proclivity in existence as there are at the present day. Our children, one may say, are almost born scientific. But our esteem for facts has not neutralized in us all religiousness. It is itself almost religious. Our scientific temper is devout. Now take a man of this type, and let him be also a philosophic amateur, unwilling to mix a hodge-podge system after the fashion of a common layman, and what does he find his situation to be, in this blessed year of our Lord 1906? He wants facts; he wants science; but he also wants a religion. And being an amateur and not an independent originator in philosophy he naturally looks for guidance to the experts and professionals whom he finds already in the field. A very large number of you here present, possibly a majority of you, are amateurs of just this sort.

Now what kinds of philosophy do you find actually offered to meet your need? You find an empirical philosophy that is not religious enough, and a religious philosophy that is not empirical enough for your purpose. If you look to the quarter where facts are most considered you find the whole tough-minded program in operation, and the 'conflict between science and religion' in full blast. Either it is that Rocky Mountain tough of a Haeckel with his materialistic monism, his ether-god and his jest at your God as a 'gaseous vertebrate'; or it is Spencer treating the world's history as a redistribution of matter and motion solely, and bowing religion politely out at the front door: – she may indeed continue to exist, but she must never show her face inside the temple.

For a hundred and fifty years past the progress of science has seemed to mean the enlargement of the material universe and the diminution of man's importance. The result is what one may call the growth of naturalistic or positivistic feeling. Man is no lawgiver to nature, he is an absorber. She it is who stands firm; he it is who must accommodate himself. Let him record truth, inhuman though it be; and submit to it! The romantic spontaneity and courage are gone, the vision is materialistic and depressing. Ideals appear as inert by-products of physiology; what is higher is explained by what is lower and treated forever as a case of 'nothing but' – nothing but something else of a quite inferior sort. You get, in short, a materialistic universe, in which only the tough-minded find themselves congenially at home.

If now, on the other hand, you turn to the religious quarter for consolation, and take counsel of the tender-minded philosophies, what do you find?

Religious philosophy in our day and generation is, among us English-reading people, of two main types. One of these is more radical and aggressive, the other has more the air of fighting a slow retreat. By the more radical wing of religious philosophy I mean the so-called transcendental idealism of the Anglo-Hegelian school, the philosophy of such men as Green, the Cairds, Bosanquet, and Royce. This philosophy has greatly influenced the more studious members of our protestant ministry. It is pantheistic, and undoubtedly it has already blunted the edge of the traditional theism in protestantism at large.

That theism remains, however. It is the lineal descendant, through one stage of concession after another, of the dogmatic scholastic theism still taught rigorously in the seminaries of the catholic church. For a long time it used to be called among us the philosophy of the Scottish school. It is what I meant by the philosophy that has the air of fighting a slow retreat. Between the encroachments of the Hegelians and other philosophers of the 'Absolute,' on the one hand, and those of the scientific evolutionists and agnostics, on the other, the men that give us this kind of a philosophy, James Martineau, Professor Bowne, Professor Ladd and others, must feel themselves rather tightly squeezed. Fair-minded and candid as you like, this philosophy is not radical in temper. It is eclectic, a thing of compromises, that seeks a *modus vivendi* above all things. It accepts the facts of Darwinism, the facts of cerebral physiology, but it does nothing active or enthusiastic with them. It lacks the victorious and aggressive note. It lacks *prestige* in consequence; whereas absolutism has a certain *prestige* due to the more radical style of it.

These two systems are what you have to choose between if you turn to the tender-minded school. And if you are the lovers of facts I have supposed you to be, you find the trail of the serpent of rationalism, of intellectualism, over everything that lies on that side of the line. You escape indeed the materialism that goes with the reigning empiricism; but you pay for your escape by losing contact with the concrete parts of life. The more absolutistic philosophers dwell on so high a level of abstraction that they never even try to come down. The absolute mind which they offer us, the mind that makes our universe by thinking it, might, for aught they show us to the contrary, have made any one of a million other universes just as well as this. You can deduce no single actual particular from the notion of it. It is compatible with any state of things whatever being true here below. And the theistic God is almost as sterile a principle. You have to go to the world which he has created to get any inkling of his actual character: he is the kind of god that has once for all made that kind of a world. The God of the theistic writers lives on as purely abstract heights as does the Absolute. Absolutism has a certain sweep and dash about it, while the usual theism is more insipid, but both are equally remote and vacuous. What *you* want is a philosophy that will not only exercise your powers of intellectual abstraction, but that will make some positive connexion with this actual world of finite human lives.

You want a system that will combine both things, the scientific loyalty to facts and willingness to take account of them, the spirit of adaptation and accommodation, in short, but also the old confidence in human values and the resultant spontaneity, whether of the religious or of the romantic type. And this is then your dilemma: you find the two parts of your *quaesitum* hopelessly separated. You find empiricism with inhumanism and irreligion; or else you find a rationalistic philosophy that indeed may call itself religious, but that keeps out of all definite touch with concrete facts and joys and sorrows.

I am not sure how many of you live close enough to philosophy to realize fully what I mean by this last reproach, so I will dwell a little longer on that unreality in all rationalistic systems by which your serious believer in facts is so apt to feel repelled.

I wish that I had saved the first couple of pages of a thesis which a student handed me a year or two ago. They illustrated my point so clearly that I am sorry I can not read them to you now. This young man, who was a graduate of some Western college, began by saying that he had always taken for granted that when you entered a philosophic classroom you had to open relations with a universe entirely distinct from the one you left behind you in the street. The two were supposed, he said, to have so little to do with each other, that you could not possibly occupy your mind with them at the same time. The world of concrete personal experiences to which the street belongs is multitudinous beyond imagination, tangled, muddy, painful and perplexed. The world to which your philos-

28

ophy-professor introduces you is simple, clean and noble. The contradictions of real life are absent from it. Its architecture is classic. Principles of reason trace its outlines, logical necessities cement its parts. Purity and dignity are what it most expresses. It is a kind of marble temple shining on a hill.

In point of fact it is far less an account of this actual world than a clear addition built upon it, a classic sanctuary in which the rationalist fancy may take refuge from the intolerably confused and gothic character which mere facts present. It is no *explanation* of our concrete universe, it is another thing altogether, a substitute for it, a remedy, a way of escape.

Its temperament, if I may use the word temperament here, is utterly alien to the temperament of existence in the concrete. *Refinement* is what characterizes our intellectualist philosophies. They exquisitely satisfy that craving for a refined object of contemplation which is so powerful an appetite of the mind. But I ask you in all seriousness to look abroad on this colossal universe of concrete facts, on their awful bewilderments, their surprises and cruelties, on the wildness which they show, and then to tell me whether 'refined' is the one inevitable descriptive adjective that springs to your lips.

Refinement has its place in things, true enough. But a philosophy that breathes out nothing but refinement will never satisfy the empiricist temper of mind. It will seem rather a monument of artificiality. So we find men of science preferring to turn their backs on metaphysics as on something altogether cloistered and spectral, and practical men shaking philosophy's dust off their feet and following the call of the wild.

Truly there is something a little ghastly in the satisfaction with which a pure but unreal system will fill a rationalist mind. Leibnitz was a rationalist mind, with infinitely more interest in facts than most rationalist minds can show. Yet if you wish for superficiality incarnate, you have only to read that charmingly written 'Théodicée' of his, in which he sought to justify the ways of God to man, and to prove that the world we live in is the best of possible worlds. Let me quote a specimen of what I mean.

Among other obstacles to his optimistic philosophy, it falls to Leibnitz to consider the number of the eternally damned. That it is infinitely greater, in our human case, than that of those saved, he assumes as a premise from the theologians, and then proceeds to argue in this way. Even then, he says:

29

"The evil will appear as almost nothing in comparison with the good, if we once consider the real magnitude of the City of God. Coelius Secundus Curio has written a little book, 'De Amplitudine Regni Coelestis', which was reprinted not long ago. But he failed to compass the extent of the kingdom of the heavens. The ancients had small ideas of the works of God. . . . It seemed to them that only our earth had inhabitants, and even the notion of our antipodes gave them pause. The rest of the world for them consisted of some shining globes and a few crystalline spheres. But to-day, whatever be the limits that we may grant or refuse to the Universe we must recognize in it a countless number of globes, as big as ours or bigger, which have just as much right as it has to support rational inhabitants, tho it does not follow that these need all be men. Our earth is only one among the six principal satellites of our sun. As all the fixed stars are suns, one sees how small a place among visible things our earth takes up, since it is only a satellite of one among them. Now all these suns *may* be inhabited by none but happy creatures; and nothing obliges us to believe that the number of damned persons is very great; for *a very few instances and samples suffice for the utility which good draws from evil.* Moreover, since there is no reason to suppose that there are stars everywhere, may there not be a great space beyond the region of the stars? And this immense space, surrounding all this region . . . may be replete with happiness and glory. . . . What now becomes of the consideration of our Earth and of its denizens? Does it not dwindle to something incomparably less than a physical point, since our Earth is but a point compared with the distance of the fixed stars. Thus the part of the Universe which we know, being almost lost in nothingness compared with that which is unknown to us, but which we are yet obliged to admit; and all the evils that we know lying in this almost-nothing; it follows that the evils may be almost-nothing in comparison with the goods that the Universe contains."

Leibnitz continues elsewhere:

"There is a kind of justice which aims neither at the amendment of the criminal, nor at furnishing an example to others, nor at the reparation of the injury. This justice is founded in pure fitness, which finds a certain satisfaction in the expiation of a wicked deed. The Socinians and Hobbes objected to this punitive justice, which is properly vindictive justice, and which God has reserved for himself at many junctures. . . . It is always founded in the fitness of things, and satisfies not only the offended party, but all wise lookers-on, even as beautiful music or a fine piece of architecture satisfies a well-constituted mind. It is thus that the torments of the damned continue, even tho' they serve no longer to turn any one away from sin, and that the rewards of the blest continue, even tho they con-firm no one in good ways. The damned draw to themselves ever new penalties by their continuing sins, and the blest attract ever fresh joys by their unceasing progress in good. Both facts are founded on the principle of fitness, . . . for God has made all things harmonious in perfection as I have already said."

Leibnitz's feeble grasp of reality is too obvious to need com-ment from me. It is evident that no realistic image of the ex-perience of a damned soul had ever approached the portals of his mind. Nor had it occurred to him that the smaller is the number of 'samples' of the genus 'lost-soul' whom God throws as a sop to the eternal fitness, the more unequitably grounded is the glory of the blest. What he gives us is a cold literary exer-cise, whose cheerful substance even hell-fire does not warm.

And do not tell me that to show the shallowness of ration-alist philosophizing I have had to go back to a shallow wig-pated age. The optimism of present-day rationalism sounds just as shallow to the fact-loving mind. The actual universe is a thing wide open, but rationalism makes systems, and systems must be closed. For men in practical life perfection is something far off and still in process of achievement. This for rationalism is but the illusion of the finite and relative: the absolute ground of things is a perfection eternally complete.

I find a fine example of revolt against the airy and shallow optimism of current religious philosophy in a publication of that valiant anarchistic writer Morrison I. Swift. Mr. Swift's anarchism goes a little farther than mine does, but I confess that I sympathize a good deal, and some of you, I know, will sym-pathize heartily with his dissatisfaction with the idealistic opti-misms now in vogue. He begins his pamphlet on 'Human Submission' with a series of city reporter's items from news-papers (suicides, deaths from starvation, and the like) as speci-mens of our civilized régime. For instance:

"After trudging through the snow from one end of the city to the other in the vain hope of securing employment, and with his wife and six children without food and ordered to leave their home in an upper east-side tenement-house because of non-payment of rent, John Corcoran, a clerk, to-day ended his life by drinking carbolic acid. Corcoran lost his position three weeks ago through illness, and during the period of idleness his scanty savings disappeared. Yesterday he obtained work with a gang of city snow-shovelers, but he was too weak from illness, and was forced to quit after an hour's trial with the shovel. Then the weary task of looking for employment was again resumed. Thoroughly discouraged, Corcoran returned to his home last night to find his wife and children without food and the notice of dispossession on the door. On the following morning he drank the poison.

"The records of many more such cases lie before me [Mr. Swift goes on]; an encyclopedia might easily be filled with their kind. These few I cite as an interpretation of the Universe. 'We are aware of the presence of God in his world,' says a writer in a recent English review. [The very presence of ill in the temporal order is the condition of the perfection of the eternal order, writes Professor Royce ('The World and the Individual', II, 385).] 'The Absolute is the richer for every discord and for all the diversity which it embraces,' says F. H. Bradley ('Appearance and Reality', 204). He means that these slain men make the universe richer, and that is philosophy. But while Professors Royce and Bradley and a whole host of guileless thoroughfed thinkers are unveiling Reality and the Absolute and explaining away evil and pain, this is the condition of the only beings known to us anywhere in the universe with a developed consciousness of what the universe is. What these people experience *is* Reality. It gives us an absolute phase of the universe. It is the personal experience of those best qualified in our circle of knowledge to *have* experience, to tell us *what is*. Now what does *thinking about* the experience of these persons come to, compared to directly and personally feeling it as they feel it? The philosophers are dealing in shades, while those who live and feel know truth. And the mind of mankind – not yet the mind of philosophers and of the proprietary class – but of the great mass of the silently thinking men and feeling men, is coming to this view. They are judging the universe as they

They are judging the universe as they have hitherto permitted the hierophants of religion and learning to judge *them*. . . . .

"This Cleveland workingman, killing his children and himself [another of the cited cases] is one of the elemental stupendous facts of this modern world and of this universe. It cannot be glozed over or minimized away by all the treatises on God, and Love, and Being, helplessly existing in their monumental vacuity. This is one of the simple irreducible elements of this world's life, after millions of years of opportunity and twenty centuries of Christ. It is in the mental world what atoms or sub-atoms are in the physical, primary, indestructible. And what it blazons to man is the imposture of all philosophy which does not see in such events the consummate factor of all conscious experience. These facts invincibly prove religion a nullity. Man will not give religion two thousand centuries or twenty centuries more to try itself and waste human time. Its time is up; its probation is ended; its own record ends it. Mankind has not aeons and eternities to spare for trying out discredited systems."[1]

Such is the reaction of an empiricist mind upon the rationalist bill of fare. It is an absolute 'No, I thank you.' 'Religion,' says Mr. Swift, 'is like a sleep-walker to whom actual things are blank.' And such, tho possibly less tensely charged with feeling, is the verdict of every seriously inquiring amateur in philosophy to-day who turns to the philosophy-professors for the wherewithal to satisfy the fulness of his nature's needs. Empiricist writers give him a materialism, rationalists give him something religious, but to that religion 'actual things are blank.' He becomes thus the judge of us philosophers. Tender or tough, he finds us wanting. None of us may treat his verdicts disdainfully, for after all, his is the typically perfect mind, the mind the sum of whose demands is greatest, the mind whose criticisms and dissatisfactions are fatal in the long run.

It is at this point that my own solution begins to appear. I offer the oddly-named thing pragmatism as a philosophy that can satisfy both kinds of demand. It can remain religious like the rationalisms, but at the same time, like the empiricisms, it can preserve the richest intimacy with facts. I hope I may be

1 Morrison I. Swift, *Human Submission*, Part Second, Philadelphia, Liberty Press, 1905, pp. 4–10.

able to leave many of you with as favorable an opinion of it as I preserve myself. Yet, as I am near the end of my hour, I will not introduce pragmatism bodily now. I will begin with it on the stroke of the clock next time. I prefer at the present moment to return a little on what I have said.

If any of you here are professional philosophers, and some of you I know to be such, you will doubtless have felt my discourse so far to have been crude in an unpardonable, nay, in an almost incredible degree. Tender-minded and tough-minded, what a barbaric disjunction! And, in general, when philosophy is all compacted of delicate intellectualities and subtleties and scrupulosities, and when every possible sort of combination and transition obtains within its bounds, what a brutal caricature and reduction of highest things to the lowest possible expression is it to represent its field of conflict as a sort of rough-and-tumble fight between two hostile temperaments! What a childishly external view! And again, how stupid it is to treat the abstractness of rationalist systems as a crime, and to damn them because they offer themselves as sanctuaries and places of escape, rather than as prolongations of the world of facts. Are not all our theories just remedies and places of escape? And, if philosophy is to be religious, how can she be anything else than a place of escape from the crassness of reality's surface? What better thing can she do than raise us out of our animal senses and show us another and a nobler home for our minds in that great framework of ideal principles subtending all reality, which the intellect divines? How can principles and general views ever be anything but abstract outlines? Was Cologne cathedral built without an architect's plan on paper? Is refinement in itself an abomination? Is concrete rudeness the only thing that's true?

Believe me, I feel the full force of the indictment. The picture I have given is indeed monstrously over-simplified and rude. But like all abstractions, it will prove to have its use. If philosophers can treat the life of the universe abstractly, they must not complain of an abstract treatment of the life of philosophy itself. In point of fact the picture I have given is, however coarse and sketchy, literally true. Temperaments with their cravings and refusals do determine men in their philosophies, and always will. The details of systems may be reasoned out piecemeal, and when the student is working at a system, he may often forget the forest for the single tree. But when the

labor is accomplished, the mind always performs its big summarizing act, and the system forthwith stands over against one
like a living thing, with that strange simple note of individu-
ality which haunts our memory, like the wraith of the man,
when a friend or enemy of ours is dead.

Not only Walt Whitman could write 'who touches this book
touches a man.' The books of all the great philosophers are like
so many men. Our sense of an essential personal flavor in each
one of them, typical but indescribable, is the finest fruit of our
own accomplished philosophic education. What the system pretends to be is a picture of the great universe of God. What it is,
– and oh so flagrantly! – is the revelation of how intensely odd
the personal flavor of some fellow creature is. Once reduced to
these terms (and all our philosophies get reduced to them in
minds made critical by learning) our commerce with the systems reverts to the informal, to the instinctive human reaction
of satisfaction or dislike. We grow as peremptory in our rejection or admission, as when a person presents himself as a candi-
date for our favor; our verdicts are couched in as simple
adjectives of praise or dispraise. We measure the total character
of the universe as we feel it, against the flavor of the philosophy proffered us, and one word is enough.

'Statt der lebendigen Natur,' we say, 'da Gott die Menschen
schuf hinein,' – that nebulous concoction, that wooden, that
straight-laced thing, that crabbled artificiality, that musty
schoolroom product, that sick man's dream! Away with it.
Away with all of them! Impossible! Impossible!

Our work over the details of his system is indeed what gives
us our resultant impression of the philosopher, but it is on the
resultant impression itself that we react. Expertness in philosophy is measured by the definiteness of our summarizing reactions, by the immediate perceptive epithet with which the
expert hits such complex objects off. But great expertness is not
necessary for the epithet to come. Few people have definitely
articulated philosophies of their own. But almost every one has
his own peculiar sense of a certain total character in the
universe, and of the inadequacy fully to match it of the peculiar
systems that he knows. They don't just cover *his* world. One
will be too dapper, another too pedantic, a third too much of a
job-lot of opinions, a fourth too morbid, and a fifth too artificial, or what not. At any rate he and we know off-hand that

such philosophies are out of plumb and out of key and out of 'whack,' and have no business to speak up in the universe's name. Plato, Locke, Spinoza, Mill, Caird, Hegel – I prudently avoid names nearer home! – I am sure that to many of you, my hearers, these names are little more than reminders of as many curious personal ways of falling short. It would be an obvious absurdity if such ways of taking the universe were actually true.

We philosophers have to reckon with such feelings on your part. In the last resort, I repeat, it will be by them that all our philosophies shall ultimately be judged. The finally victorious way of looking at things will be the most completely *impressive* way to the normal run of minds.

One word more – namely about philosophies necessarily being abstract outlines. There are outlines and outlines, outlines of buildings that are *fat*, conceived in the cube by their planner, and outlines of buildings invented flat on paper, with the aid of ruler and compass. These remain skinny and emaciated even when set up in stone and mortar, and the outline already suggests that result. An outline in itself is meagre, truly, but it does not necessarily suggest a meagre thing. It is the essential meagreness of *what is suggested* by the usual rationalistic philosophies that moves empiricists to their gesture of rejection. The case of Herbert Spencer's system is much to the point here. Rationalists feel his fearful array of insufficiencies. His dry schoolmaster temperament, the hurdy-gurdy monotony of him, his preference for cheap makeshifts in argument, his lack of education even in mechanical principles, and in general the vagueness of all his fundamental ideas, his whole system wooden, as if knocked together out of cracked hemlock boards – and yet the half of England wants to bury him in Westminster Abbey.

Why? Why does Spencer call out so much reverence in spite of his weakness in rationalistic eyes? Why should so many educated men who feel that weakness, you and I perhaps, wish to see him in the Abbey notwithstanding?

Simply because we feel his heart to be *in the right place* philosophically. His principles may be all skin and bone, but at any rate his books try to mould themselves upon the particular shape of this particular world's carcase. The noise of facts resounds through all his chapters, the citations of fact never cease, he emphasizes facts, turns his face towards their quarter; and that is enough. It means the right *kind* of thing for the empiricist mind.

The pragmatistic philosophy of which I hope to begin talking in my next lecture preserves as cordial a relation with facts, and, unlike Spencer's philosophy, it neither begins nor ends by turning positive religious constructions out of doors – it treats them cordially as well.

I hope I may lead you to find it just the mediating way of thinking that you require.

LECTURE II
WHAT PRAGMATISM MEANS

Some years ago, being with a camping party in the mountains, I returned from a solitary ramble to find every one engaged in a ferocious metaphysical dispute. The *corpus* of the dispute was a squirrel supposed to be clinging to one side of a tree-trunk; while over against the tree's opposite side a human being was imagined to stand. This human witness tries to get sight of the squirrel by moving rapidly round the tree, but no matter how fast he goes, the squirrel moves as fast in the opposite direction, and always keeps the tree between himself and the man, so that never a glimpse of him is caught. The resultant metaphysical problem now is this: *Does the man go round the squirrel or not?* He goes round the tree, sure enough, and the squirrel is on the tree; but does he go round the squirrel? In the unlimited leisure of the wilderness, discussion had been worn threadbare. Every one had taken sides, and was obstinate; and the numbers on both sides were even. Each side, when I appeared therefore appealed to me to make it a majority. Mindful of the scholastic adage that whenever you meet a contradiction you must make a distinction, I immediately sought and found one, as follows: "Which party is right," I said, "depends on what you *practically mean* by 'going round' the squirrel. If you mean passing from the north of him to the east, then to the south, then to the west, and then to the north of him again, obviously the man does go round him, for he occupies these successive positions. But if on the contrary you mean being first in front of him, then on his right of him, then behind him, then on his left, and finally in front again, it is quite as obvious that the man fails to go round him, for by the compensating movements the squirrel makes, he keeps his belly turned towards the man all the time, and his back turned away. Make the distinction, and there is no occasion for any farther dispute. You are both right and both wrong according as you conceive the verb 'to go round' in one practical fashion or the other."

Although one or two of the hotter disputants called my speech a shuffling evasion, saying they wanted no quibbling or scholastic hair-splitting, but meant just plain honest English 'round,' the majority seemed to think that the distinction had assuaged the dispute.

I tell this trivial anecdote because it is a peculiarly simple example of what I wish now to speak of as *the pragmatic method*. The pragmatic method is primarily a method of settling metaphysical disputes that otherwise might be interminable. Is the world one or many? – fated or free? – material or spiritual? – here are notions either of which may or may not hold good of the world; and disputes over such notions are unending. The pragmatic method in such cases is to try to interpret each notion by tracing its respective practical consequences. What difference would it practically make to any one if this notion rather than that notion were true? If no practical difference whatever can be traced, then the alternatives mean practically the same thing, and all dispute is idle. Whenever a dispute is serious, we ought to be able to show some practical difference that must follow from one side or the other's being right.

A glance at the history of the idea will show you still better what pragmatism means. The term is derived from the same Greek word πράγμα, meaning action, from which our words 'practice' and 'practical' come. It was first introduced into philosophy by Mr. Charles Peirce in 1878. In an article entitled 'How to Make Our Ideas Clear,' in the 'Popular Science Monthly' for January of that year[1] Mr. Peirce, after pointing out that our beliefs are really rules for action, said that, to develop a thought's meaning, we need only determine what conduct it is fitted to produce: that conduct is for us its sole significance. And the tangible fact at the root of all our thought–distinctions, however subtle, is that there is no one of them so fine as to consist in anything but a possible difference of practice. To attain perfect clearness in our thoughts of an object, then, we need only consider what conceivable effects of a practical kind the object may involve – what sensations we are to expect from it, and what reactions we must prepare. Our conception of these effects, whether immediate or remote, is then for us the whole of our conception of the object, so far as that conception has positive significance at all.

This is the principle of Peirce, the principle of pragmatism. It lay entirely unnoticed by any one for twenty years, until I, in an address before Professor Howison's philosophical union at the university of California, brought it forward again and made a

---

1   Translated in the *Revue Philosophique* for January, 1879 (vol. vii).

special application of it to religion. By that date (1898) the times seemed ripe for its reception. The word 'pragmatism' spread, and at present it fairly spots the pages of the philosophic journals. On all hands we find the 'pragmatic movement' spoken of, sometimes with respect, sometimes with contumely, seldom with clear understanding. It is evident that the term applies itself conveniently to a number of tendencies that hitherto have lacked a collective name, and that it has 'come to stay.'

To take in the importance of Peirce's principle, one must get accustomed to applying it to concrete cases. I found a few years ago that Ostwald, the illustrious Leipzig chemist, had been making perfectly distinct use of the principle of pragmatism in his lectures on the philosophy of science, though he had not called it by that name.

"All realities influence our practice," he wrote me, "and that influence is their meaning for us. I am accustomed to put questions to my classes in this way: in what respects would the world be different if this alternative or that were true? If I can find nothing that would become different, then the alternative has no sense."

That is, the rival views mean practically the same thing, and meaning, other than practical, there is for us none. Ostwald in a published lecture gives this example of what he means. Chemists have long wrangled over the inner constitution of certain bodies called 'tautomerous.' Their properties seemed equally consistent with the notion that an instable hydrogen atom oscillates inside of them, or that they are instable mixtures of two bodies. Controversy raged, but never was decided. "It would never have begun," says Ostwald, "if the combatants had asked themselves what particular experimental fact could have been made different by one or the other view being correct. For it would then have appeared that no difference of fact could possibly ensue; and the quarrel was as unreal as if, theorising in primitive times about the raising of dough by yeast, one party should have invoked a 'brownie', while another insisted on an 'elf' as the true cause of the phenomenon."[2]

2 'Theorie und Praxis,' *Zeitsch. des Oesterreichischen Ingenieur u. Architecten-Vereines*, 1905, Nr 4 u. 6. I find a still more radical pragmatism than Ostwald's in an address by Professor W. S. Franklin: "I think that the sickliest notion of physics, even if a student gets it, is that it is 'the science of masses, molecules, and the ether'. And I think that the healthiest notion, even if a student does not wholly get it, is that physics is the science of the ways of taking hold of bodies and pushing them!" (*Science*, January 2, 1903.)

It is astonishing to see how many philosophical disputes collapse into insignificance the moment you subject them to this simple test of tracing a concrete consequence. There can *be* no difference anywhere that does n't *make* a difference elsewhere – no difference in abstract truth that does n't express itself in a difference in concrete fact and in conduct consequent upon that fact, imposed on somebody, somehow, somewhere, and somewhen. The whole function of philosophy ought to be to find out what definite difference it will make to you and me, at definite instants of our life, if this world-formula or that world-formula be the true one.

There is absolutely nothing new in the pragmatic method. Socrates was an adept at it. Aristotle used it methodically. Locke, Berkeley, and Hume made momentous contributions to truth by its means. Shadworth Hodgson keeps insisting that realities are only what they are 'known as.' But these forerunners of pragmatism used it in fragments: they were a prelude only. Not until in our time has it generalized itself, become conscious of a universal mission, pretended to a conquering destiny. I believe in that destiny, and I hope I may end by inspiring you with my belief.

Pragmatism represents a perfectly familiar attitude in philosophy, the empiricist attitude, but it represents it, as it seems to me, both in a more radical and in a less objectionable form than it has ever yet assumed. A pragmatist turns his back resolutely and once for all upon a lot of inveterate habits dear to professional philosophers. He turns away from abstraction and insufficiency, from verbal solutions, from bad *a priori* reasons, from fixed principles, closed systems, and pretended absolutes and origins. He turns towards concreteness and adequacy, towards facts, towards action and towards power. That means the empiricist temper regnant and the rationalist temper sincerely given up. It means the open air and possibilities of nature, as against dogma, artificiality, and the pretence of finality in truth.

At the same time it does not stand for any special results. It is a method only. But the general triumph of that method would mean an enormous change in what I called in my last lecture the 'temperament' of philosophy. Teachers of the ultra-rationalistic type would be frozen out, much as the courtier type is frozen out in republics, as the ultramontane type of priest is frozen out in protestant lands. Science and metaphysics would come much nearer together, would in fact work absolutely hand in hand.

Metaphysics has usually followed a very primitive kind of quest.

You know how men have always hankered after unlawful magic, and you know what a great part in magic *words* have always played. If you have his name, or the formula of incantation that binds him, you can control the spirit, genie, afrite, or whatever the power may be. Solomon knew the names of all the spirits, and having their names, he held them subject to his will. So the universe has always appeared to the natural mind as a kind of enigma, of which the key must be sought in the shape of some illuminating or power-bringing word or name. That word names the universe's *principle*, and to possess it is after a fashion to possess the universe itself. 'God,' 'Matter,' 'Reason,' 'the Absolute,' 'Energy,' are so many solving names. You can rest when you have them. You are at the end of your metaphysical quest.

But if you follow the pragmatic method, you cannot look on any such word as closing your quest. You must bring out of each word its practical cash-value, set it at work within the stream of your experience. It appears less as a solution, then, than as a program for more work, and more particularly as an indication of the ways in which existing realities may be *changed*.

Theories thus become instruments, not answers to enigmas, in which we can rest. We don't lie back upon them, we move forward, and, on occasion, make nature over again by their aid. Pragmatism un-stiffens all our theories, limbers them up and sets each one at work. Being nothing essentially new, it harmonizes with many ancient philosophic tendencies. It agrees with nominalism, for instance, in always appealing to particulars; with utilitarianism in emphasizing practical aspects; with positivism in its disdain for verbal solutions, useless questions and metaphysical abstractions.

All these, you see, are *anti-intellectualist* tendencies. Against rationalism as a pretension and a method pragmatism is fully armed and militant. But, at the outset, at least, it stands for no particular results. It has no dogmas, and no doctrines save its method. As the young Italian pragmatist Papini has well said, it lies in the midst of our theories, like a corridor in a hotel. Innumerable chambers open out of it. In one you may find a man writing an atheistic volume; in the next some one on his knees praying for faith and strength; in a third a chemist investigating a body's properties. In a fourth a system of idealistic metaphysics is being excogitated; in a fifth the impossibility of metaphysics is being shown. But they all own the corridor, and all must pass through it if they want a practicable way of getting into or out of their respective rooms.

No particular results then, so far, but only an attitude of orientation, is what the pragmatic method means. *The attitude of looking away from first things, principles, 'categories,' supposed necessities; and of looking towards last things, fruits, consequences, facts.*

So much for the pragmatic method! You may say that I have been praising it rather than explaining it to you, but I shall presently explain it abundantly enough by showing how it works on some familiar problems. Meanwhile the word pragmatism has come to be used in a still wider sense, as meaning also a certain *theory of truth.* I mean to give a whole lecture to the statement of that theory, after first paving the way, so I can be very brief now. But brevity is hard to follow, so I ask for your redoubled attention for a quarter of an hour. If much remains obscure, I hope to make it clearer in the later lectures.

One of the most successfully cultivated branches of philosophy in our time is what is called inductive logic, the study of the conditions under which our sciences have evolved. Writers on this subject have begun to show a singular unanimity as to what the laws of nature and elements of fact mean, when formulated by mathematicians, physicists and chemists. When the first mathematical, logical and natural uniformities, the first *laws*, were discovered, men were so carried away by the clearness, beauty and simplification that resulted, that they believed themselves to have deciphered authentically the eternal thoughts of the Almighty. His mind also thundered and reverberated in syllogisms. He also thought in conic sections, squares and roots and ratios, and geometrized like Euclid. He made Kepler's laws for the planets to follow; he made velocity increase proportionally to the time in falling bodies; he made the law of the sines for light to obey when refracted; he established the classes, orders, families and genera of plants and animals, and fixed the distances between them. He thought the archetypes of all things, and devised their variations; and when we rediscover any one of these his wondrous institutions, we seize his mind in its very literal intention.

But as the sciences have developed farther, the notion has gained ground that most, perhaps all, of our laws are only approximations. The laws themselves, moreover, have grown so numerous that there is no counting them; and so many rival formulations are proposed in all the branches of science that investigators have become accustomed to the notion that no theory is absolutely a transcript of reality, but that any one of them may from some point

43

of view be useful. Their great use is to summarize old facts and to lead to new ones. They are only a man-made language, a conceptual shorthand, as some one calls them, in which we write our reports of nature; and languages, as is well known, tolerate much choice of expression and many dialects.

Thus human arbitrariness has driven divine necessity from scientific logic. If I mention the names of Sigwart, Mach, Ostwald, Pearson, Milhaud, Poincaré, Duhem, Heymans, those of you who are students will easily identify the tendency I speak of, and will think of additional names.

Riding now on the front of this wave of scientific logic Messrs. Schiller and Dewey appear with their pragmatistic account of what truth everywhere signifies. Everywhere, these teachers say, 'truth' in our ideas and beliefs means the same thing that it means in science. It means, they say, nothing but this, *that ideas (which themselves are but parts of our experience) become true just in so far as they help us to get into satisfactory relation with other parts of our experience*, to summarize them and get about among them by conceptual short-cuts instead of following the interminable succession of particular phenomena. Any idea upon which we can ride, so to speak; any idea that will carry us prosperously from any one part of our experience to any other part, linking things satisfactorily, working securely, simplifying, saving labor; is true for just so much, true in so far forth, true *instrumentally*. This is the 'instrumental' view of truth taught so successfully at Chicago, the view that truth in our ideas means their power to 'work,' promulgated so brilliantly at Oxford.

Messrs. Dewey, Schiller and their allies, in reaching this general conception of all truth, have only followed the example of geologists, biologists and philologists. In the establishment of these other sciences, the successful stroke was always to take some simple process actually observable in operation – as denudation by weather, say, or variation from parental type, or change of dialect by incorporation of new words and pronunciations – and then to generalize it, making it apply to all times, and produce great results by summating its effects through the ages.

The observable process which Schiller and Dewey particularly singled out for generalization is the familiar one by which any individual settles into *new opinions*. The process here is always the same. The individual has a stock of old opinions already, but he meets a new experience that puts them to a strain. Somebody contradicts them; or in a reflective moment he discovers that they contradict each other; or he hears of facts with which they are incompatible; or desires arise in him which they cease to satisfy. The result is an inward trouble to which his mind till then had been a stranger, and from which he seeks to escape by modifying his previous mass of opinions. He saves as much of it as he can, for in this matter of belief we are all extreme conservatives. So he tries to change first this opinion, and then that (for they resist change very variously), until at last some new idea comes up which he can graft upon the ancient stock with a minimum of disturbance of the latter, some idea that mediates between the stock and the new experience and runs them into one another most felicitously and expediently.

This new idea is then adopted as the true one. It preserves the older stock of truths with a minimum of modification, stretching them just enough to make them admit the novelty, but conceiving that in ways as familiar as the case leaves possible. An *outrée* explanation, violating all our preconceptions, would never pass for a true account of a novelty. We should scratch round industriously till we found something less excentric. The most violent revolutions in an individual's beliefs leave most of his old order standing. Time and space, cause and effect, nature and history, and one's own biography remain untouched. New truth is always a go-between, a smoother-over of transitions. It marries old opinion to new fact so as ever to show a minimum of jolt, a maximum of continuity. We hold a theory true just in proportion to its success in solving this 'problem of maxima and minima.' But success in solving this problem is eminently a matter of approximation. We say this theory solves it on the whole more satisfactorily than that theory; but that means more satisfactorily to ourselves, and individuals will emphasize their points of satisfaction differently. To a certain degree, therefore, everything here is plastic.

The point I now urge you to observe particularly is the part played by the older truths. Failure to take account of it is the source of much of the unjust criticism levelled against pragmatism. Their influence is absolutely controlling. Loyalty to them is the first principle – in most cases it is the only principle; for by far the most usual way of handling phenomena so novel that they would make for a serious rearrangement of our preconception is to ignore them altogether, or to abuse those who bear witness for them.

You doubtless wish examples of this process of truth's growth, and the only trouble is their superabundance. The simplest case of new truth is of course the mere numerical addition of new kinds of facts, or of new single facts of old kinds, to our experience – an addition that involves no alteration in the old beliefs. Day follows day, and its contents are simply added. The new contents themselves are not true, they simply *come* and *are*. Truth is *what we say about* them, and when we say that they have come, truth is satisfied by the plain additive formula.

But often the day's contents oblige a rearrangement. If I should now utter piercing shrieks and act like a maniac on this platform, it would make many of you revise your ideas as to the probable worth of my philosophy. 'Radium' came the other day as part of the day's content, and seemed for a moment to contradict our ideas of the whole order of nature, that order having come to be identified with what is called the conservation of energy. The mere sight of radium paying heat away indefinitely out of its own pocket seemed to violate that conservation. What to think? If the radiations from it were nothing but an escape of unsuspected 'potential' energy, pre-existent inside of the atoms, the principle of conservation would be saved. The discovery of 'helium' as the radiation's outcome, opened a way to this belief. So Ramsay's view is generally held to be true, because, although it extends our old ideas of energy, it causes a minimum of alteration in their nature.

I need not multiply instances. A new opinion counts as 'true' just in proportion as it gratifies the individual's desire to assimilate the novel in his experience to his beliefs in stock. It must both lean on old truth and grasp new fact; and its success (as I said a moment ago) in doing this, is a matter for the individual's appreciation. When old truth grows, then, by new truth's addition, it is for subjective reasons. We are in the process and obey the reasons. That new idea is truest which performs most felicitously its function of satisfying our double urgency. It makes itself true, gets itself classed as true, by the way it works; grafting itself then upon the ancient body of truth, which thus grows much as a tree grows by the activity of a new layer of cambium.

Now Dewey and Schiller proceed to generalize this observation and to apply it to the most ancient parts of truth. They also once were plastic. They also were called true for human reasons. They also mediated between still earlier truths and what in those days were novel observations. Purely objective truth, truth in whose establishment the function of giving human satisfaction in marrying previous parts of experience with newer parts played no rôle whatever, is nowhere to be found. The reasons why we call things true is the reason why they *are* true, for 'to be true' *means* only to perform this marriage-function.

The trail of the human serpent is thus over everything. Truth independent; truth that we *find* merely; truth no longer malleable to human need; truth incorrigible, in a word; such truth exists indeed superabundantly – or is supposed to exist by rationalistically minded thinkers; but then it means only the dead heart of the living tree, and its being there means only that truth also has its paleontology, and its 'prescription,' and may grow stiff with years of veteran service and petrified in men's regard by sheer antiquity. But how plastic even the oldest truths nevertheless really are has been vividly shown in our day by the transformation of logical and mathematical ideas, a transformation which seems even to be invading physics. The ancient formulas are reinterpreted as special expressions of much wider principles, principles that our ancestors never got a glimpse of in their present shape and formulation.

Mr. Schiller still gives to all this view of truth the name of 'Humanism,' but, for this doctrine too, the name of pragmatism seems fairly to be in the ascendant, so I will treat it under the name of pragmatism in these lectures.

Such then would be the scope of pragmatism – first, a method; and second, a genetic theory of what is meant by truth. And these two things must be our future topics.

What I have said of the theory of truth will, I am sure, have appeared obscure and unsatisfactory to most of you by reason of its brevity. I shall make amends for that hereafter. In a lecture on 'common sense' I shall try to show what I mean by truths grown petrified by antiquity. In another lecture I shall expatiate on the idea that our thoughts become true in proportion as they successfully exert their go-between function. In a third I shall show how hard it is to discriminate subjective from objective factors in Truth's development. You may not follow me wholly in these lectures; and if you do, you may not wholly agree with me. But you will, I know, regard me at least as serious, and treat my effort with respectful consideration.

You will probably be surprised to learn, then, that Messrs. Schiller's and Dewey's theories have suffered a hailstorm of contempt and ridicule. All rationalism has risen against them. In influential quarters Mr. Schiller, in particular, has been treated like an impudent schoolboy who deserves a spanking. I should not mention this, but for the fact that it throws so much sidelight upon that rationalistic temper to which I have opposed the temper of pragmatism. Pragmatism is uncomfortable away from facts. Rationalism is comfortable only in the presence of abstractions. This pragmatist talk about truths in the plural, about their utility and satisfactoriness, about the success with which they 'work,' etc., suggests to the typical intellectualist mind a sort of coarse lame second-rate makeshift article of truth. Such truths are not real truth. Such tests are merely subjective. As against this, objective truth must be something non-utilitarian, haughty, refined, remote, august, exalted. It must be an absolute correspondence of our thoughts with an equally absolute reality. It must be what we *ought* to think unconditionally. The conditioned ways in which we *do* think are so much irrelevance and matter for psychology. Down with psychology, up with logic, in all this question!

See the exquisite contrast of the types of mind! The pragmatist clings to facts and concreteness, observes truth at its work in particular cases, and generalizes. Truth, for him, becomes a class-name for all sorts of definite working-values in experience. For the rationalist it remains a pure abstraction, to the bare name of which we must defer. When the pragmatist undertakes to show in detail just *why* we must defer, the rationalist is unable to recognize the concretes from which his own abstraction is taken. He accuses us of *denying* truth; whereas we have only sought to trace exactly why people follow it and always ought to follow it. Your typical ultra-abstractionist fairly shudders at concreteness: other things equal, he positively prefers the pale and spectral. If the two universes were offered, he would always choose the skinny outline rather than the rich thicket of reality. It is so much purer, clearer, nobler.

I hope that as these lectures go on, the concreteness and closeness to facts of the pragmatism which they advocate may be what approves itself to you as its most satisfactory peculiarity. It only follows here the example of the sister-sciences, interpreting the unobserved by the observed. It brings old and new harmoniously together. It converts the absolutely empty notion of a static relation of 'correspondence' (what that may mean we must ask later) be-tween our minds and reality, into that of a rich and active com-merce (that any one may follow in detail and understand) between particular thoughts of ours, and the great universe of other experi-ences in which they play their parts and have their uses.

But enough of this at present? The justification of what I say

48

must be postponed. I wish now to add a word in further explanation of the claim I made at our last meeting, that pragmatism may be a happy harmonizer of empiricist ways of thinking with the more religious demands of human beings.

Men who are strongly of the fact-loving temperament, you may remember me to have said, are liable to be kept at a distance by the small sympathy with facts which that philosophy from the present-day fashion of idealism offers them. It is far too intellectualistic. Old-fashioned theism was bad enough, with its notion of God as an exalted monarch, made up of a lot of unintelligible or preposterous 'attributes'; but, so long as it held strongly by the argument from design, it kept some touch with concrete realities. Since, however, Darwinism has once for all displaced design from the minds of the 'scientific,' theism has lost that foothold; and some kind of an immanent or pantheistic deity working *in* things rather than above them is, if any, the kind recommended to our contemporary imagination. Aspirants to a philosophic religion turn, as a rule, more hopefully nowadays towards idealistic pantheism than towards the older dualistic theism, in spite of the fact that the latter still counts able defenders.

But, as I said in my first lecture, the brand of pantheism offered is hard for them to assimilate if they are lovers of facts, or empirically minded. It is the absolutistic brand, spurning the dust and reared upon pure logic. It keeps no connexion whatever with concreteness. Affirming the Absolute Mind, which is its substitute for God, to be the rational presupposition of all particulars of fact, whatever they may be, it remains supremely indifferent to what the particular facts in our world actually are. Be they what they may, the Absolute will father them. Like the sick lion in Esop's fable, all footprints lead into his den, but *nulla vestigia retrorsum*. You cannot redescend into the world of particulars by the Absolute's aid, or deduce any necessary consequences of detail important for your life from your idea of his nature. He gives you indeed the assurance that all is well with *Him*, and for his eternal way of thinking; but thereupon he leaves you to be finitely saved by your own temporal devices.

Far be it from me to deny the majesty of this conception, or its capacity to yield religious comfort to a most respectable class of minds. But from the human point of view, no one can pretend that it does n't suffer from the faults of remoteness and abstractness. It

49

is eminently a product of what I have ventured to call the rationalistic temper. It disdains empiricism's needs. It substitutes a pallid outline for the real world's richness. It is dapper, it is noble in the bad sense, in the sense in which to be noble is to be inapt for humble service. In this real world of sweat and dirt, it seems to me that when a view of things is 'noble,' that ought to count as a presumption against its truth, and as a philosophic disqualification. The prince of darkness may be a gentleman, as we are told he is, but whatever the God of earth and heaven is, he can surely be no gentleman. His menial services are needed in the dust of our human trials, even more than his dignity is needed in the empyrean.

Now pragmatism, devoted though she be to facts, has no such materialistic bias as ordinary empiricism labors under. Moreover, she has no objection whatever to the realizing of abstractions, so long as you get about among particulars with their aid and they actually carry you somewhere. Interested in no conclusions but those which our minds and our experiences work out together, she has no *a priori* prejudices against theology. *If theological ideas prove to have a value for concrete life, they will be true, for pragmatism, in the sense of being good for so much. For how much more they are true, will depend entirely on their relations to the other truths that also have to be acknowledged.*

What I said just now about the Absolute, of transcendental idealism, is a case in point. First, I called it majestic and said it yielded religious comfort to a class of minds, and then I accused it of remoteness and sterility. But so far as it affords such comfort, it surely is not sterile; it has that amount of value; it performs a concrete function. As a good pragmatist, I myself ought to call the Absolute true 'in so far forth,' then; and I unhesitatingly now do so.

But what does *true in so far forth* mean in this case? To answer, we need only apply the pragmatic method. What do believers in the Absolute mean by saying that their belief affords them comfort? They mean that since, in the Absolute finite evil is 'overruled' already, we may, therefore, whenever we wish, treat the temporal as if it were potentially the eternal, be sure that we can trust its outcome, and, without sin, dismiss our fear and drop the worry of our finite responsibility. In short, they mean that we have a right ever and anon to take a moral holiday, to let the world wag in its own way, feeling that its issues are in better hands than ours and are none of our business.

The universe is a system of which the individual members may relax their anxieties occasionally, in which the don't-care mood is also right for men, and moral holidays in order – that, if I mistake not, is part, at least, of what the Absolute is 'known-as,' that is the great difference in our particular experiences which his being true makes, for us, that is his cash-value when he is pragmatically interpreted. Farther than that the ordinary lay-reader in philosophy who thinks favorably of absolute idealism does not venture to sharpen his conceptions. He can use the Absolute for so much, and so much is very precious. He is pained at hearing you speak incredulously of the Absolute, therefore, and disregards your criticisms because they deal with aspects of the conception that he fails to follow.

If the Absolute means this, and means no more than this, who can possibly deny the truth of it? To deny it would be to insist that men should never relax, and that holidays are never in order.

I am well aware how odd it must seem to some of you to hear me say that an idea is 'true' so long as to believe it is profitable to our lives. That it is *good*, for as much as it profits, you will gladly admit. If what we do by its aid is good, you will allow the idea itself to be good in so far forth, for we are the better for possessing it. But is it not a strange misuse of the word 'truth,' you will say, to call ideas also 'true' for this reason?

To answer this difficulty fully is impossible at this stage of my account. You touch here upon the very central point of Messrs. Schiller's, Dewey's and my own doctrine of truth, which I can not discuss with detail until my sixth lecture. Let me now say only this, that truth is *one species of good*, and not, as is usually supposed, a category distinct from good, and co-ordinate with it. *The true is the name of whatever proves itself to be good in the way of belief, and good, too, for definite, assignable reasons.* Surely you must admit this, that if there were *no* good for life in true ideas, or if the knowledge of them were positively disadvantageous and false ideas the only useful ones, then the current notion that truth is divine and precious, and its pursuit a duty, could never have grown up or become a dogma. In a world like that, our duty would be to *shun* truth, rather. But in this world, just as certain foods are not only agreeable to our taste, but good for our teeth, our stomach, and our tissues; so certain ideas are not only agreeable to think about, or agreeable as supporting other ideas that we are fond of, but they are also helpful in life's practical struggles. If there be any life that it is really better we should lead, and if there be any idea which, if believed in, would help us to lead that life, then it would be really *better for us* to believe in that idea, *unless, indeed, belief in it incidentally clashed with other greater vital benefits.*

'What would be better for us to believe'! This sounds very like a definition of truth. It comes very near to saying 'what we *ought* to believe': and in *that* definition none of you would find any oddity. Ought we ever not to believe what it is *better for us* to believe? And can we then keep the notion of what is better for us, and what is true for us, permanently apart?

Pragmatism says no, and I fully agree with her. Probably you also agree, so far as the abstract statement goes, but with a suspicion that if we practically did believe everything that made for good in our own personal lives, we should be found indulging all kinds of fancies about this world's affairs, and all kinds of sentimental superstitions about a world hereafter. Your suspicion here is undoubtedly well founded, and it is evident that something happens when you pass from the abstract to the concrete that complicates the situation.

I said just now that what is better for us to believe is true *unless the belief incidentally clashes with some other vital benefit.* Now in real life what vital benefits is any particular belief of ours most liable to clash with? What indeed except the vital benefits yielded by *other beliefs* when these prove incompatible with the first ones? In other words, the greatest enemy of any one of our truths may be the rest of our truths. Truths have once for all this desperate instinct of self-preservation and of desire to extinguish whatever contradicts them. My belief in the Absolute, based on the good it does me, must run the gauntlet of all my other beliefs. Grant that it may be true in giving me a moral holiday. Nevertheless, as I conceive it, – and let me speak now confidentially, as it were, and merely in my own private person, – it clashes with other truths of mine whose benefits I hate to give up on its account. It happens to be associated with a kind of logic of which I am the enemy, I find that it entangles me in metaphysical paradoxes that are inacceptable, etc., etc. But as I have enough trouble in life already without adding the trouble of carrying these intellectual inconsistencies, I personally just give up the Absolute. I just *take* my moral holidays; or else as a professional philosopher, I try to justify them by some other principle.

If I could restrict my notion of the Absolute to its bare holiday-giving value, it would n't clash with my other truths. But we can not easily thus restrict our hypotheses. They carry supernumerary features, and these it is that clash so. My disbelief in the Absolute means then disbelief in those other supernumerary features, for I fully believe in the legitimacy of taking moral holidays.

You see by this what I meant when I called pragmatism a mediator and reconciler and said, borrowing the word from Papini, that she 'unstiffens' our theories. She has in fact no prejudices whatever, no obstructive dogmas, no rigid canons of what shall count as proof. She is completely genial. She will entertain any hypothesis, she will consider any evidence. It follows that in the religious field she is at a great advantage both over positivistic empiricism, with its anti-theological bias, and over religious rationalism, with its exclusive interest in the remote, the noble, the simple, and the abstract in the way of conception.

In short, she widens the field of search for God. Rationalism sticks to logic and the empyrean. Empiricism sticks to the external senses. Pragmatism is willing to take anything, to follow either logic or the senses and to count the humblest and most personal experiences. She will count mystical experiences if they have practical consequences. She will take a God who lives in the very dirt of private fact – if that should seem a likely place to find him.

Her only test of probable truth is what works best in the way of leading us, what fits every part of life best and combines with the collectivity of experience's demands, nothing being omitted. If theological ideas should do this, if the notion of God, in particular, should prove to do it, how could pragmatism possibly deny God's existence? She could see no meaning in treating as 'not true' a notion that was pragmatically so successful. What other kind of truth could there be, for her, than all this agreement with concrete reality?

In my last lecture I shall return again to the relations of pragmatism with religion. But you see already how democratic she is. Her manners are as various and flexible, her resources as rich and endless, and her conclusions as friendly as those of mother nature.

LECTURE III
SOME METAPHYSICAL PROBLEMS
PRAGMATICALLY CONSIDERED

I am now to make the pragmatic method more familiar by giving you some illustrations of its application to particular problems. I will begin with what is driest, and the first thing I shall take will be the problem of *Substance*. Every one uses the old distinction between substance and attribute, enshrined as it is in the very structure of human language, in the difference between grammatical subject and predicate. Here is a bit of blackboard crayon. Its modes, attributes, properties, accidents, or affections, – use which term you will, – are whiteness, friability, cylindrical shape, insolubility in water, etc., etc. But the bearer of these attributes is so much *chalk*, which thereupon is called the substance in which they inhere. So the attributes of this desk inhere in the substance 'wood,' those of my coat in the substance 'wool,' and so forth. Chalk, wood and wool, show again, in spite of their differences, common properties, and in so far forth they are themselves counted as modes of a still more primal substance, *matter*, the attributes of which are space-occupancy and impenetrability. Similarly our thoughts and feelings are affections or properties of our several *souls*, which are substances, but again not wholly in their own right, for they are modes of the still deeper substance 'spirit.'

Now it was very early seen that all *we know* of the chalk is the whiteness, friability, etc., all *we know* of the wood is the combustibility and fibrous structure. A group of attributes is what each substance here is known-as, they form its sole cash-value for our actual experience. The substance is in every case revealed through *them*; if we were cut off from *them* we should never suspect its existence; and if God should keep sending them to us in an unchanged order, miraculously annihilating at a certain moment the substance that supported them, we never could detect the moment, for our experiences themselves would be unaltered. Nominalists accordingly adopt the opinion that substance is a spurious idea due to our inveterate human trick of turning names into things. Phenomena come in groups – the chalk-group, the wood-group, etc., – and each group gets its name. The name we then treat as in a way supporting the group of phenomena. The low thermometer to-day, for instance, is supposed to come from something called the 'climate.' Climate is really only the name for a certain group of days, but it is treated as if it lay *behind* the day, and in general we place the name, as if it were a being, behind the facts it is the name of. But the phenomenal properties of things, nominalists say, surely do not really inhere in names, and if not in names then they do not inhere in anything. They *ad*here, or *co*here, rather, *with each other*, and the notion of a substance inaccessible to us, which we think accounts for such cohesion by supporting it, as cement might support pieces of mosaic, must be abandoned. The fact of the bare cohesion itself is all that the notion of the substance signifies. Behind that fact is nothing.

Scholasticism has taken the notion of substance from common sense and made it very technical and articulate. Few things would seem to have fewer pragmatic consequences for us than substances, cut off as we are from every contact with them. Yet in one case scholasticism has proved the importance of the substance-idea by treating it pragmatically. I refer to certain disputes about the mystery of the Eucharist. Substance here would appear to have momentous pragmatic value. Since the accidents of the wafer don't change in the Lord's supper, and yet it has become the very body of Christ, it must be that the change is in the substance solely. The bread-substance must have been withdrawn, and the divine substance substituted miraculously without altering the immediate sensible properties. But tho these don't alter, a tremendous difference has been made, no less a one than this, that we who take the sacrament, now feed upon the very substance of divinity. The substance-notion breaks into life, then, with tremendous effect, if once you allow that substances can separate from their accidents, and exchange these latter.

This is the only pragmatic application of the substance-idea with which I am acquainted; and it is obvious that it will only be treated seriously by those who already believe in the 'real presence' on independent grounds.

Material substance was criticised by Berkeley with such telling effect that his name has reverberated through all subsequent philosophy. Berkeley's treatment of the notion of matter is so well known as to need hardly more than a mention. So far from denying the external world which we know, Berkeley corroborated it. It was the scholastic notion of a material substance unapproachable by us, *behind* the external world, deeper and more real than it, and needed to support it, which Berkeley maintained to be the most effective of all reducers of the external world to unreality. Abolish

that substance, he said, believe that God, whom you can understand and approach, sends you the sensible world directly, and you
confirm the latter and back it up by his divine authority. Berkeley's
criticism of 'matter' was consequently absolutely pragmatistic.
Matter is known as our sensations of colour, figure, hardness and
the like. They are the cash-value of the term. The difference matter
makes to us by truly being is that we then get such sensations; by
not being, is that we lack them. These sensations then are its sole
meaning. Berkeley does n't deny matter, then; he simply tells us
what it consists of. It is a true name for just so much in the way of
sensations.

Locke, and later Hume, applied a similar pragmatic criticism to
the notion of *spiritual substance*. I will only mention Locke's treatment of our 'personal identity,' He immediately reduces this notion
to its pragmatic value in terms of experience. It means, he says, so
much 'consciousness,' namely the fact that at one moment of life
we remember other moments, and feel them all as parts of one and
the same personal history. Rationalism had explained this practical
continuity in our life by the unity of our soul-substance. But Locke
says: suppose that God should take away the consciousness, should
we be any the better for having still the soul-principle? Suppose he
annexed the same consciousness to different souls, should *we*, as we
realize *ourselves*, be any the worse for that fact? In Locke's day the
soul was chiefly a thing to be rewarded or punished. See how
Locke, discussing it from this point of view, keeps the question
pragmatic:

"Suppose," he says, "one to think himself to be the same *soul*
that once was Nestor or Thersites. Can he think their actions his
own any more than the actions of any other man that ever
existed? But let him once find himself *conscious* of any of the
actions of Nestor, he then finds himself the same person with
Nestor . . . In this personal identity is founded all the right and
justice of reward and punishment. It may be reasonable to think,
no one shall be made to answer for what he knows nothing of,
but shall receive his doom, his consciousness accusing or excus-
ing. Supposing a man punished now for what he had done in
another life, whereof he could be made to have no consciousness
at all, what difference is there between that punishment and
being created miserable?"

Our personal identity, then, consists, for Locke, solely in pragmatically definable particulars. Whether, apart from these verifiable

facts, it also inheres in a spiritual principle, is a merely curious speculation. Locke, compromiser that he was, passively tolerated the belief in a substantial soul behind our consciousness. But his successor Hume, and most empirical psychologists after him, have denied the soul, save as the name for verifiable cohesions in our inner life. They redescend into the stream of experience with it, and cash it into so much small-change value in the way of 'ideas' and their peculiar connexions with each other. As I said of Berkeley's matter, the soul is good or 'true' for just *so much*, but no more.

The mention of material substance naturally suggests the doctrine of 'materialism,' but philosophical materialism is not necessarily knit up with belief in 'matter,' as a metaphysical principle. One may deny matter in that sense, as strongly as Berkeley did, one may be a phenomenalist like Huxley, and yet one may still be a materialist in the wider sense, of explaining higher phenomena by lower ones, and leaving the destinies of the world at the mercy of its blinder parts and forces. It is in this wider sense of the word that materialism is opposed to spiritualism or theism. The laws of physical nature are what run things, materialism says. The highest productions of human genius might be ciphered by one who had complete acquaintance with the facts, out of their physiological conditions, regardless whether nature be there only for our minds, as idealists contend, or not. Our minds in any case would have to record the kind of nature it is, and write it down as operating through blind laws of physics. This is the complexion of present-day materialism, which may better be called naturalism. Over against it stands 'theism,' or what in a wide sense may be termed 'spiritualism.' Spiritualism says that mind not only witnesses and records things, but also runs and operates them: the world being thus guided, not by its lower, but by its higher element.

Treated as it often is, this question becomes little more than a conflict between aesthetic preferences. Matter is gross, coarse, crass, muddy; spirit is pure, elevated, noble; and since it is more consonant with the dignity of the universe to give the primacy in it to what appears superior, spirit must be affirmed as the ruling principle. To treat abstract principles as finalities, before which our intellects may come to rest in a state of admiring contemplation, is the great rationalist failing. Spiritualism, as often held, may be simply a state of admiration for one kind, and of dislike for another kind, of abstraction. I remember a worthy spiritualist professor

57

who always referred to materialism as the 'mud-philosophy,' and deemed it thereby refuted.

To such spiritualism as this there is an easy answer, and Mr. Spencer makes it effectively. In some well-written pages at the end of the first volume of his *Psychology* he shows us that a 'matter' so infinitely subtle, and performing motions as inconceivably quick and fine as those which modern science postulates in her explanations, has no trace of grossness left. He shows that the conception of spirit, as we mortals hitherto have framed it, is itself too gross to cover the exquisite tenuity of nature's facts. Both terms, he says, are but symbols, pointing to that one unknowable reality in which their oppositions cease.

To an abstract objection an abstract rejoinder suffices; and so far as one's opposition to materialism springs from one's disdain of matter as something 'crass,' Mr. Spencer cuts the ground from under one. Matter is indeed infinitely and incredibly refined. To any one who has ever looked on the face of a dead child or parent the mere fact that matter *could* have taken for a time that precious form, ought to make matter sacred ever after. It makes no difference what the *principle* of life may be, material or immaterial, matter at any rate co-operates, lends itself to all life's purposes. That beloved incarnation was among matter's possibilities.

But now, instead of resting in principles, after this stagnant intellectualist fashion, let us apply the pragmatic method to the question. What do we *mean* by matter? What practical difference can it make *now* that the world should be run by matter or by spirit? I think we find that the problem takes with this a rather different character.

And first of all I call your attention to a curious fact. It makes not a single jot of difference so far as the *past* of the world goes, whether we deem it to have been the work of matter or whether we think a divine spirit was its author.

Imagine, in fact, the entire contents of the world to be once for all irrevocably given. Imagine it to end this very moment, and to have no future; and then let a theist and a materialist apply their rival explanations to its history. The theist shows how a God made it; the materialist shows, and we will suppose with equal success, how it resulted from blind physical forces. Then let the pragmatist be asked to choose between their theories. How can he apply his test if a world is already completed? Concepts for him are things to come back into experience with, things to make us look for differences. But by hypothesis there is to be no more experience and no possible differences can now be looked for. Both theories have shown all their consequences and, by the hypothesis we are adopting, these are identical. The pragmatist must consequently say that the two theories, in spite of their different-sounding names, mean exactly the same thing, and that the dispute is purely verbal. [I am supposing, of course, that the theories *have* been equally successful in their explanations of what is.]

For just consider the case sincerely, and say what would be the *worth* of a God if he *were* there, with his work accomplished and his world run down. He would be worth no more than just that world was worth. To that amount of result, with its mixed merits and defects, his creative power could attain but go no farther. And since there is to be no future; since the whole value and meaning of the world has been already paid in and actualized in the feelings that went with it in the passing, and now go with it in the ending; since it draws no supplemental significance (such as our real world draws) from its function of preparing something yet to come; why then, by it we take God's measure, as it were. He is the Being who could once for all do *that*; and for that much we are thankful to him, but for nothing more. But now, on the contrary hypothesis, namely, that the bits of matter following their laws could make that world and do no less, should we not be just as thankful to them? Wherein should we suffer loss, then, if we dropped God as an hypothesis and made the matter alone responsible? Where would any special deadness, or crassness, come in? And how, experience being what is once for all, would God's presence in it make it any more living or richer?

Candidly, it is impossible to give any answer to this question. The actually experienced world is supposed to be the same in its details on either hypothesis, 'the same, for our praise or blame,' as Browning says. It stands there indefeasibly: a gift which can't be taken back. Calling matter the cause of it retracts no single one of the items that have made it up, nor does calling God the cause augment them. They are the God or the atoms, respectively, of just that and no other world. The God, if there, has been doing just what atoms could do – appearing in the character of atoms, so to speak – earning such gratitude as is due to atoms, and no more. If his presence lends no different turn or issue to the performance, it surely can lend it no increase of dignity. Nor would indignity come to it were he absent, and did the atoms remain the only actors on the stage. When a play is once over, and the curtain down, you really make it no better by claiming an illustrious genius for its author, just as you make it no worse by calling him a common hack.

Thus if no future detail of experience or conduct is to be deduced from our hypothesis, the debate between materialism and theism becomes quite idle and insignificant. Matter and God in that event mean exactly the same thing – the power, namely, neither more nor less, that could make just this completed world – and the wise man is he who in such a case would turn his back on such a supererogatory discussion. Accordingly, most men instinctively, and positivists and scientists deliberately, do turn their backs on philosophical disputes from which nothing in the line of definite future consequences can be seen to follow. The verbal and empty character of philosophy is surely a reproach with which we are but too familiar. If pragmatism be true, it is a perfectly sound reproach unless the theories under fire can be shown to have alternative practical outcomes, however delicate and distant these may be. The common man and the scientist say they discover no such outcomes, and if the metaphysician can discern none either, the others certainly are in the right of it, as against him. His science is then but pompous trifling; and the endowment of a professorship for such a being would be silly.

Accordingly, in every genuine metaphysical debate some practical issue, however conjectural and remote, is involved. To realize this, revert with me to our question, and place yourselves this time in the world we live in, in the world that *has* a future, that is yet uncompleted whilst we speak. In this unfinished world the alternative of 'materialism or theism?' is intensely practical; and it is worth while for us to spend some minutes of our hour in seeing that it is so.

How, indeed, does the program differ for us, according as we consider that the facts of experience up to date are purposeless configurations of blind atoms moving according to eternal laws, or that on the other hand they are due to the providence of God? As far as the past facts go, indeed, there is no difference. Those facts are in, are bagged, are captured; and the good that's in them is gained, be the atoms or be the God their cause. There are accordingly many materialists about us to-day who, ignoring altogether the future and practical aspects of the question, seek to eliminate the odium attaching to the word materialism, and even to eliminate the word itself, by showing that, if matter could give birth to all these gains, why then matter, functionally considered, is just as divine an entity as God, in fact coalesces with God, is what you mean by God. Cease, these persons advise us, to use either of these terms, with their outgrown opposition. Use a term free of the clerical connotations, on the one hand; of the suggestion of grossness, coarseness, ignobility, on the other. Talk of the primal mystery, of the unknowable energy, of the one and, only power, instead of saying either God or matter. This is the course to which Mr. Spencer urges us; and if philosophy were purely retrospective, he would thereby proclaim himself an excellent pragmatist.

But philosophy is prospective also, and, after finding what the world has been and done, and yielded, still asks the further question 'what does the world *promise*?' Give us a matter that promises *success*, that is bound by its laws to lead our world ever nearer to perfection, and any rational man will worship that matter as readily as Mr. Spencer worships his own so-called unknowable power. It not only has made for righteousness up to date, but it will make for righteousness forever; and that is all we need. Doing practically all that a God can do, it is equivalent to God, its function, and in a world in which a God would be superfluous; from such a world a God could never lawfully be missed. 'Cosmic emotion' would here be the right name for religion.

But *is* the matter by which Mr. Spencer's process of cosmic evolution is carried on any such principle of never-ending perfection as this? Indeed it is not, for the future end of every cosmically evolved thing or system of things is foretold by science to be death and tragedy; and Mr. Spencer, in confining himself to the aesthetic and ignoring the practical side of the controversy, has really contributed nothing serious to its relief. But apply now our principle of practical results, and see what a vital significance the question of materialism or theism immediately acquires.

Theism and materialism, so indifferent when taken retrospectively, point, when we take them prospectively, to wholly different outlooks of experience. For, according to the theory of mechanical evolution, the laws of redistribution of matter and motion, though they are certainly to thank for all the good hours which our organisms have ever yielded us and for all the ideals which our minds now frame, are yet fatally certain to undo their work again, and to redissolve everything that they have once evolved. You all know the picture of the last state of the universe, which evolutionary science foresees. I can not state it better than in Mr. Balfour's words: "The energies of our system will decay, the glory of the sun will be dimmed, and the earth, tideless and inert, will no longer tolerate the race which has for a moment disturbed its solitude. Man will go down into the pit, and all his thoughts will perish. The uneasy consciousness which in this obscure corner has for a brief space broken the contented silence of the universe, will be at rest. Matter will know itself no longer. 'Imperishable monuments' and 'immortal deeds,' death itself, and love stronger than death, will be as if they had not been. Nor will anything that is, be better or worse for all that the labor, genius, devotion, and suffering of man have striven through countless ages to effect."[1]

That is the sting of it, that in the vast driftings of the cosmic weather, though many a jewelled shore appears, and many an enchanted cloud-bank floats away, long lingering ere it be dissolved – even as our world now lingers, for our joy – yet when these transient products are gone, nothing, absolutely *nothing* remains, to represent those particular qualities, those elements of preciousness which they may have enshrined. Dead and gone are they, gone utterly from the very sphere and room of being. Without an echo; without a memory; without an influence on aught that may come after, to make it care for similar ideals. This utter final wreck and tragedy is of the essence of scientific materialism as at present understood. The lower and not the higher forces are the eternal forces, or the last surviving forces within the only cycle of evolution which we can definitely see. Mr. Spencer believes this as much as anyone; so why should he argue with us as if we were making silly aesthetic objections to the 'grossness' of 'matter and motion,' the principles of his philosophy, when what really dismays us is the disconsolateness of its ulterior practical results?

No, the true objection to materialism is not positive but negative. It would be farcical at this day to make complaint of it for what it *is*, for 'grossness.' Grossness is what grossness *does* – we now know *that*. We make complaint of it, on the contrary, for what it is *not* – not a permanent warrant for our more ideal interests, not a fulfiller of our remotest hopes.

1 *The Foundations of Belief,* p. 30.

The notion of God, on the other hand, however inferior it may be in clearness to those mathematical notions so current in mechanical philosophy, has at least this practical superiority over them, that it guarantees an ideal order that shall be permanently preserved. A world with a God in it to say the last word, may indeed burn up or freeze, but we then think of him as still mindful of the old ideals and sure to bring them elsewhere to fruition; so that, where he is, tragedy is only provisional and partial, and shipwreck and dissolution not the absolutely final things. This need of an eternal moral order is one of the deepest needs of our breast. And those poets, like Dante and Wordsworth, who live on the conviction of such an order, owe to that fact the extraordinary tonic and consoling power of their verse. Here then, in these different emotional and practical appeals, in these adjustments of our concrete attitudes of hope and expectation, and all the delicate consequences which their differences entail, lie the real meanings of materialism and spiritualism – not in hair-splitting abstractions about matter's inner essence, or about the metaphysical attributes of God. Materialism means simply the denial that the moral order is eternal, and the cutting off of ultimate hopes; spiritualism means the affirmation of an eternal moral order and the letting loose of hope. Surely here is an issue genuine enough, for any one who feels it; and, as long as men are men, it will yield matter for a serious philosophic debate.

But possibly some of you may still rally to their defence. Even whilst admitting that spiritualism and materialism make different prophecies of the world's future, you may yourselves pooh-pooh the difference as something so infinitely remote as to mean nothing for a sane mind. The essence of a sane mind, you may say, is to take shorter views, and to feel no concern about such chimaeras as the latter end of the world. Well, I can only say that if you say this, you do injustice to human nature. Religious melancholy is not disposed of by a simple flourish of the word insanity. The absolute things, the last things, the overlapping things, are the truly philosophic concerns; all superior minds feel seriously about them, and the mind with the shortest views is simply the mind of the more shallow man.

The issues of fact at stake in the debate are of course vaguely enough conceived by us at present. But spiritualistic faith in all its forms deals with a world of *promise*, while materialism's sun sets in a sea of disappointment. Remember what I said of the Absolute: it

63

grants us moral holidays. Any religious view does this. It not only incites our more strenuous moments, but it also takes our joyous, careless, trustful moments, and it justifies them. It paints the grounds of justification vaguely enough, to be sure. The exact features of the saving future facts that our belief in God insures, will have to be ciphered out by the interminable methods of science: we can *study* our God only by studying his Creation. But we can *enjoy* our God, if we have one, in advance of all that labor. I myself believe that the evidence for God lies primarily in inner personal experiences. When they have once given you your God, his name means at least the benefit of the holiday. You remember what I said yesterday about the way in which truths clash and try to 'down' each other. The truth of 'God' has to run the gauntlet of all our other truths. It is on trial by them and they on trial by it. Our *final* opinion about God can be settled only after all the truths have straightened themselves out together. Let us hope that they shall find a *modus vivendi*!

Let me pass to a very cognate philosophic problem, the *question of design in nature*. God's existence has from time immemorial been held to be proved by certain natural facts. Many facts appear as if expressly designed in view of one another. Thus the woodpecker's bill, tongue, feet, tail, etc., fit him wondrously for a world of trees, with grubs hid in their bark to feed upon. The parts of our eye fit the laws of light to perfection, leading its rays to a sharp picture on our retina. Such mutual fitting of things diverse in origin argued design, it was held; and the designer was always treated as a man-loving deity.

The first step in these arguments was to prove that the design *existed*. Nature was ransacked for results obtained through separate things being co-adapted. Our eyes, for instance, originate in intra-uterine darkness, and the light originates in the sun, yet see how they fit each other. They are evidently made *for* each other. Vision is the end designed, light and eyes the separate means devised for its attainment.

It is strange, considering how unanimously our ancestors felt the force of this argument, to see how little it counts for since the triumph of the Darwinian theory. Darwin opened our minds to the power of chance-happenings to bring forth 'fit' results if only they have time to add themselves together. He showed the enormous waste of nature in producing results that get destroyed because of their unfitness. He also emphasized the number of adaptations which, if designed, would argue an evil rather than a good designer. *Here*, all depends upon the point of view. To the grub under the bark the exquisite fitness of the woodpecker's organism to extract him would certainly argue a diabolical designer.

Theologians have by this time stretched their minds so as to embrace the Darwinian facts, and yet to interpret them as still showing divine purpose. It used to be a question of purpose against mechanism, of one *or* the other. It was as if one should say "My shoes are evidently designed to fit my feet, hence it is impossible that they should have been produced by machinery." We know that they are both: they are made by a machinery itself designed to fit the feet with shoes. Theology need only stretch similarly the designs of God. As the aim of a football-team is not merely to get the ball to a certain goal (if that were so, they would simply get up on some dark night and place it there), but to get it there by a fixed *machinery of conditions* – the game's rules and the opposing players; so the aim of God is not merely, let us say, to make men and to save them, but rather to get this done through the sole agency of nature's vast machinery. Without nature's stupendous laws and counter-forces, man's creation and perfection, we might suppose, would be too insipid achievements for God to have proposed them.

This saves the form of the design-argument at the expense of its old easy human content. The designer is no longer the old man-like deity. His designs have grown so vast as to be incomprehensible to us humans. The *what* of them so overwhelms us that to establish the mere *that* of a designer for them becomes of very little conse-quence in comparison. We can with difficulty comprehend the *character* of a cosmic mind whose purposes are fully revealed by the strange mixture of goods and evils that we find in this actual world's particulars. Or rather we cannot by any possibility com-prehend it. The mere word 'design' by itself has no consequences and explains nothing. It is the barrenest of principles. The old question of *whether* there is design is idle. The real question is what *is* the world, whether or not it have a designer – and that can be revealed only by the study of all nature's particulars.

Remember that *no matter what* nature may have produced or may be producing, the means must necessarily have been adequate, must have been *fitted to that production*. The argument from fitness to design would consequently always apply, whatever were the prod-uct's character. The recent Mont-Pelée eruption, for example, required all previous history to produce that exact combination of ruined houses, human and animal corpses, sunken ships, volcanic ashes, etc., in just that one hideous configuration of positions. France had to be a nation and colonize Martinique. Our country had to exist and send our ships there. *If* God aimed at just that result, the means by which the centuries bent their influences towards it, showed exquisite intelligence. And so of any state of things whatever, either in nature or in history, which we find actually realized. For the parts of things must always make *some* definite resultant, be it chaotic or harmonious. When we look at what has actually come, the conditions must always appear perfectly designed to ensure it. We can always say, therefore, in any conceivable world, of any conceivable character, that the whole cosmic machinery *may* have been designed to produce it.

Pragmatically, then, the abstract word 'design' is a blank cartridge. It carries no consequences, it does no execution. *What* design? and *what* designer? are the only serious questions, and the study of facts is the only way of getting even approximate answers. Meanwhile, pending the slow answer from facts, anyone who insists that there *is* a designer and who is sure he is a divine one, gets a certain pragmatic benefit from the term – the same, in fact, which we saw that the terms God, Spirit, or the Absolute, yield us. 'Design,' worthless tho it be as a mere rationalistic principle set above or behind things for our admiration, becomes, if our faith concretes it into something theistic, a term of *promise*. Returning with it into experience, we gain a more confiding outlook on the future. If not a blind force but a seeing force runs things, we may reasonably expect better issues. This vague confidence in the future is the sole pragmatic meaning at present discernible in the terms design and designer. But if cosmic confidence is right not wrong, better not worse, that is a most important meaning. That much at least of possible 'truth' the terms will then have in them.

Let me take up another well-worn controversy, *the free-will problem*. Most persons who believe in what is called their free-will do so after the rationalistic fashion. It is a principle, a positive faculty or virtue added to man, by which his dignity is enigmatically augmented. He ought to believe it for this reason. Determinists, who deny it, who say that individual men originate nothing, but merely transmit to the future the whole push of the past cosmos of which they are so small an expression, diminish man. He is less admirable, stripped of this creative principle. I imagine that more than half of you share our instinctive belief in free-will, and that admiration of it as a principle of dignity has much to do with your fidelity.

But free-will has also been discussed pragmatically, and, strangely enough, the same pragmatic interpretation has been put upon it by both disputants. You know how large a part questions of *accountability* have played in ethical controversy. To hear some persons, one would suppose that all that ethics aims at is a code of merits and demerits. Thus does the old legal and theological leaven, the interest in crime and sin and punishment abide with us. 'Who's to blame? whom can we punish? whom will God punish?' – these preoccupations hang like a bad dream over man's religious history.

So both free-will and determinism have been inveighed against and called absurd, because each, in the eyes of its enemies, has seemed to prevent the 'imputability' of good or bad deeds to their authors. Queer antinomy this! Free-will means novelty, the grafting on to the past of something not involved therein. If our acts were predetermined, if we merely transmitted the push of the whole past, the free-willists say, how could we be praised or blamed for anything? We should be 'agents' only, not 'principals,' and where then would be our precious imputability and responsibility?

But where would it be if we *had* free-will? rejoin the determinists. If a 'free' act be a sheer novelty, that comes not *from* me, the previous me, but *ex nihilo*, and simply tacks itself on to me, how can I, the previous I, be responsible? How can I have any permanent *character* that will stand still long enough for praise or blame to be awarded? The chaplet of my days tumbles into a cast of disconnected beads as soon as the thread of inner necessity is drawn out by the preposterous indeterminist doctrine. Messrs. Fullerton and McTaggart have recently laid about them doughtily with this argument.

It may be good *ad hominem*, but otherwise it is pitiful. For I ask you, quite apart from other reasons, whether any man, woman or child, with a sense for realities, ought not to be ashamed to plead such principles as either dignity or imputability. Instinct and utility between them can safely be trusted to carry on the social business of punishment and praise. If a man does good acts we shall praise him, if he does bad acts we shall punish him, – anyhow, and quite apart from theories as to whether the acts result from what was previous in him or are novelties in a strict sense. To make our human ethics revolve about the question of 'merit' is a piteous unreality – God alone can know our merits, if we have any. The real ground for supposing free-will is indeed pragmatic, but it has nothing to do with this contemptible right to punish which has made such a noise in past discussions of the subject.

Free-will pragmatically means *novelties in the world*, the right to expect that in its deepest elements as well as in its surface phenomena, the future may not identically repeat and imitate the past. That imitation *en masse* is there, who can deny? The general 'uniformity of nature' is presupposed by every lesser law. But nature may be only approximately uniform; and persons in whom knowledge of the world's past has bred pessimism (or doubts as to the world's good character, which become certainties if that character be supposed eternally fixed) may naturally welcome free-will as a *melioristic* doctrine. It holds up improvement as at least possible; whereas determinism assures us that our whole notion of possibility is born of human ignorance, and that necessity and impossibility between them rule the destinies of the world.

Free-will is thus a general cosmological theory of *promise*, just like the Absolute, God, Spirit or Design. Taken abstractly, no one of these terms has any inner content, none of them gives us any picture, and no one of them would retain the least pragmatic value in a world whose character was obviously perfect from the start. Elation at mere existence, pure cosmic emotion and delight, would, it seems to me, quench all interest in those speculations, if the world were nothing but a lubberland of happiness already. Our interest in religious metaphysics arises in the fact that our empirical future feels to us unsafe, and needs some higher guarantee. If the past and present were purely good, who could wish that the future might possibly not resemble them? Who could desire free-will? Who would not say, with Huxley, 'let me be wound up every day like a watch, to go right fatally, and I ask no better freedom.' 'Freedom' in a world already perfect could only mean freedom to *be worse*, and who could be so insane as to wish that? To be necessarily what it is, to be impossibly aught else, would put the last touch of perfection upon optimism's universe. Surely the only *possibility* that one can rationally claim is the possibility that things may be *better*. That possibility, I need hardly say, is one that, as the actual world goes, we have ample grounds for desiderating.

Free-will thus has no meaning unless it be a doctrine of *relief*. As such, it takes its place with other religious doctrines. Between them, they build up the old wastes and repair the former desolations. Our spirit, shut within this courtyard of sense-experience, is always saying to the intellect upon the tower: 'Watchman, tell us of the night, if it aught of promise bear,' and the intellect gives it then these terms of promise.

Other than this practical significance, the words God, free-will, design, etc., have none. Yet dark tho they be in themselves, or intellectualistically taken, when we bear them into life's thicket with us the darkness *there* grows light about us. If you stop, in dealing with such words, with their definition, thinking that to be an intellectual finality, where are you? Stupidly staring at a pretentious sham! "Deus est Ens, a se, extra et supra omne genus, necessarium, unum, infinite perfectum, simplex, immutabile, immensum, aeternum, intelligens," etc., – wherein is such a definition really instructive? It means less than nothing, in its pompous robe of adjectives. Pragmatism alone can read a positive meaning into it, and for that she turns her back upon the intellectualist point of view altogether. 'God's in his heaven; all's right with the world!' – *That's* the real heart of your theology, and for that you need no rationalist definitions.

Why should n't all of us, rationalists as well as pragmatists, confess this? Pragmatism, so far from keeping her eyes bent on the immediate practical foreground, as she is accused of doing, dwells just as much upon the world's remotest perspectives.

See then how all these ultimate questions turn, as it were, upon their hinges; and from looking backwards upon principles, upon an *erkenntnisstheoretische Ich*, a God, a *Kausalitätsprinzip*, a Design, a Free-will, taken in themselves, as something august and exalted above facts, – see, I say, how pragmatism shifts the emphasis and looks forward into facts themselves. The really vital question for us all is, What is this world going to be? What is life eventually to make of itself? The centre of gravity of philosophy must therefore alter its place. The earth of things, long thrown into shadow by the glories of the upper ether, must resume its rights. To shift the emphasis in this way means that philosophic questions will fall to be treated by minds of a less abstractionist type than heretofore, minds more scientific and individualistic in their tone yet not irreligious either. It will be an alteration in 'the seat of authority' that reminds one almost of the protestant reformation. And as, to papal minds, protestantism has often seemed a mere mess of anarchy and confusion, such, no doubt, will pragmatism often seem to ultra-rationalist minds in philosophy. It will seem so much sheer trash, philosophically. But life wags on, all the same, and compasses its ends, in protestant countries. I venture to think that philosophic protestantism will compass not dissimilar prosperity.

LECTURE IV
THE ONE AND THE MANY

We saw in the last lecture that the pragmatic method, in its dealings with certain concepts, instead of ending with admiring contemplation, plunges forward into the river of experience with them and prolongs the perspective by their means. Design, free-will, the absolute mind, spirit instead of matter, have for their sole meaning a better promise as to this world's outcome. Be they false or be they true, the meaning of them is this meliorism. I have sometimes thought of the phenomenon called 'total reflexion' in Optics as a good symbol of the relation between abstract ideas and concrete realities, as pragmatism conceives it. Hold a tumbler of water a little above your eyes and look up through the water at its surface – or better still look similarly through the flat wall of an aquarium. You will then see an extraordinarily brilliant reflected image say of a candle-flame, or any other clear object, situated on the opposite side of the vessel. No ray, under these circumstances, gets beyond the water's surface: every ray is totally reflected back into the depths again. Now let the water represent the world of sensible facts, and let the air above it represent the world of abstract ideas. Both worlds are real, of course, and interact; but they interact only at their boundary, and the *locus* of everything that lives, and happens to us, so far as full experience goes, is the water. We are like fishes swimming in the sea of sense, bounded above by the superior element, but unable to breathe it pure or penetrate it. We get our oxygen from it, however, we touch it incessantly, now in this part, now in that, and every time we touch it, we turn back into the water with our course re-determined and re-energized. The abstract ideas of which the air consists are indispensable for life, but irrespirable by themselves, as it were, and only active in their re-directing function. All similes are halting, but this one rather takes my fancy. It shows how something, not sufficient for life in itself, may nevertheless be an effective determinant of life elsewhere.

In this present hour I wish to illustrate the pragmatic method by one more application. I wish to turn its light upon the ancient problem of 'the one and the many.' I suspect that in but few of you has this problem occasioned sleepless nights, and I should not be astonished if some of you told me it had never vexed you at all. I myself have come, by long brooding over it, to consider it the most

71

central of all philosophic problems, central because so pregnant. I mean by this that if you know whether a man is a decided monist or a decided pluralist, you perhaps know more about the rest of his opinions than if you give him any other name ending in *ist*. To believe in the one or in the many, that is the classification with the maximum number of consequences. So bear with me for an hour while I try to inspire you with my own interest in this problem.

Philosophy has often been defined as the quest or the vision of the world's unity. Few persons ever challenge this definition, which is true as far as it goes, for philosophy has indeed manifested above all things its interest in unity. But how about the *variety* in things? Is that such an irrelevant matter? If instead of using the term philosophy, we talk in general of our intellect and its needs, we quickly see that unity is only one of them. Acquaintance with the details of fact is always reckoned, along with their reduction to system, as an indispensable mark of mental greatness. Your 'scholarly' mind, of encyclopedic, philological type, your man essentially of *learning*, has never lacked for praise along with your philosopher. What our intellect really aims at is neither variety nor unity taken singly, but *totality*.[1] In this, acquaintance with reality's diversities is as important as understanding their connexion. Curiosity goes *pari passu* with the systematizing passion.

In spite of this obvious fact the unity of things has always been considered more *illustrious*, as it were, than their variety. When a young man first conceives the notion that the whole world forms one great fact, with all its parts moving abreast, as it were, and interlocked, he feels as if he were enjoying a great insight, and looks superciliously on all who still fall short of this sublime conception. Taken thus abstractly as it first comes to one, the monistic insight is so vague as hardly to seem worth defending intellectually. Yet probably every one in this audience in some way cherishes it. A certain abstract monism, a certain emotional response to the character of oneness, as if it were a feature of the world not co-ordinate with its manyness, but vastly more excellent and eminent, is so prevalent in educated circles that we might almost call it a part of philosophic common sense. Of *course* the world is One, we say. How else could it be a world at all? Empiricists as a rule, are as stout monists of this abstract kind as rationalists are.

---

1 Compare A. Bellanger, *Les concepts de Cause, et l'activité intentionelle de l'Esprit*, Paris, Alcan, 1905, p. 79 ff.

The difference is that the empiricists are less dazzled. Unity doesn't blind them to everything else, doesn't quench their curiosity for special facts, whereas there is a kind of rationalist who is sure to interpret abstract unity mystically and to forget everything else, to treat it as a principle; to admire and worship it; and thereupon to come to a full stop intellectually.

'The world is One!' – the formula may become a sort of number-worship. 'Three' and 'seven' have, it is true, been reckoned sacred numbers; but, abstractly taken, why is 'one' more excellent than 'forty-three,' or than 'two million and ten'? In this first vague conviction of the world's unity, there is so little to take hold of that we hardly know what we mean by it.

The only way to get forward with our notion is to treat it pragmatically. Granting the oneness to exist, what facts will be different in consequence? What will the unity be known as? The world is One – yes, but *how* one. What is the practical value of the oneness for *us*.

Asking such questions, we pass from the vague to the definite, from the abstract to the concrete. Many distinct ways in which a oneness predicated of the universe might make a difference, come to view. I will note succesively the more obvious of these ways.

1. First, the world is at least *one subject of discourse*. If its manyness were so irremediable as to permit *no* union whatever of its parts, not even our minds could 'mean' the whole of it at once: they would be like eyes trying to look in opposite directions. But in point of fact we mean to cover the whole of it by our abstract term 'world' or 'universe,' which expressly intends that no part shall be left out. Such unity of discourse carries obviously no farther monistic specifications. A 'chaos,' once so named, has as much unity of discourse as a cosmos. It is an odd fact that many monists consider a great victory scored for their side when pluralists say 'the universe is many.' " 'The Universe'!" they chuckle – "his speech bewrayeth him. He stands confessed of monism out of his own mouth." Well, let things be one in so far forth! You can then fling such a word as universe at the whole collection of them, but what matters it? It still remains to be ascertained whether they are one in any further or more valuable sense.

2. Are they, for example, *continuous*? Can you pass from one to another, keeping always in your one universe without any danger of falling out? In other words, do the parts of our universe *hang together*, instead of being like detached grains of sand?

73

Even grains of sand hang together through the space in which they are embedded, and if you can in any way move through such space, you can pass continuously from number one of them to number two. Space and time are thus vehicles of continuity by which the world's parts hang together. The practical difference to us, resultant from these forms of union, is immense. Our whole motor life is based upon them.

3. There are innumerable other paths of practical continuity among things. Lines of *influence* can be traced by which they hang together. Following any such line you pass from one thing to another till you may have covered a good part of the universe's extent. Gravity and heat-conduction are such all-uniting influences, so far as the physical world goes. Electric, luminous and chemical influences follow similar lines of influence. But opaque and inert bodies interrupt the continuity here, so that you have to step round them, or change your mode of progress if you wish to get farther on that day. Practically, you have then lost your universe's unity, *so far as it was constituted by those first lines of influence.*

There are innumerable kinds of connexion that special things have with other special things; and the *ensemble* of any one of these connexions forms one sort of *system* by which things are conjoined. Thus men are conjoined in a vast network of *acquaintanceship*. Brown knows Jones, Jones knows Robinson, etc.; and *by choosing your farther intermediaries rightly* you may carry a message from Jones to the Empress of China, or the Chief of the African Pigmies, or to any one else in the inhabited world. But you are stopped short, as by a non-conductor, when you choose one man wrong in this experiment. What may be called love-systems are grafted on the acquaintance-system. A loves (or hates) B; B loves (or hates) C, etc. But these systems are smaller than the great acquaintance-system that they presuppose.

Human efforts are daily unifying the world more and more in definite systematic ways. We found colonial, postal, consular, commercial systems, all the parts of which obey definite influences that propagate themselves within the system but not to facts outside of it. The result is innumerable little hangings-together of the world's parts within the larger hangings-together, little worlds, not only of discourse but of operation, within the wider universe. Each system exemplifies one type or grade of union, its parts being strung on that peculiar kind of relation, and the same part may figure in many different systems, as a man may hold various offices and belong to several clubs. From this 'systematic' point of view, therefore, the pragmatic value of the world's unity is that all these definite networks actually and practically exist. Some are more enveloping and extensive, some less so; they are superposed upon each other; and between them all they let no individual elementary part of the universe escape. Enormous as is the amount of discon-nexion among things (for these systematic influences and conjunc-tions follow rigidly exclusive paths), everything that exists is influenced in *some* way by something else, if you can only pick the way out rightly. Loosely speaking, and in general, it may be said that all things cohere and adhere to each other *somehow*, and that the universe exists practically in reticulated or concatenated forms which make of it a continuous or 'integrated' affair. Any kind of influence whatever helps to make the world one, so far as you can follow it from next to next. You may then say that 'the world *is* One,' – meaning in these respects, namely, and just so far as they obtain. But just as definitely is it *not* One, so far as they do not obtain; and there is no species of connexion which will not fail, if, instead of choosing conductors for it you choose non-conductors. You are then arrested at your very first step and have to write the world down as a pure *many* from that particular point of view. If our intellect had been as much interested in disjunctive as it is in conjunctive relations, philosophy would have equally successfully celebrated the world's *disunion*.

The great point is to notice that the oneness and the manyness are absolutely co-ordinate here. Neither is primordial or more essential or excellent than the other. Just as with space, whose separating of things seems exactly on a par with its uniting of them, but some-times one function and sometimes the other is what comes home to us most, so, in our general dealings with the world of influences, we now need conductors and now need non-conductors, and wisdom lies in knowing which is which at the appropriate moment.

4. All these systems of influence or non-influence may be listed under the general problem of the world's *causal unity*. If the minor causal influences among things should converge towards one com-mon causal origin of them in the past, one great first cause for all that is, one might then speak of the absolute causal unity of the world. God's *fiat* on creation's day has figured in traditional philos-ophy as such an absolute cause and origin. Transcendental Idealism, translating 'creation' into 'thinking' (or 'willing to think')

calls the divine act 'eternal' rather than 'first'; but the union of the many here is absolute, just the same – the many would not *be*, save for the One. Against this notion of the unity of origin of all things there has always stood the pluralistic notion of an eternal self-existing many in the shape of atoms or even of spiritual units of some sort. The alternative has doubtless a pragmatic meaning, but perhaps, as far as these lectures go, we had better leave the question of unity of origin unsettled.

5. The most important sort of union that obtains among things, pragmatically speaking, is their *generic unity*. Things exist in kinds, there are many specimens in each kind, and what the 'kind' implies for one specimen, it implies also for every other specimen of that kind. We can easily conceive that every fact in the world might be singular, that is, unlike any other fact and sole of its kind. In such a world of singulars our logic would be useless, for logic works by predicating of the single instance what is true of all its kind. With no two things alike in the world, we should be unable to reason from our past experiences to our future ones. The existence of so much generic unity in things is thus perhaps the most momentous pragmatic specification of what it may mean to say 'the world is One.' *Absolute* generic unity would obtain if there were one *summum genus* under which all things without exception could be eventually subsumed. 'Beings,' 'thinkables,' 'experiences,' would be candidates for this position. Whether the alternatives expressed by such words have any pragmatic significance or not, is another question which I prefer to leave unsettled just now.

6. Another specification of what the phrase 'the world is one' may mean is *unity of purpose*. An enormous number of things in the world subserve a common purpose. All the man-made systems, administrative, industrial, military, or what not, exist each for its controlling purpose. Every living being pursues its own peculiar purposes. They co-operate, according to the degree of their development, in collective or tribal purposes, larger ends thus enveloping lesser ones, until an absolutely single, final and climacteric purpose subserved by all things without exception might conceivably be reached. It is needless to say that the appearances conflict with such a view. Any resultant, as I said in my third lecture, *may* have been purposed in advance, but none of the results we actually know in this world have in point of fact been purposed in advance in all their details. Men and nations start with a vague notion of being rich, or great, or good. Each step they make brings unfore-

seen chances into sight, and shuts out older vistas, and the specifications of the general purpose have to be daily changed. What is
reached in the end may be better or worse than what was proposed,
but it is always more complex and different.

Our different purposes also are at war with each other. Where
one can't crush the other out, they compromise; and the result is
again different from what any one distinctly proposed beforehand.
Vaguely and generally, much of what was purposed may be
gained; but everything makes strongly for the view that our world
is incompletely unified teleologically and is still trying to get its
unification better organized.

Whoever claims *absolute* teleological unity, saying that there is
one purpose that every detail of the universe subserves, dogmatizes
at his own risk. Theologians who dogmatize thus find it more and
more impossible, as our acquaintance with the warring interests of
the world's parts grows more concrete, to imagine what the one
climacteric purpose may possibly be like. We see indeed that certain
evils minister to ulterior goods, that the bitter makes the cocktail
better, and that a bit of danger or hardship puts us agreeably to our
trumps. We can vaguely generalize this into the doctrine that all the
evil in the universe is but instrumental to its greater perfection. But
the scale of the evil actually in sight defies all human tolerance; and
transcendental idealism, in the pages of a Bradley or a Royce,
brings us no farther than the book of Job did – God's ways are not
our ways, so let us put our hands upon our mouth. A God who can
relish such superfluities of horror is no God for human beings to
appeal to. His animal spirits are too high. In other words the
'Absolute' with his one purpose, is not the man-like God of common people.

7. *Aesthetic union* among things also obtains, and is very analogous to teleological union. Things tell a story. Their parts hang
together so as to work out a climax. They play into each other's
hands expressively. Retrospectively, we can see that altho no definite purpose presided over a chain of events, yet the events fell into
a dramatic form, with a start, a middle and a finish. In point of fact
all stories end; and here again the point of view of a many is the
more natural one to take. The world is full of partial stories that run
parallel to one another, beginning and ending at odd times. They
mutually interlace and interfere at points, but we can not unify them
completely in our minds. In following your life-history, I must
temporarily turn my attention from my own. Even a biographer of

twins would have to press them alternately upon his reader's attention.

It follows that whoever says that the whole world tells one story utters another of those monistic dogmas that a man believes at his risk. It is easy to see the world's history pluralistically, as a rope of which each fibre tells a separate tale; but to conceive of each cross-section of the rope as an absolutely single fact, and to sum the whole longitudinal series into one being living an undivided life, is harder. We have indeed the analogy of embryology to help us. The microscopist makes a hundred flat cross-sections of a given embryo, and mentally unites them into one solid whole. But the great world's ingredients, so far as they are beings, seem, like the rope's fibres, to be discontinuous, cross-wise, and to cohere only in the longitudinal direction. Followed in that direction they are many. Even the embryologist, when he follows the *development* of his object, has to treat the history of each single organ in turn. *Absolute* aesthetic union is thus another barely abstract ideal. The world appears as something more epic than dramatic.

So far, then, we see how the world is unified by its many systems, kinds, purposes, and dramas. That there is more union in all these ways than openly appears is certainly true. That there *may* be one sovereign purpose, system, kind, and story, is a legitimate hypothesis. All I say here is that it is rash to affirm this dogmatically without better evidence than we possess at present.

8. The *great* monistic *denkmittel* for a hundred years past has been the notion of *the one Knower*. The many exist only as objects for his thought – exist in his dream, as it were, and *as he knows* them, they have one purpose, form one system, tell one tale for him. This notion of an *all enveloping noetic unity* in things is the sublimest achievement of intellectualist philosophy. Those who believe in the Absolute, as the all-knower is termed, usually say that they do so for coercive reasons, which clear thinkers can not evade. The Absolute has far-reaching practical consequences, to some of which I drew attention in my second lecture. Many kinds of difference important to us would surely follow from its being true. I can not here enter into all the logical proofs of such a Being's existence, farther than to say that none of them seem to me sound. I must therefore treat the notion of an All-Knower simply as an hypothesis, exactly on a par logically with the pluralist notion that there is no point of view, no focus of information extant, from which the entire content of the universe is visible at once. "God's

conscience," says Professor Royce,[2] "forms in its wholeness one luminously transparent conscious moment" – this is the type of noetic unity on which rationalism insists. Empiricism on the other hand is satisfied with the type of noetic unity that is humanly familiar. Everything gets known by *some* knower along with something else; but the knowers may in the end be irreducibly many, and the greatest knower of them all may yet not know the whole of everything, or even know what he does know at one single stroke: – he may be liable to forget. Whichever type obtained, the world would still be a universe noetically. Its parts would be conjoined by knowledge, but in the one case the knowledge would be absolutely unified, in the other it would be strung along and overlapped.

The notion of one instantaneous or eternal Knower – either adjective here means the same thing – is, as I said, the great intellectualist achievement of our time. It has practically driven out that conception of 'Substance' which earlier philosophers set such store by, and by which so much unifying work used to be done – universal substance which alone has being in and from itself, and of which all the particulars of experience are but forms to which it gives support. Substance has succumbed to the pragmatic criticisms of the English school. It appears now only as another name for the fact that phenomena as they come are actually grouped and given in coherent forms, the very forms in which we finite knowers experience or think them together. These forms of conjunction are as much parts of the tissue of experience as are the terms which they connect; and it is a great pragmatic achievement for recent idealism to have made the world hang together in these directly representable ways instead of drawing its unity from the 'inherence' of its parts – whatever that may mean – in an unimaginable principle behind the scenes.

'The world is One,' therefore, just so far as we experience it to be concatenated, One by as many definite conjunctions as appear. But then also *not* One by just as many definite *dis*junctions as we find. The oneness and the manyness of it thus obtain in respects which can be separately named. It is neither a universe pure and simple nor a multiverse pure and simple. And its various manners of being One suggest, for their accurate ascertainment, so many distinct programs of scientific work. Thus the pragmatic question 'What is the oneness known as? What practical difference will it make?'

2 *The Conception of God*, New York, 1897, p. 292.

saves us from all feverish excitement over it as a principle of sublimity and carries us forward into the stream of experience with a cool head. The stream may indeed reveal far more connexion and union than we now suspect, but we are not entitled on pragmatic principles to claim absolute oneness in any respect in advance.

It is so difficult to see definitely what absolute oneness can mean, that probably the majority of you are satisfied with the sober attitude which we have reached. Nevertheless there are possibly some radically monistic souls among you who are not content to leave the one and the many on a par. Union of various grades, union of diverse types, union that stops at non-conductors, union that merely goes from next to next, and means in many cases outer nextness only, and not a more internal bond, union of concatenation, in short; all that sort of thing seems to you a halfway stage of thought. The oneness of things, superior to their manyness, you think must also be more deeply true, must be the more real aspect of the world. The pragmatic view, you are sure, gives us a universe imperfectly rational. The real universe must form an unconditional unit of being, something consolidated, with its parts co-implicated through. Only then could we consider our estate completely rational.

There is no doubt whatever that this ultra-monistic way of thinking means a great deal to many minds. "One Life, One Truth, one Love, one Principle, One Good, One God" – I quote from a Christian Science leaflet which the day's mail brings into my hands – beyond doubt such a confession of faith has pragmatically an emotional value, and beyond doubt the word 'one' contributes to the value quite as much as the other words. But if we try to realize *intellectually* what we can possibly *mean* by such a glut of oneness we are thrown right back upon our pragmatistic determinations again. It means either the mere name One, the universe of discourse; or it means the sum total of all the ascertainable particular conjunctions and concatenations; or, finally, it means some one vehicle of conjunction treated as all-inclusive, like one origin, one purpose, or one knower. In point of fact it always means one *knower* to those who take it intellectually to-day. The one knower involves, they think, the other forms of conjunction. His world must have all its parts co-implicated in the one logical-aesthetical-teleological unit-picture which is his eternal dream.

The character of the absolute knower's picture is however so impossible for us to represent clearly, that we may fairly suppose that the authority which absolute monism undoubtedly possesses, and probably always will possess over some persons, draws its strength far less from intellectual than from mystical grounds. To interpret absolute monism worthily, be a mystic. Mystical states of mind in every degree are shown by history, usually tho not always, to make for the monistic view. This is no proper occasion to enter upon the general subject of mysticism, but I will quote one mystical pronouncement to show just what I mean. The paragon of all monistic systems is the Vedânta philosophy of Hindostan, and the paragon of Vedântist missionaries was the late Swami Vivekanda who visited our shores some years ago. The method of Vedântism is the mystical method. You do not reason, but after going through a certain discipline *you see*, and having seen, you can report the truth. Vivekanda thus reports the truth in one of his lectures here:

"Where is there any more misery for him who sees this Oneness in the universe, this Oneness of life, Oneness of everything? . . . This separation between man and man, man and woman, man and child, nation from nation, earth from moon, moon from sun, this separation between atom and atom is the cause really of all the misery, and the Vedânta says this separation does not exist, it is not real. It is merely apparent, on the surface. In the heart of things there is unity still. If you go inside you find that unity between man and man, women and children, races and races, high and low, rich and poor, the gods and men: all are One, and animals too, if you go deep enough, and he who has attained to that has no more delusion. . . . Where is there any more delusion for him? What can delude him? He knows the reality of everything, the secret of everything. Where is there any more misery for him? What does he desire? He has traced the reality of everything unto the Lord, that centre, that Unity of everything, and that is Eternal Bliss, Eternal Knowledge, Eternal Existence. Neither death nor disease nor sorrow nor misery nor discontent is There. . . . In the Centre, the reality, there is no one to be mourned for, no one to be sorry for. He has penetrated everything, the Pure One, the Formless, the Bodiless, the Stainless, He the Knower, He the great Poet, the Self-Existent, He who is giving to every one what he deserves."

Observe how radical the character of the monism here is.

Separation is not simply overcome by the One, it is denied to exist. There is no many. We are not parts of the One; It has no parts; and since in a sense we undeniably *are*, it must be that each of us *is* the One, indivisibly and totally. *An Absolute One, and I that One*, – surely we have here a religion which, emotionally considered, has a high pragmatic value; it imparts a perfect sumptuosity of security. As our Swami says in another place:

"When man has seen himself as One with the infinite Being of the universe, when all separateness has ceased, when all men, all women, all angels, all gods, all animals, all plants, the whole universe has been melted into that oneness, then all fear disappears. Whom to fear? Can I hurt myself? Can I kill myself? Can I injure myself? Do you fear yourself? Then will all sorrow disappear. What can cause me sorrow? I am the One Existence of the universe. Then all jealousies will disappear; of whom to be jealous? Of myself? Then all bad feelings disappear. Against whom shall I have this bad feeling? Against myself? There is none in the universe but me . . . kill out this differentiation, kill out this superstition that there are many. 'He who, in this world of many, sees that One; he who, in this mass of insentiency, sees that One Sentient Being; he who in this world of shadow, catches that Reality, unto him belongs eternal peace, unto none else, unto none else.' "

We all have some ear for this monistic music: it elevates and reassures. We all have at least the germ of mysticism in us. And when our idealists recite their arguments for the Absolute, saying that the slightest union admitted anywhere carries logically absolute Oneness with it, and that the slightest separation admitted anywhere logically carries disunion remediless and complete, I cannot help suspecting that the palpable weak places in the intellectual reasonings they use are protected from their own criticism by a mystical feeling that, logic or no logic, absolute Oneness must somehow at any cost be true. Oneness overcomes *moral* separateness at any rate. In the passion of love we have the mystic germ of what might mean a total union of all sentient life. This mystical germ wakes up in us on hearing the monistic utterances, acknowledges their authority, and assigns to intellectual considerations a secondary place.

I will dwell no longer on these religious and moral aspects of the question in this lecture. When I come to my final lecture there will be something more to say.

Leave then out of consideration for the moment the authority which mystical insights may be conjectured eventually to possess; treat the problem of the One and the Many in a purely intellectual way; and we see clearly enough where pragmatism stands. With her criterion of the practical differences that theories make, we see that she must equally abjure absolute monism and absolute pluralism. The world is One just so far as its parts hang together by any definite connexion. It is many just so far as any definite connexion fails to obtain. And finally it is growing more and more unified by those systems of connexion at least which human energy keeps framing as time goes on.

It is possible to imagine alternative universes to the one we know, in which the most various grades and types of union should be embodied. Thus the lowest grade of universe would be a world of mere *withness*, of which the parts were only strung together by the conjunction 'and.' Such a universe is even now the collection of our several inner lives. The spaces and times of your imagination, the objects and events of your day-dreams are not only more or less incoherent *inter se*, but are wholly out of definite relation with the similar contents of any one else's mind. Our various reveries now as we sit here compenetrate each other idly without influencing or interfering. They coexist, but in no order and in no receptacle, being the nearest approach to an absolute 'many' that we can conceive. We can not even imagine any reason why they *should* be known all together, and we can imagine even less, if they were known together, how they could be known as one systematic whole.

But add our sensations and bodily actions, and the union mounts to a much higher grade. Our *audita et visa* and our acts fall into those receptacles of time and space in which each event finds its date and place. They form 'things' and are of 'kinds' too, and can be classed. Yet we can imagine a world of things and of kinds in which the causal interactions with which we are so familiar should not exist. Everything there might be inert towards everything else, and refuse to propagate its influence. Or gross mechanical influences might pass, but no chemical action. Such worlds would be far less unified than ours. Again there might be complete physico-chemical interaction, but no minds; or minds, but altogether private ones, with no social life; or social life limited to acquaintance, but no love; or love, but no customs or institutions that should systematize it. No one of these grades of universe would be absolutely irrational or disintegrated, inferior tho it might appear when looked at from the higher grades. For instance, if our minds should ever become 'telepathically' connected, so that we knew immediately, or could under certain conditions know immediately, each what the other was thinking, the world we now live in would appear to the thinkers in that world to have been of an inferior grade.

With the whole of past eternity open for our conjectures to range in, it may be lawful to wonder whether the various kinds of union now realized in the universe that we inhabit may not possibly have been successively evolved after the fashion in which we now see human systems evolving in consequence of human needs. If such an hypothesis were legitimate, total oneness would appear at the end of things rather than at their origin. In other words the notion of the 'Absolute' would have to be replaced by that of the 'Ultimate'. The two notions would have the same content – the maximally unified content of fact, namely – but their time-relations would be positively reversed.[3]

After discussing the unity of the universe in this pragmatic way, you ought to see why I said in my second lecture, borrowing the word from my friend G. Papini, that pragmatism tends to *unstiffen* all our theories. The world's oneness has generally been affirmed abstractly only, and as if any one who questioned it must be an idiot. The temper of monists has been so vehement, as almost at times to be convulsive; and this way of holding a doctrine does not easily go with reasonable discussion and the drawing of distinctions. The theory of the Absolute, in particular, has had to be an article of faith, affirmed dogmatically and exclusively. The One and All, first in the order of being and of knowing, logically necessary itself, and uniting all lesser things in the bonds of mutual necessity, how could it allow of any mitigation of its inner rigidity? The slightest suspicion of pluralism, the minutest wiggle of independence of any one of its parts from the control of the totality would ruin it. Absolute unity brooks no degrees, – as well might you claim absolute purity for a glass of water because it contains but a single little cholera-germ. The independence, however infini-

3 Compare on the Ultimate, Mr. Schiller's essay "Activity and Substance," in his book entitled *Humanism*, p. 204.

tesimal, of a part, however small, would be to the Absolute as fatal as a cholera-germ.

Pluralism on the other hand has no need of this dogmatic rigoristic temper. Provided you grant *some* separation among things, some tremor of independence, some free play of parts on one another, some real novelty or chance, however minute, she is amply satisfied, and will allow you any amount, however great, of real union. How much of union there may be is a question that she thinks can only be decided empirically. The amount may be enormous, colossal; but absolute monism is shattered if, along with all the union, there has to be granted the slightest modicum, the most incipient nascency, or the most residual trace, of a separation that is not 'overcome.'

Pragmatism, pending the final empirical ascertainment of just what the balance of union and disunion among things may be, must obviously range herself upon the pluralistic side. Some day, she admits, even total union, with one knower, one origin, and a universe consolidated in every conceivable way, may turn out to be the most acceptable of all hypotheses. Meanwhile the opposite hypothesis, of a world imperfectly unified still, and perhaps always to remain so, must be sincerely entertained. This latter hypothesis is pluralism's doctrine. Since absolute monism forbids its being even considered seriously, branding it as irrational from the start, it is clear that pragmatism must turn its back on absolute monism, and follow pluralism's more empirical path.

This leaves us with the common-sense world, in which we find things partly joined and partly disjoined. 'Things,' then, and their 'conjunctions' – what do such words mean, pragmatically handled? In my next lecture, I will apply the pragmatic method to the stage of philosophizing known as Common Sense.

LECTURE V
PRAGMATISM AND COMMON SENSE

In the last lecture we turned ourselves from the usual way of talking of the universe's oneness as a principle, sublime in all its blankness, towards a study of the special kinds of union which the universe enfolds. We found many of these to coexist with kinds of separation equally real. 'How far am I verified?' is the question which each kind of union and each kind of separation asks us here, so as good pragmatists we have to turn our face towards experience, towards 'facts.'

Absolute oneness remains, but only as an hypothesis, and that hypothesis is reduced nowadays to that of an omniscient knower who sees all things without exception as forming one single systematic fact. But the knower in question may still be conceived either as an Absolute or as an Ultimate; and over against the hypothesis of him in either form the counter-hypothesis that the widest field of knowledge that ever was or will be still contains some ignorance, may be legitimately held. Some bits of information always may escape.

This is the hypothesis of *noetic pluralism*, which monists consider so absurd. Since we are bound to treat it as respectfully as noetic monism, until the facts shall have tipped the beam, we find that our pragmatism, tho originally nothing but a method, has forced us to be friendly to the pluralistic view. It *may* be that some parts of the world are connected so loosely with some other parts as to be strung along by nothing but the copula *and*. They might even come and go without those other parts suffering any internal change. This pluralistic view, of a world of *additive* constitution, is one that pragmatism is unable to rule out from serious consideration. But this view leads one to the farther hypothesis that the actual world, instead of being complete 'eternally,' as the monists assure us, may be eternally incomplete, and at all times subject to addition or liable to loss.

It *is* at any rate incomplete in one respect, and flagrantly so. The very fact that we debate this question shows that *our knowledge* is incomplete at present and subject to addition. In respect of the knowledge it contains the world does genuinely change and grow. Some general remarks on the way in which our knowledge completes itself – when it does complete itself – will lead us very conveniently into our subject for this lecture, which is 'Common Sense.'

To begin with, our knowledge grows *in spots*. The spots may be large or small, but the knowledge never grows all over: some old knowledge always remains what it was. Your knowledge of pragmatism, let us suppose, is growing now. Later, its growth may involve considerable modification of opinions which you previously held to be true. But such modifications are apt to be gradual. To take the nearest possible example, consider these lectures of mine. What you first gain from them is probably a small amount of new information, a few new definitions, or distinctions, or points of view. But while these special ideas are being added, the rest of your knowledge stands still, and only gradually will you 'line up' your previous opinions with the novelties I am trying to instil, and modify to some slight degree their mass.

You listen to me now, I suppose, with certain prepossessions as to my competency, and these affect your reception of what I say, but were I suddenly to break off lecturing, and to begin to sing 'We won't go home till morning' in a rich baritone voice, not only would that new fact be added to your stock, but it would oblige you to define me differently, and that might alter your opinion of the pragmatic philosophy, and in general bring about a rearrangement of a number of your ideas. Your mind in such processes is strained, and sometimes painfully so, between its older beliefs and the novelties which experience brings along.

Our minds thus grow in spots; and like grease-spots, the spots spread. But we let them spread as little as possible: we keep unaltered as much of our old knowledge, as many of our old prejudices and beliefs, as we can. We patch and tinker more than we renew. The novelty soaks in; it stains the ancient mass; but it is also tinged by what absorbs it. Our past apperceives and co-operates; and in the new equilibrium in which each step forward in the process of learning terminates, it happens relatively seldom that the new fact is added *raw*. More usually it is embedded cooked, as one might say, or stewed down in the sauce of the old.

New truths thus are resultants of new experiences and of old truths combined and mutually modifying one another. And since this is the case in the changes of opinion of to-day, there is no reason to assume that it has not been so at all times. It follows that very ancient modes of thought may have survived through all the later changes in men's opinions. The most primitive ways of thinking may not yet be wholly expunged. Like our five fingers, our ear-bones, our rudimentary caudal appendage, or our other 'vestigial' peculiarities, they may remain as indelible tokens of events in our race-history. Our ancestors may at certain moments have struck into ways of thinking which they might conceivably not have found. But once they did so, and after the fact, the inheritance continues. When you begin a piece of music in a certain key, you must keep the key to the end. You may alter your house *ad libitum*, but the ground-plan of the first architect persists – you can make great changes, but you can not change a Gothic church into a Doric temple. You may rinse and rinse the bottle, but you can't get the taste of the medicine or whiskey that first filled it wholly out.

My thesis now is this, that *our fundamental ways of thinking about things are discoveries of exceedingly remote ancestors, which have been able to preserve themselves throughout the experience of all subsequent time.* They form one great stage of equilibrium in the human mind's development, the stage of *common sense.* Other stages have grafted themselves upon this stage, but have never succeeded in displacing it. Let us consider this common-sense stage first, as if it might be final.

In practical talk, a man's common sense means his good judgment, his freedom from excentricity, his *gumption*, to use the vernacular word. In philosophy it means something entirely different, it means his use of certain intellectual forms or categories of thought. Were we lobsters, or bees, it might be that our organization would have led to our using quite different modes from these of apprehending our experiences. It *might* be too (we can not dogmatically deny this) that such categories, unimaginable by us to-day, would have proved on the whole as serviceable for handling our experiences mentally as those which we actually use.

If this sounds paradoxical to any one, let him think of analytical geometry. The identical figures which Euclid defined by intrinsic relations were defined by Descartes by the relations of their points to adventitious co-ordinates, the result being an absolutely different and vastly more potent way of handling curves. All our conceptions are what the Germans call *Denkmittel*, means by which we handle facts by thinking them. Experience merely as such doesn't come ticketed and labelled, we have first to discover what it is. Kant speaks of it as being in its first intention a *gewühl der erschein-*

ungen, a *rhapsodie der wahrnehmungen*, a mere motley which we have to unify by our wits. What we usually do is first to frame some system of concepts mentally classified, serialized, or connected in some intellectual way, and then to use this as a tally by which we 'keep tab' on the impressions that present themselves. When each is referred to some possible place in the conceptual system, it is thereby 'understood.' This notion of parallel 'manifolds' with their elements standing reciprocally in 'one-to-one relation,' is proving so convenient nowadays in mathematics and logic as to supersede more and more the older classificatory conceptions. There are many conceptual systems of this sort; and the sense manifold is also such a system. Find a one-to-one relation for your sense-impressions *anywhere* among the concepts, and in so far forth you rationalize the impressions. But obviously you can rationalize them by using various conceptual systems.

The old common-sense way of rationalizing them is by a set of concepts of which the most important are these:

Thing;
The same or different;
Kinds;
Minds;
Bodies;
One Time;
One Space;
Subjects and attributes;
Causal influences;
The fancied;
The real.

We are now so familiar with the order that these notions have woven for us out of the everlasting weather of our perceptions that we find it hard to realize how little of a fixed routine the perceptions follow when taken by themselves. The word weather is a good one to use here. In Boston, for example, the weather has almost no routine, the only law being that if you have had any weather for two days, you will probably but not certainly have another weather on the third. Weather-experience as it thus comes to Boston is discontinuous, and chaotic. In point of temperature, of wind, rain or sunshine, it *may* change three times a day. But the Washington weather-bureau intellectualizes this disorder by making each successive bit of Boston weather *episodic*. It refers it to its place and moment in a continental cyclone, on the history of which the local changes everywhere are strung as beads are strung upon a cord.

Now it seems almost certain that young children and the inferior animals take all their experiences very much as uninstructed Bostonians take their weather. They know no more of time, or space, as world-receptacles, or of permanent subjects and changing predicates, or of causes, or kinds, or thoughts, or things, than our common people know of continental cyclones. A baby's rattle drops out of his hand, but the baby looks not for it. It has 'gone out' for him, as a candle-flame goes out; and it comes back, when you replace it in his hand, as the flame comes back when relit. The idea of its being a 'thing,' whose permanent existence by itself he might interpolate between its successive apparitions, has evidently not occurred to him. It is the same with dogs. Out of sight, out of mind, with them. It is pretty evident that they have no *general* tendency to interpolate 'things.' Let me quote here a passage from my colleague G. Santayana's book.

"If a dog, while sniffing about contentedly, sees his master arriving after a long absence . . . the poor brute asks for no reason why his master went, why he has come again, why he should be loved, or why presently while lying at his feet you forget him and begin to grunt and dream of the chase – all that is an utter mystery, utterly unconsidered. Such experience has variety, scenery, and a certain vital rhythm; its story might be told in dithyrambic verse. It moves wholly by inspiration; every event is providential, every act unpremeditated. Absolute freedom and absolute helplessness have met together: you depend wholly on divine favor, yet that unfathomable agency is not distinguishable from your own life . . . [But] the figures even of that disordered drama have their exits and their entrances; and their cues can be gradually discovered by a being capable of fixing his attention and retaining the order of events. . . . In proportion as such understanding advances, each moment of experience becomes consequential and prophetic of the rest. The calm places in life are filled with power and its spasms with resource. No emotion can overwhelm the mind, for of none is the basis or issue wholly hidden; no event can disconcert it altogether, because it sees beyond. Means can be looked for to escape from the worst predicament; and whereas each moment had been formerly filled with nothing but its own adventures and surprised emotion, each now makes room for the lesson of what went before and surmises what may be the plot of the whole. "[1]

Even to-day science and philosophy are still laboriously trying to part fancies from realities in our experience; and in primitive times they made only the most incipient distinctions in this line. Men believed whatever they thought with any liveliness, and they mixed their dreams with their realities inextricably. The categories of 'thought' and 'things' are indispensable here – instead of being realities we now call certain experiences only 'thoughts.' There is not a category, among those enumerated, of which we may not imagine the use to have thus originated historically and only gradually spread.

That one Time which we all believe in and in which each event has its definite date, that one Space in which each thing has its position, these abstract notions unify the world incomparably; but in their finished shape as concepts how different they are from the loose unordered time-and-space experiences of natural men! Everything that happens to us brings its own duration and extension, and both are vaguely surrounded by a marginal 'more' that runs into the duration and extension of the next thing that comes. But we soon lose all our definite bearings; and not only do our children make no distinction between yesterday and the day before yesterday, the whole past being churned up together, but we adults still do so whenever the times are large. It is the same with spaces. On a map I can distinctly see the relation of London, Constantinople and Pekin to the place where I am; in reality I utterly fail to *feel* the facts which the map symbolizes. The directions and distances are vague, confused and mixed. Cosmic space and cosmic time, so far from being the intuitions that Kant said they were, are constructions as patently artificial as any that science can show. The great majority of the human race never use these notions, but live in plural times and spaces, interpenetrant and *durcheinander*.

Permanent 'things' again; the 'same' thing and its various 'appearances' and 'alterations'; the different 'kinds' of thing; with the 'kind' used finally as a 'predicate,' of which the thing remains the 'subject' – what a straightening of the tangle of our experience's immediate flux and sensible variety does this list of terms suggest! And it is only the smallest part of his experience's flux that any one

1 *The Life of Reason: Reason in Common Sense*, 1905, p. 59.

actually does straighten out by applying to it these conceptual instruments. Out of them all our lowest ancestors probably used only, and then most vaguely and inaccurately, the notion of 'the same again'. But even then if you had asked them whether the same were a 'thing' that had endured throughout the unseen interval, they would probably have been at a loss, and would have said that they had never asked that question, or considered matters in that light.

Kinds, and sameness of kind – what colossally useful *denkmittel* for finding our way among the many! The manyness might conceivably have been absolute. Experiences might have all been singulars, no one of them occurring twice. In such a world logic would have had no application; for kind and sameness of kind are logic's only instruments. Once we know that whatever is of a kind is also of that kind's kind, we can travel through the universe as if with seven-league boots. Brutes surely never use these abstractions, and civilized men use them in most various amounts.

Causal influence, again! This, if anything, seems to have been an antediluvian conception; for we find primitive men thinking that almost everything is significant and can exert influence of some sort. The search for the more definite influences seems to have started in the question: "Who, or what, is to blame?" – for any illness, namely, or disaster, or untoward thing. From this centre the search for causal influences has spread. Hume and 'Science' together have tried to eliminate the whole notion of influence, substituting the entirely different *denkmittel* of 'law.' But law is a comparatively recent invention, and influence reigns supreme in the older realm of common sense.

The 'possible,' as something less than the actual and more than the wholly unreal, is another of these magisterial notions of common sense. Criticise them as you may, they persist; and we fly back to them the moment critical pressure is relaxed. 'Self,' 'body,' in the substantial or metaphysical sense – no one escapes subjection to *those* forms of thought. In practice, the common-sense *denkmittel* are uniformly victorious. Every one, however instructed, still thinks of a 'thing' in the common-sense way, as a permanent unit-subject that 'supports' its attributes interchangeably. No one stably or sincerely uses the more critical notion, of a group of sense-qualities united by a law. With these categories in our hand, we make our plans and plot together, and connect all the remoter parts of experience with what lies before our eyes. Our later and more critical philosophies are mere fads and fancies compared with this natural mother-tongue of thought.

Common sense appears thus as a perfectly definite stage in our understanding of things, a stage that satisfies in an extraordinarily successful way the purposes for which we think. 'Things' do exist, even when we do not see them. Their 'kinds' also exist. Their 'qualities' are what they act by, and are what we act on; and these also exist. These lamps shed their quality of light on every object in this room. We intercept *it* on its way whenever we hold up an opaque screen. It is the very sound that my lips emit that travels into your ears. It is the sensible heat of the fire that migrates into the water in which we boil an egg; and we can change the heat into coolness by dropping in a lump of ice. At this stage of philosophy all non-European men without exception have remained. It suffices for all the necessary practical ends of life; and, among our race even, it is only the highly sophisticated specimens, the minds debauched by learning, as Berkeley calls them, who have ever even suspected common sense of not being absolutely true.

But when we look back, and speculate as to how the common-sense categories may have achieved their wonderful supremacy, no reason appears why it may not have been by a process just like that by which the conceptions due to Democritus, Berkeley, or Darwin, achieved their similar triumphs in more recent times. In other words, they may have been successfully *discovered* by prehistoric geniuses whose names the night of antiquity has covered up; they may have been verified by the immediate facts of experience which they first fitted; and then from fact to fact and from man to man they may have *spread*, until all language rested on them and we are now incapable of thinking naturally in any other terms. Such a view would only follow the rule that has proved elsewhere so fertile, of assuming the vast and remote to conform to the laws of formation that we can observe at work in the small and near.

For all utilitarian practical purposes these conceptions amply suffice; but that they began at special points of discovery and only gradually spread from one thing to another, seems proved by the exceedingly dubious limits of their application to-day. We assume for certain purposes one 'objective' Time that *aequabiliter fluit*, but we don't livingly believe in or realize any such equally-flowing time. 'Space' is a less vague notion; but 'things,' what are they? Is a constellation properly a thing? or an army? or is an *ens rationis* such as space or justice a thing? Is a knife whose handle and blade are changed the 'same'? Is the 'changeling,' whom Locke so seriously discusses, of the human 'kind'? Is 'telepathy' a 'fancy' or a 'fact'? The moment you pass beyond the practical use of these categories (a use usually suggested sufficiently by the circumstances of the special case) to a merely curious or speculative way of thinking, you find it impossible to say within just what limits of fact any one of them shall apply.

The peripatetic philosophy, obeying rationalist propensities, has tried to eternalize the common-sense categories by treating them very technically and articulately. A 'thing' for instance is a being, or *ens*. An *ens* is a subject in which qualities 'inhere.' A subject is a substance. Substances are of kinds, and kinds are definite in number, and discrete. These distinctions are fundamental and eternal. As terms of *discourse* they are indeed magnificently useful, but what they mean, apart from their use in steering our discourse to profitable issues, does not appear. If you ask a scholastic philosopher what a substance may be in itself, apart from its being the support of attributes, he simply says that your intellect knows perfectly what the word means.

But what the intellect knows clearly is only the word itself and its steering function. So it comes about that intellects *sibi permissi*, intellects only curious and idle, have forsaken the common-sense level for what in general terms may be called the 'critical' level of thought. Not merely *such* intellects either – your Humes and Berkeleys and Hegels; but practical observers of facts, your Galileos, Daltons, Faradays, have found it impossible to treat the *naïfs* sense-termini of common sense as ultimately real. As common sense interpolates her constant 'things' between our intermittent sensations, so science *extra*polates her world of 'primary' qualities, her atoms, her ether, her magnetic fields, and the like, beyond the common-sense world. The 'things' are now invisible impalpable things; and the old visible common-sense things are supposed to result from the mixture of these invisibles. Or else the whole *naïf* conception of thing gets superseded, and a thing's name is interpreted as denoting only the law or *regel der verbindung* by which certain of our sensations habitually succeed or coexist.

Science and critical philosophy thus burst the bounds of common sense. With science *naïf* realism ceases: 'Secondary' qualities become unreal; primary ones alone remain. With critical philosophy, havoc is made of everything. The common-sense categories one and all cease to represent anything in the way of *being*; they are but sublime tricks of human thought, our ways of escaping bewilderment in the midst of sensation's irremediable flow.

But the scientific tendency in critical thought, tho inspired at first by purely intellectual motives, has opened an entirely unexpected range of practical utilities to our astonished view. Galileo gave us accurate clocks and accurate artillery-practice; the chemists flood us with new medicines and dye-stuffs; Ampère and Faraday have endowed us with the New York subway and with Marconi telegrams. The hypothetical things that such men have invented, defined as they have defined them, are showing an extraordinary fertility in consequences verifiable by sense. Our logic can deduce from them a consequence due under certain conditions, we can then bring about the conditions, and presto, the consequence is there before our eyes. The scope of the practical control of nature newly put into our hand by scientific ways of thinking vastly exceeds the scope of the old control grounded on common sense. Its rate of increase accelerates so that no one can trace the limit; one may even fear that the *being* of man may be crushed by his own powers, that his fixed nature as an organism may not prove adequate to stand the strain of the ever increasingly tremendous functions, almost divine creative functions, which his intellect will more and more enable him to wield. He may drown in his wealth like a child in a bath-tub, who has turned on the water and who can not turn it off.

The philosophic stage of criticism, much more thorough in its negations than the scientific stage, so far gives us no new range of practical power. Locke, Hume, Berkeley, Kant, Hegel, have all been utterly sterile, so far as shedding any light on the details of nature goes, and I can think of no invention or discovery that can be directly traced to anything in their peculiar thought, for neither with Berkeley's tar-water nor with Kant's nebular hypothesis had their respective philosophic tenets anything to do. The satisfactions they yield to their disciples are intellectual, not practical; and even then we have to confess that there is a large minus-side to the account.

There are thus at least three well-characterized levels, stages or types of thought about the world we live in, and the notions of one stage have one kind of merit, those of another stage another kind. It is impossible, however, to say that any stage as yet in sight is absolutely more *true* than any other. Common sense is the more *consolidated* stage, because it got its innings first, and made all language into its ally. Whether it or science be the more *august* stage may be left to private judgment. But neither consolidation nor augustness are decisive marks of truth. If common sense were true, why should science have had to brand the secondary qualities, to which our world owes all its living interest, as false, and to invent an invisible world of points and curves, and mathematical equations instead? Why should it have needed to transform causes and activities into laws of 'functional variation'? Vainly did scholasticism, common sense's college-trained younger sister, seek to stereotype the forms the human family had always talked with, to make them definite and fix them for eternity. Substantial forms (in other words our secondary qualities) hardly outlasted the year of our Lord 1600. People were already tired of them then; and Galileo, and Descartes, with his 'new philosophy,' gave them only a little later their *coup de grâce*.

But now if the new kinds of scientific 'thing,' the corpuscular and etheric world, were essentially more 'true,' why should they have excited so much criticism within the body of science itself? Scientific logicians are saying on every hand that these entities and their determinations, however definitely conceived, should not be held for literally real. It is *as if* they existed; but in reality they are like co-ordinates or logarithms, only artificial short-cuts for taking us from one part to another of experience's flux. We can cipher fruitfully with them; they serve us wonderfully; but we must not be their dupes.

There is no *ringing* conclusion possible when we compare these types of thinking, with a view to telling which is the more absolutely true. Their naturalness, their intellectual economy, their fruitfulness for practice, all start up as distinct tests of their veracity, and as a result we get confused. Common sense is *better* for one sphere of life, science for another, philosophic criticism for a third; but whether either be *truer* absolutely, Heaven only knows. Just now, if I understand the matter rightly, we are witnessing a curious reversion to the common sense way of looking at physical nature, in the philosophy of science favored by such men as Mach, Ostwald and Duhem. According to these teachers no hypothesis is truer than any other in the sense of being a more literal copy of reality. They are all but ways of talking on our part, to be compared solely from the point of view of their *use*. The only literally true thing is *reality*; and the only reality we know is, for these logicians, sensible reality, the flux of our sensations and emotions as they pass. 'Energy' is the collective name (according to Ostwald) for the sensations just as they present themselves (the movement, heat, magnetic pull, or light, or whatever it may be) when they are measured in certain ways. So measuring them, we are enabled to describe the correlated changes which they show us, in formulas matchless for their simplicity and fruitfulness for human use. They are sovereign triumphs of economy in thought.

No one can fail to admire the 'energetic' philosophy. But the hypersensible entities, the corpuscles and vibrations, hold their own with most physicists and chemists, in spite of its appeal. It seems too economical to be all-sufficient. Profusion, not economy, may after all be reality's key-note.

I am dealing here with highly technical matters, hardly suitable for popular lecturing, and in which my own competence is small. All the better for my conclusion, however, which at this point is this. The whole notion of truth, which naturally and without reflexion we assume to mean the simple duplication by the mind of a ready-made and given reality, proves hard to understand clearly. There is no simple test available for adjudicating off-hand between the divers types of thought that claim to possess it. Common sense, common science or corpuscular philosophy, ultra-critical science, or energetic, and critical or idealistic philosophy, all seem insufficiently true in some regard and leave some dissatisfaction. It is evident that the conflict of these so widely differing systems obliges us to overhaul the very idea of truth, for at present we have no definite notion of what the word may mean. I shall face that task in my next lecture, and will add but a few words, in finishing the present one.

There are only two points that I wish you to retain from the present lecture. The first one relates to common sense. We have seen reason to suspect it, to suspect that in spite of their being so venerable, of their being so universally used and built into the very structure of language, its categories may after all be only a collection of extraordinarily successful hypotheses (historically discovered or invented by single men, but gradually communicated, and used by everybody) by which our forefathers have from time immemorial unified and straightened the discontinuity of their immediate experiences, and put themselves into an equilibrium with the surface of nature so satisfactory for ordinary practical purposes that it certainly would have lasted forever, but for the excessive intellectual vivacity of Democritus, Archimedes, Galileo,

Berkeley, and of other excentric geniuses whom the example of such men inflamed. Retain, I pray you, this suspicion about common sense.

The other point is this. Ought not the existence of the various types of thinking which we have reviewed, each so splendid for certain purposes, yet all conflicting still, and neither one of them able to support a claim of absolute veracity, to awaken a presumption favorable to the pragmatistic view that all our theories are *instrumental*, are mental modes of *adaptation* to reality, rather than revelations or gnostic answers to some divinely instituted world-enigma? I expressed this view as clearly as I could in the second of these lectures. Certainly the restlessness of the actual theoretic situation, the value for some purposes of each thought-level, and the inability of either to expel the others decisively, suggest this pragmatistic view, which I hope that the next lectures may soon make entirely convincing. May there not after all be a possible ambiguity in truth?

LECTURE VI
PRAGMATISM'S CONCEPTION OF TRUTH

When Clerk-Maxwell was a child it is written that he had a mania for having everything explained to him, and that when people put him off with vague verbal accounts of any phenomenon he would interrupt them impatiently by saying, 'Yes; but I want you to tell me the *particular go* of it!' Had his question been about truth, only a pragmatist could have told him the particular go of it. I believe that our contemporary pragmatists, especially Messrs. Schiller and Dewey, have given the only tenable account of this subject. It is a very ticklish subject, sending subtle rootlets into all kinds of crannies, and hard to treat in the sketchy way that alone befits a public lecture. But the Schiller–Dewey view of truth has been so ferociously attacked by rationalistic philosophers, and so abominably misunderstood, that here, if anywhere, is the point where a clear and simple statement should be made.

I fully expect to see the pragmatist view of truth run through the classic stages of a theory's career. First, you know, a new theory is attacked as absurd; then it is admitted to be true, but obvious and insignificant; finally it is seen to be so important that its adversaries claim that they themselves discovered it. Our doctrine of truth is at present in the first of these three stages, with symptoms of the second stage having begun in certain quarters. I wish that this lecture might help it beyond the first stage in the eyes of many of you.

Truth, as any dictionary will tell you, is a property of certain of our ideas. It means their 'agreement,' as falsity means their disagreement, with 'reality.' Pragmatists and intellectualists both accept this definition as a matter of course. They begin to quarrel only after the question is raised as to what may precisely be meant by the term 'agreement,' and what by the term 'reality,' when reality is taken as something for our ideas to agree with.

In answering these questions the pragmatists are more analytic and painstaking, the intellectualists more offhand and irreflective. The popular notion is that a true idea must copy its reality. Like other popular views, this one follows the analogy of the most usual experience. Our true ideas of sensible things do indeed copy them. Shut your eyes and think of yonder clock on the wall, and you get just such a true picture or copy of its dial. But your idea of its 'works' (unless you are a clockmaker) is much less of a copy, yet it passes muster, for it in no way clashes with the reality. Even though it should shrink to the mere word 'works,' that word still serves you truly; and when you speak of the 'time-keeping function' of the clock, or of its spring's 'elasticity,' it is hard to see exactly what your ideas can copy.

You perceive that there is a problem here. Where our ideas cannot copy definitely their object, what does agreement with that object mean? Some idealists seem to say that they are true whenever they are what God means that we ought to think about that object. Others hold the copy-view all through, and speak as if our ideas possessed truth just in proportion as they approach to being copies of the Absolute's eternal way of thinking.

These views, you see, invite pragmatistic discussion. But the great assumption of the intellectualists is that truth means essentially an inert static relation. When you've got your true idea of anything, there's an end of the matter. You're in possession; you *know*; you have fulfilled your thinking destiny. You are where you ought to be mentally; you have obeyed your categorical imperative; and nothing more need follow on that climax of your rational destiny. Epistemologically you are in stable equilibrium.

Pragmatism, on the other hand, asks its usual question. "Grant an idea or belief to be true," it says, "what concrete difference will its being true make in any one's actual life? How will the truth be realized? What experiences will be different from those which would obtain if the belief were false? What, in short, is the truth's cash-value in experiential terms?"

The moment pragmatism asks this question, it sees the answer: *True ideas are those that we can assimilate, validate, corroborate and verify. False ideas are those that we can not.* That is the practical difference it makes to us to have true ideas; that, therefore, is the meaning of truth, for it is all that truth is known-as.

This thesis is what I have to defend. The truth of an idea is not a stagnant property inherent in it. Truth *happens* to an idea. It *becomes* true, is *made* true by events. Its verity *is* in fact an event, a process: the process namely of its verifying itself, its veri-*fication*. Its validity is the process of its valid-*ation*.

But what do the words verification and validation themselves pragmatically mean? They again signify certain practical consequences of the verified and validated idea. It is hard to find any one phrase that characterizes these consequences better than the ordinary agreement-formula – just such consequences being what we have in mind whenever we say that our ideas 'agree' with reality. They lead us, namely, through the acts and other ideas which they instigate, into or up to, or towards, other parts of experience with which we feel all the while – such feeling being among our potentialities – that the original ideas remain in agreement. The connexions and transitions come to us from point to point as being progressive, harmonious, satisfactory. This function of agreeable leading is what we mean by an idea's verification. Such an account is vague and it sounds at first quite trivial, but it has results which it will take the rest of my hour to explain.

Let me begin by reminding you of the fact that the possession of true thoughts means everywhere the possession of invaluable instruments of action; and that our duty to gain truth, so far from being a blank command from out of the blue, or a 'stunt' self-imposed by our intellect, can account for itself by excellent practical reasons.

The importance to human life of having true beliefs about matters of fact is a thing too notorious. We live in a world of realities that can be infinitely useful or infinitely harmful. Ideas that tell us which of them to expect count as the true ideas in all this primary sphere of verification, and the pursuit of such ideas is a primary human duty. The possession of truth, so far from being here an end in itself, is only a preliminary means towards other vital satisfactions. If I am lost in the woods and starved, and find what looks like a cow-path, it is of the utmost importance that I should think of a human habitation at the end of it, for if I do so and follow it, I save myself. The true thought is useful here because the house which is its object is useful. The practical value of true ideas is thus primarily derived from the practical importance of their objects to us. Their objects are, indeed, not important at all times. I may on another occasion have no use for the house; and then my idea of it, however verifiable, will be practically irrelevant, and had better remain latent. Yet since almost any object may some day become temporarily important, the advantage of having a general stock of *extra* truths, of ideas that shall be true of merely possible situations, is obvious. We store such extra truths away in our memories, and with the overflow we fill our books of reference. Whenever such an extra truth becomes practically relevant to one of our emergencies, it passes from cold-storage to do work in the world and our belief in it grows active. You can say of it then either that 'it is useful because it is true' or that 'it is true because it is useful.' Both these phrases mean exactly the same thing, namely that here is an idea that gets fulfilled and can be verified. True is the name for whatever idea starts the verification-process, useful is the name for its completed function in experience. True ideas would never have been singled out as such, would never have acquired a class-name, least of all a name suggesting value, unless they had been useful from the outset in this way.

From this simple cue pragmatism gets her general notion of truth as something essentially bound up with the way in which one moment in our experience may lead us towards other moments which it will be worth while to have been led to. Primarily, and on the common-sense level, the truth of a state of mind means this function of *a leading that is worth while*. When a moment in our experience, of any kind whatever, inspires us with a thought that is true, that means that sooner or later we dip by that thought's guidance into the particulars of experience again and make advantageous connexion with them. This is a vague enough statement, but I beg you to retain it, for it is essential.

Our experience meanwhile is all shot through with regularities. One bit of it can warn us to get ready for another bit, can 'intend' or be 'significant of' that remoter object. The object's advent is the significance's verification. Truth, in these cases, meaning nothing but eventual verification, is manifestly incompatible with waywardness on our part. Woe to him whose beliefs play fast and loose with the order which realities follow in his experience; they will lead him nowhere or else make false connexions.

By 'realities' or 'objects' here, we mean either things of common sense, sensibly present, or else common-sense relations, such as dates, places, distances, kinds, activities. Following our mental image of a house along the cow-path, we actually come to see the house; we get the image's full verification. *Such simply and fully verified leadings are certainly the originals and prototypes of the truth-process.* Experience offers indeed other forms of truth-process, but they are all conceivable as being primary verifications arrested, multiplied or substituted one for another.

Take, for instance, yonder object on the wall. You and I consider it to be a 'clock,' altho no one of us has seen the hidden works that make it one. We let our notion pass for true without attempting to verify. If truths mean verification-process essentially, ought we then to call such unverified truths as this abortive? No, for they form the overwhelmingly large number of the truths we live by. Indirect as well as direct verifications pass muster. Where circumstantial evidence is sufficient, we can go without eye-witnessing. Just as we here assume Japan to exist without ever having been there, because it *works* to do so, everything we know conspiring with the belief, and nothing interfering, so we assume that thing to be a clock. We *use* it as a clock, regulating the length of our lecture by it. The verification of the assumption here means its leading to no frustration or contradiction. Verifi*ability* of wheels and weights and pendulum is as good as verification. For one truth-process completed there are a million in our lives that function in this state of nascency. They turn us *towards* direct verification; lead us into the *surroundings* of the objects they envisage; and then, if everything runs on harmoniously, we are so sure that verification is possible that we omit it, and are usually justified by all that happens.

Truth lives, in fact, for the most part on a credit system. Our thoughts and beliefs 'pass,' so long as nothing challenges them, just as bank-notes pass so long as nobody refuses them. But this all points to direct face-to-face verifications somewhere, without which the fabric of truth collapses like a financial system with no cash-basis whatever. You accept my verification of one thing, I yours of another. We trade on each other's truth. But beliefs verified concretely by *somebody* are the posts of the whole superstructure.

Another great reason – beside economy of time – for waiving complete verification in the usual business of life is that all things exist in kinds and not singly. Our world is found once for all to have that peculiarity. So that when we have once directly verified our ideas about one specimen of a kind, we consider ourselves free to apply them to other specimens without verification. A mind that habitually discerns the kind of thing before it, and acts by the law of the kind immediately, without pausing to verify, will be a 'true' mind in ninety-nine out of a hundred emergencies, proved so by its conduct fitting everything it meets, and getting no refutation.

Indirectly or only potentially verifying processes may thus be true as well as full verification-processes. They work as true processes would work, give us the same advantages, and claim our recognition for the same reasons. All this on the common-sense level of matters of fact, which we are alone considering.

But matters of fact are not our only stock in trade. *Relations among purely mental ideas* form another sphere where true and false beliefs obtain, and here the beliefs are absolute, or unconditional. When they are true they bear the name either of definitions or of principles. It is either a principle or a definition that 1 and 1 make 2, that 2 and 1 make 3, and so on; that white differs less from gray than it does from black; that when the cause begins to act the effect also commences. Such propositions hold of all possible 'ones,' of all conceivable 'whites' and 'grays' and 'causes.' The objects here are mental objects. Their relations are perceptually obvious at a glance, and no sense-verification is necessary. Moreover, once true, always true, of those same mental objects. Truth here has an 'eternal' character. If you can find a concrete thing anywhere that is 'one' or 'white' or 'gray' or an 'effect,' then your principles will everlastingly apply to it. It is but a case of ascertaining the kind, and then applying the law of its kind to the particular object. You are sure to get truth if you can but name the kind rightly, for your mental relations hold good of everything of that kind without exception. If you then, nevertheless, failed to get truth concretely, you would say that you had classed your real objects wrongly.

In this realm of mental relations, truth again is an affair of leading. We relate one abstract idea with another, framing in the end great systems of logical and mathematical truth, under the respective terms of which the sensible facts of experience eventually arrange themselves, so that our eternal truths hold good of realities also. This marriage of fact and theory is endlessly fertile. What we say is here already true in advance of special verification, *if we have subsumed our objects rightly.* Our ready-made ideal framework for all sorts of possible objects follows from the very structure of our thinking. We can no more play fast and loose with these abstract relations than we can do so with our sense-experiences. They coerce us; we must treat them consistently, whether or not we like the results. The rules of addition apply to our debts as rigorously as to our assets. The hundredth decimal of π, the ratio of the circumference to its diameter, is predetermined ideally now, tho no one may have computed it. If we should ever need the figure in our dealings with an actual circle we should need to have it given rightly, calculated by the usual rules; for it is the same kind of truth that those rules elsewhere calculate.

Between the coercions of the sensible order and those of the ideal order, our mind is thus wedged tightly. Our ideas must agree with realities, be such realities concrete or abstract, be they facts or be they principles, under penalty of endless inconsistency and frustration.

So far, intellectualists can raise no protest. They can only say that we have barely touched the skin of the matter.

Realities mean, then, either concrete facts, or abstract kinds of thing and relations perceived intuitively between them. They furthermore and thirdly mean, as things that new ideas of ours must no less take account of, the whole body of other truths already in our possession. But what now does 'agreement' with such three-fold realities mean? – to use again the definition that is current.

Here it is that pragmatism and intellectualism begin to part company. Primarily, no doubt, to agree means to copy, but we saw that the mere word 'clock' would do instead of a mental picture of its works, and that of many realities our ideas can only be symbols and not copies. 'Past time,' 'power,' 'spontaneity,' – how can our mind copy such realities?

To 'agree' in the widest sense with a reality *can only mean to be guided either straight up to it or into its surroundings, or to be put into such working touch with it as to handle either it or something connected with it better than if we disagreed.* Better either intellectually or practically! And often agreement will only mean the negative fact that nothing contradictory from the quarter of that reality comes to interfere with the way in which our ideas guide us elsewhere. To copy a reality is, indeed, one very important way of agreeing with it, but it is far from being essential. The essential thing is the process of being guided. Any idea that helps us to *deal*, whether practically or intellectually, with either the reality or its belongings, that doesn't entangle our progress in frustrations, that *fits*, in fact, and adapts our life to the reality's whole setting, will agree sufficiently to meet the requirement. It will hold true of that reality.

Thus, *names* are just as 'true' or 'false' as definite mental pictures are. They set up similar verification-processes, and lead to fully equivalent practical results.

All human thinking gets discursified; we exchange ideas; we lend and borrow verifications, get them from one another by means of social intercourse. All truth thus gets verbally built out, stored up, and made available for every one. Hence, we must *talk* consistently just as we must *think* consistently: for both in talk and thought we deal with kinds. Names are arbitrary, but once understood they must be kept to. We mustn't now call Abel 'Cain' or Cain 'Abel.' If we do, we un-gear ourselves from the whole book of Genesis, and from all its connexions with the universe of speech and fact down to the present time. We throw ourselves out of whatever truth that entire system of speech and fact may embody.

The overwhelming majority of our true ideas admit of no direct or face-to-face verification – those of past history, for example, as of Cain and Abel. The stream of time can be remounted only verbally, or verified indirectly by the present prolongations or effects of what the past harbored. Yet if they agree with these verbalities and effects, we can know that our ideas of the past are true. *As true as past time itself was*, so true was Julius Caesar, so true were antediluvian monsters, all in their proper dates and settings. That past time itself was, is guaranteed by its coherence with everything that's present. True as the present *is*, the past *was* also.

Agreement thus turns out to be essentially an affair of leading – leading that is useful because it is into quarters that contain objects that are important. True ideas lead us into useful verbal and conceptual quarters as well as directly up to useful sensible termini. They lead to consistency, stability and flowing human intercourse. They lead away from excentricity and isolation, from foiled and barren thinking. The untrammelled flowing of the leading-process, its general freedom from clash and contradiction, passes for its indirect verification; but all roads lead to Rome, and in the end and eventually, all true processes must lead to the face of directly verifying sensible experiences *somewhere*, which somebody's ideas have copied.

Such is the large loose way in which the pragmatist interprets the word agreement. He treats it altogether practically. He lets it cover any process of conduction from a present idea to a future terminus, provided only it run prosperously. It is only thus that 'scientific' ideas, flying as they do beyond common sense, can be said to agree with their realities. It is, as I have already said, *as if* reality were made of ether, atoms or electrons, but we must n't think so literally. The term 'energy' does n't even pretend to stand for anything 'objective.' It is only a way of measuring the surface of phenomena so as to string their changes on a simple formula.

Yet in the choice of these man-made formulas we can not be capricious with impunity any more than we can be capricious on the common-sense practical level. We must find a theory that will *work*; and that means something extremely difficult; for our theory must mediate between all previous truths and certain new experiences. It must derange common sense and previous belief as little as possible, and it must lead to some sensible terminus or other that can be verified exactly. To 'work' means both these things; and the squeeze is so tight that there is little loose play for any hypothesis. Our theories are wedged and controlled as nothing else is. Yet sometimes alternative theoretic formulas are equally compatible with all the truths we know, and then we choose between them for subjective reasons. We choose the kind of theory to which we are already partial; we follow 'elegance' or 'economy.' Clerk-Maxwell somewhere says it would be 'poor scientific taste' to choose the more complicated of two equally well-evidenced conceptions; and you will all agree with him. Truth in science is what gives us the maximum possible sum of satisfactions, taste included, but consistency both with previous truth and with novel fact is always the most imperious claimant.

I have led you through a very sandy desert. But now, if I may be allowed so vulgar an expression, we begin to taste the milk in the cocoanut. Our rationalist critics here discharge their batteries upon us, and to reply to them will take us out from all this dryness into full sight of a momentous philosophical alternative.

Our account of truth is an account of truths in the plural, of processes of leading, realized *in rebus*, and having only this quality in common, that they *pay*. They pay by guiding us into or towards some part of a system that dips at numerous points into sense-percepts, which we may copy mentally or not, but with which at any rate we are now in the kind of commerce vaguely designated as verification. Truth for us is simply a collective name for verification-processes, just as health, wealth, strength, etc., are names for other processes connected with life, and also pursued because it pays to pursue them. Truth is *made*, just as health, wealth and strength are made, in the course of experience.

Here rationalism is instantaneously up in arms against us. I can imagine a rationalist to talk as follows:

"Truth is not made", he will say; "it absolutely obtains, being a unique relation that does not wait upon any process, but shoots straight over the head of experience, and hits its reality every time. Our belief that yon thing on the wall is a clock is true already, altho' no one in the whole history of the world should

107

verify it. The bare quality of standing in that transcendent relation is what makes any thought true that possesses it, whether or not there be verification. You pragmatists put the cart before the horse in making truth's being reside in verification-processes. These are merely signs of its being, merely our lame ways of ascertaining after the fact, which of our ideas already has possessed the wondrous quality. The quality itself is timeless, like all essences and natures. Thoughts partake of it directly, as they partake of falsity or of irrelevancy. It can't be analyzed away into pragmatic consequences."

The whole plausibility of this rationalist tirade is due to the fact to which we have already paid so much attention. In our world, namely, abounding as it does in things of similar kinds and similarly associated, one verification serves for others of its kind, and one great use of knowing things is to be led not so much to them as to their associates, especially to human talk about them. The quality of truth, obtaining *ante rem*, pragmatically means, then, the fact that in such a world innumerable ideas work better by their indirect or possible than by their direct and actual verification. Truth *ante rem* means only verifiability, then; or else it is a case of the stock rationalist trick of treating the *name* of a concrete phenomenal reality as an independent prior entity, and placing it behind the reality as its explanation. Professor Mach quotes somewhere an epigram of Lessing's:

Sagt Hänschen Schlau zu Vetter Fritz,
"Wie kommt es, Vetter Fritzen,
Dass grad' die Reichsten in der Welt,
Das meiste Geld besitzen?"

Hänschen Schlau here treats the principle 'wealth' as something distinct from the facts denoted by the man's being rich. It antedates them; the facts become only a sort of secondary coincidence with the rich man's essential nature.

In the case of 'wealth' we all see the fallacy. We know that wealth is but a name for concrete processes that certain men's lives play a part in, and not a natural excellence found in Messrs. Rockefeller and Carnegie, but not in the rest of us.

Like wealth, health also lives *in rebus*. It is a name for processes, as digestion, circulation, sleep, etc., that go on happily, tho in this instance we are more inclined to think of it as a principle and to say the man digests and sleeps so well *because* he is so healthy.

With 'strength' we are, I think, more rationalistic still, and decidedly inclined to treat it as an excellence pre-existing in the man and explanatory of the herculean performances of his muscles.

With 'truth' most people go over the border entirely, and treat the rationalistic account as self-evident. But really all these words in *th* are exactly similar. Truth exists *ante rem* just as much and as little as the other things do.

The scholastics, following Aristotle, made much of the distinction between habit and act. Health *in actu* means, among other things, good sleeping and digesting. But a healthy man need not always be sleeping, or always digesting, any more than a wealthy man need be always handling money, or a strong man always lifting weights. All such qualities sink to the status of 'habits' between their times of exercise; and similarly truth becomes a habit of certain of our ideas and beliefs in their intervals of rest from their verifying activities. But those activities are the root of the whole matter, and the condition of there being any habit to exist in the intervals.

'The true,' to put it very briefly, is only the expedient in the way of our thinking, just as 'the right' is only the expedient in the way of our behaving. Expedient in almost any fashion; and expedient in the long run and on the whole of course; for what meets expediently all the experience in sight won't necessarily meet all farther experiences equally satisfactorily. Experience, as we know, has ways of *boiling over*, and making us correct our present formulas.

The 'absolutely' true, meaning what no farther experience will ever alter, is that ideal vanishing-point towards which we imagine that all our temporary truths will some day converge. It runs on all fours with the perfectly wise man, and with the absolutely complete experience; and, if these ideals are ever realized, they will all be realized together. Meanwhile we have to live to-day by what truth we can get to-day, and be ready to-morrow to call it falsehood. Ptolemaic astronomy, euclidean space, aristotelian logic, scholastic metaphysics, were expedient for centuries, but human experience has boiled over those limits, and we now call these things only relatively true, or true within those borders of experience. 'Absolutely' they are false; for we know that those limits were casual, and might have been transcended by past theorists just as they are by present thinkers.

109

When new experiences lead to retrospective judgments, using the past tense, what these judgments utter *was* true, even tho no past thinker had been led there. We live forwards, a Danish thinker has said, but we understand backwards. The present sheds a backward light on the world's previous processes. They may have been truth-processes for the actors in them. They are not so for one who knows the later revelations of the story.

This regulative notion of a potential better truth to be established later, possibly to be established some day absolutely, and having powers of retroactive legislation, turns its face, like all pragmatist notions, towards concreteness of fact, and towards the future. Like the half-truths, the absolute truth will have to be *made,* made as a relation incidental to the growth of a mass of verification-experience, to which the half-true ideas are all along contributing their quota.

I have already insisted on the fact that truth is made largely out of previous truths. Men's beliefs at any time are so much experience *funded.* But the beliefs are themselves parts of the sum total of the world's experience, and become matter, therefore, for the next day's funding operations. So far as reality means experienceable reality, both it and the truths men gain about it are everlastingly in process of mutation – mutation towards a definite goal, it may be – but still mutation.

Mathematicians can solve problems with two variables. On the Newtonian theory, for instance, acceleration varies with distance, but distance also varies with acceleration. In the realm of truth-processes facts come independently and determine our beliefs provisionally. But these beliefs make us act, and as fast as they do so, they bring into sight or into existence new facts which re-determine the beliefs accordingly. So the whole coil and ball of truth, as it rolls up, is the product of a double influence. Truths emerge from facts; but they dip forward into facts again and add to them; which facts again create or reveal new truth (the word is indifferent) and so on indefinitely. The 'facts' themselves meanwhile are not *true.* They simply *are.* Truth is the function of the beliefs that start and terminate among them.

The case is like a snowball's growth, due as it is to the distribution of the snow on the one hand, and to the successive pushes of the boys on the other, with these factors co-determining each other incessantly.

The most fateful point of difference between being a rationalist

110

The most fateful point of difference between being a rationalist and being a pragmatist is now fully in sight. Experience is in mutation, and our psychological ascertainments of truth are in mutation – so much rationalism will allow; but never that either reality itself or truth itself is mutable. Reality stands complete and ready-made from all eternity, rationalism insists, and the agreement of our ideas with it is that unique unanalyzable virtue in them of which she has already told us. As that intrinsic excellence, their truth has nothing to do with our experiences. It adds nothing to the content of experience. It makes no difference to reality itself; it is supervenient, inert, static, a reflexion merely. It doesn't *exist*, it *holds* or *obtains*, it belongs to another dimension from that of either facts or fact-relations, belongs, in short, to the epistemological dimension – and with that big word rationalism closes the discussion.

Thus, just as pragmatism faces forward to the future, so does rationalism here again face backward to a past eternity. True to her inveterate habit, rationalism reverts to 'principles,' and thinks that when an abstraction once is named, we own an oracular solution.

The tremendous pregnancy in the way of consequences for life of this radical difference of outlook will only become apparent in my later lectures. I wish meanwhile to close this lecture by showing that rationalism's sublimity does not save it from inanity.

When, namely, you ask rationalists, instead of accusing pragmatism of desecrating the notion of truth, to define it themselves by saying exactly what *they* understand by it, the only positive attempts I can think of are these two:

1. "Truth is the system of propositions which have an unconditional claim to be recognized as valid."[1]
2. Truth is a name for all those judgments which we find ourselves under obligation to make by a kind of imperative duty.[2]

The first thing that strikes one in such definitions is their unutterable triviality. They are absolutely true, of course, but absolutely insignificant until you handle them pragmatically. What do you mean by 'claim' here, and what do you mean by 'duty'? As summary names for the concrete reasons why thinking in true ways is overwhelmingly expedient and good for mortal men, it is all right to talk of claims on reality's part to be agreed with, and of obligations

---

1 A. E. Taylor, *Philosophical Review*, vol. xiv, p. 288.
2 H. Rickert, *Der Gegenstand der Erkenntniss*, chapter on 'Die Urtheilsnothwendigkeit.'

on our part to agree. We feel both the claims and the obligations, and we feel them for just those reasons.

But the rationalists who talk of claim and obligation *expressly say that they have nothing to do with our practical interests or personal reasons.* Our reasons for agreeing are psychological facts, they say, relative to each thinker, and to the accidents of his life. They are his evidence merely, they are no part of the life of truth itself. That life transacts itself in a purely logical or epistemological, as distinguished from a psychological, dimension, and its claims antedate and exceed all personal motivations whatsoever. Tho neither man nor God should ever ascertain truth, the word would still have to be defined as that which *ought* to be ascertained and recognized.

There never was a more exquisite example of an idea abstracted from the concretes of experience and then used to oppose and negate what it was abstracted from.

Philosophy and common life abound in similar instances. The 'sentimentalist fallacy' is to shed tears over abstract justice and generosity, beauty, etc., and never to know these qualities when you meet them in the street, because the circumstances make them vulgar. Thus I read in the privately printed biography of an eminently rationalistic mind: "It was strange that with such admiration for beauty in the abstract, my brother had no enthusiasm for fine architecture, for beautiful painting, or for flowers." And in almost the last philosophic work I have read, I find such passages as the following: "Justice is ideal, solely ideal. Reason conceives that it ought to exist, but experience shows that it can not. . . . Truth, which ought to be can not be. . . . Reason is deformed by experience. As soon as reason enters experience it becomes contrary to reason."

The rationalist's fallacy here is exactly like the sentimentalist's. Both extract a quality from the muddy particulars of experience, and find it so pure when extracted that they contrast it with each and all its muddy instances as an opposite and higher nature. All the while it is *their* nature. It is the nature of truths to be validated, verified. It pays for our ideas to be validated. Our obligation to seek truth is part of our general obligation to do what pays. The payments true ideas bring are the sole why of our duty to follow them. Identical whys exist in the case of wealth and health.

Truth makes no other kind of claim and imposes no other kind of ought than health and wealth do. All these claims are conditional; the concrete benefits we gain are what we mean by calling the pursuit a duty. In the case of truth, untrue beliefs work as perniciously in the long run as true beliefs work beneficially. Talking abstractly, the quality 'true' may thus be said to grow absolutely precious and the quality 'untrue' absolutely damnable: the one may be called good, the other bad, unconditionally. We ought to think the true, we ought to shun the false, imperatively.

But if we treat all this abstraction literally and oppose it to its mother soil in experience, see what a preposterous position we work ourselves into.

We can not then take a step forward in our actual thinking. When shall I acknowledge this truth and when that? Shall the acknowledgment be loud? – or silent? If sometimes loud, sometimes silent, which *now*? When may a truth go into cold-storage in the encyclopedia? and when shall it come out for battle? Must I constantly be repeating the truth 'twice two are four' because of its eternal claim on recognition? or is it sometimes irrelevant? Must my thoughts dwell night and day on my personal sins and blemishes, because I truly have them? – or may I sink and ignore them in order to be a decent social unit, and not a mass of morbid melancholy and apology?

It is quite evident that our obligation to acknowledge truth, so far from being unconditional, is tremendously conditioned. Truth with a big T, and in the singular, claims abstractly to be recognized, of course; but concrete truths in the plural need be recognized only when their recognition is expedient. A truth must always be preferred to a falsehood when both relate to the situation; but when neither does, truth is as little of a duty as falsehood. If you ask me what o'clock it is and I tell you that I live at 95 Irving Street, my answer may indeed be true, but you don't see why it is my duty to give it. A false address would be as much to the purpose.

With this admission that there are conditions that limit the application of the abstract imperative, *the pragmatistic treatment of truth sweeps back upon us in its fulness.* Our duty to agree with reality is seen to be grounded in a perfect jungle of concrete expediencies.

When Berkeley had explained what people meant by matter, people thought that he denied matter's existence. When Messrs. Schiller and Dewey now explain what people mean by truth, they are accused of denying *its* existence. These pragmatists destroy all objective standards, critics say, and put foolishness and wisdom on one level. A favorite formula for describing Mr. Schiller's doctrines and mine is that we are persons who think that by saying

113

whatever you find it pleasant to say and calling it truth you fulfil every pragmatistic requirement.

I leave it to you to judge whether this be not an impudent slander. Pent in, as the pragmatist more than any one else sees himself to be, between the whole body of funded truths squeezed from the past and the coercions of the world of sense about him, who so well as he feels the immense pressure of objective control under which our minds perform their operations? If any one imagines that this law is lax, let him keep its commandment one day, says Emerson. We have heard much of late of the uses of the imagination in science. It is high time to urge the use of a little imagination in philosophy. The unwillingness of some of our critics to read any but the silliest of possible meanings into our statements is as discreditable to their imaginations as anything I know in recent philosophic history. Schiller says the true is that which 'works.' Thereupon he is treated as one who limits verification to the lowest material utilities. Dewey says truth is what gives 'satisfaction.' He is treated as one who believes in calling everything true which, if it were true, would be pleasant.

Our critics certainly need more imagination of realities. I have honestly tried to stretch my own imagination and to read the best possible meaning into the rationalist conception, but I have to confess that it still completely baffles me. The notion of a reality calling on us to 'agree' with it, and that for no reasons, but simply because its claim is 'unconditional' or 'transcendent,' is one that I can make neither head nor tail of. I try to imagine myself as the sole reality in the world, and then to imagine what more I would 'claim' if I were allowed to. If you suggest the possibility of my claiming that a mind should come into being from out of the void inane and stand and *copy* me, I can indeed imagine what the copying might mean, but I can conjure up no motive. What good it would do me to be copied, or what good it would do that mind to copy me, if further consequences are expressly and in principle ruled out as motives for the claim (as they are by our rationalist authorities) I cannot fathom. When the Irishman's admirers ran him along to the place of banquet in a sedan chair with no bottom, he said, "Faith, if it wasn't for the honor of the thing, I might as well have come on foot." So here: but for the honor of the thing, I might as well have remained uncopied. Copying is one genuine mode of knowing (which for some strange reason our contemporary transcendentalists seem to be tumbling over each other to repudiate); but when we get beyond copying, and fall back on unnamed forms of agreeing that are expressly denied to be either copyings or leadings or fittings, or any other processes pragmatically definable, the *what* of the 'agreement' claimed becomes as unintelligible as the why of it. Neither content nor motive can be imagined for it. It is an absolutely meaningless abstraction.[3]

Surely in this field of truth it is the pragmatists and not the rationalists who are the more genuine defenders of the universe's rationality.

3 I am not forgetting that Professor Rickert long ago gave up the whole notion of truth being founded on agreement with reality. Reality according to him, is whatever agrees with truth, and truth is founded solely on our primal duty. This fantastic flight, together with Mr. Joachim's candid confession of failure in his book *The Nature of Truth*, seems to me to mark the bankruptcy of rationalism when dealing with this subject. Rickert deals with part of the pragmatistic position under the head of what he calls 'Relativismus.' I can not discuss his text here. Suffice it to say that his argumentation in that chapter is so feeble as to seem almost incredible in so generally able a writer.

LECTURE VII
PRAGMATISM AND HUMANISM

What hardens the heart of every one I approach with the view of truth sketched in my last lecture is that typical idol of the tribe, the notion of *the* Truth, conceived as the one answer, determinate and complete, to the one fixed enigma which the world is believed to propound. For popular tradition, it is all the better if the answer be oracular, so as itself to awaken wonder as an enigma of the second order, veiling rather than revealing what its profundities are supposed to contain. All the great single-word answers to the world's riddle, such as God, the One, Reason, Law, Spirit, Matter, Nature, Polarity, the Dialectic Process, the Idea, the Self, the Oversoul, draw the admiration that men have lavished on them from this oracular rôle. By amateurs in philosophy and professionals alike, the universe is represented as a queer sort of petrified sphinx whose appeal to men consists in a monotonous challenge to his divining powers. *The* Truth: what a perfect idol of the rationalistic mind! I read in an old letter – from a gifted friend who died too young – these words: "In everything, in science, art, morals and religion, there *must* be one system that is right and *every* other wrong." How characteristic of the enthusiasm of a certain stage of youth! At twenty-one we rise to such a challenge and expect to find the system. It never occurs to most of us even later that the question 'what is. *the* truth?' is no real question (being irrelative to all conditions) and that the whole notion of *the* truth is an abstraction from the fact of truths in the plural, a mere useful summarizing phrase like *the* latin Language or *the* Law.

Common-law judges sometimes talk about the law, and schoolmasters talk about the latin tongue, in a way to make their hearers think they mean entities pre-existent to the decisions or to the words and syntax, determining them unequivocally and requiring them to obey. But the slightest exercise of reflexion makes us see that, instead of being principles of this kind, both law and latin are results. Distinctions between the lawful and the unlawful in conduct, or between the correct and incorrect in speech, have grown up incidentally among the interactions of men's experiences in detail; and in no other way do distinctions between the true and the false in belief ever grow up. Truth grafts itself on previous truth, modifying it in the process, just as idiom grafts itself on previous idiom, and law on previous law. Given previous law and a novel

116

case, and the judge will twist them into fresh law. Previous idiom; new slang or metaphor or oddity that hits the public taste; – and presto, a new idiom is made. Previous truth; fresh facts: – and our mind finds a new truth.

All the while, however, we pretend that the eternal is unrolling, that the one previous justice, grammar or truth are simply fulgurating and not being made. But imagine a youth in the courtroom trying cases with his abstract notion of 'the' law, or a censor of speech let loose among the theatres with his idea of 'the' mother-tongue, or a professor setting up to lecture on the actual universe with his rationalistic notion of the Truth' with a big T, and what progress do they make? Truth, law and language fairly boil away from them at the least touch of novel fact. These things *make themselves* as we go. Our rights, wrongs, prohibitions, penalties, words, forms, idioms, beliefs, are so many new creations that add themselves as fast as history proceeds. Far from being antecedent principles that animate the process, law, language, truth are but abstract names for its results.

Laws and languages at any rate are thus seen to be man-made things. Mr. Schiller applies the analogy to beliefs, and proposes the name of 'Humanism' for the doctrine that to an unascertainable extent our truths are man-made products too. Human motives sharpen all our questions, human satisfactions lurk in all our answers, all our formulas have a human twist. This element is so inextricable in the products that Mr. Schiller sometimes seems almost to leave it an open question whether there be anything else. "The world," he says, "is essentially ὕλη, it is what we make it. It is fruitless to define it by what it originally was or by what it is apart from us; it *is* what is made of it. Hence . . . the world *is plastic*."[1] He adds that we can learn the limits of the plasticity only by trying, and that we ought to start as if it were wholly plastic, acting methodically on that assumption, and stopping only when we are decisively rebuked.

This is Mr. Schiller's butt-end-foremost statement of the humanist position, and it has exposed him to severe attack. I mean to defend the humanist position in this lecture, so I will insinuate a few remarks at this point.

Mr. Schiller admits as emphatically as any one the presence of resisting factors in every actual experience of truth-making, of

---

1 *Personal Idealism*, p. 60.

which the new-made special truth must take account, and with which it has perforce to 'agree.' All our truths are beliefs about 'Reality'; and in any particular belief the reality acts as something independent, as a thing *found*, not manufactured. Let me here recall a bit of my last lecture.

'Reality' is in general what truths have to take account of;[2] and the *first* part of reality from this point of view is the flux of our sensations. Sensations are forced upon us, coming we know not whence. Over their nature, order and quantity we have as good as no control. *They* are neither true nor false; they simply *are*. It is only what we say about them, only the names we give them, our theories of their source and nature and remote relations, that may be true or not.

The *second* part of reality, as something that our beliefs must also obediently take account of, is the *relations* that obtain between our sensations or between their copies in our minds. This part falls into two sub-parts: 1) the relations that are mutable and accidental, as those of date and place; and 2) those that are fixed and essential because they are grounded on the inner natures of their terms. Both sorts of relation are matters of immediate perception. Both are 'facts.' But it is the latter kind of fact that forms the more important sub-part of reality for our theories of knowledge. Inner relations namely are 'eternal,' are perceived whenever their sensible terms are compared; and of them our thought – mathematical and logical thought so-called – must eternally take account.

The *third* part of reality, additional to these perceptions (tho largely based upon them), is the *previous truths* of which every new inquiry takes account. This third part is a much less obdurately resisting factor: it often ends by giving way. In speaking of these three portions of reality as at all times controlling our belief's formation, I am only reminding you of what we heard in our last hour.

Now however fixed these elements of reality may be, we still have a certain freedom in our dealings with them. Take our sensations. *That* they are is undoubtedly beyond our control; but *which* we attend to, note, and make emphatic in our conclusions depends on our own interests; and, according as we lay the emphasis here or there, quite different formulations of truth result. We read the same facts differently. 'Waterloo,' with the same fixed details, spells a 'victory' for an Englishman; for a Frenchman it spells a 'defeat.' So,

2   Mr. Taylor in his *Elements of Metaphysics* uses this excellent definition.

for an optimist philosopher the universe spells victory, for a pessimist, defeat.

What we say about reality thus depends on the perspective into which we throw it. The *that* of it is its own; but the *what* depends on the *which*; and the which depends on *us*. Both the sensational and the relational parts of reality are dumb; they say absolutely nothing about themselves. We it is who have to speak for them. This dumbness of sensations has led such intellectualists as T. H. Green and Edward Caird to shove them almost beyond the pale of philosophic recognition, but pragmatists refuse to go so far. A sensation is rather like a client who has given his case to a lawyer and then has passively to listen in the courtroom to whatever account of his affairs, pleasant or unpleasant, the lawyer finds it most expedient to give.

Hence, even in the field of sensation, our minds exert a certain arbitrary choice. By our inclusions and omissions we trace the field's extent; by our emphasis we mark its foreground and its background; by our order we read it in this direction or in that. We receive in short the block of marble, but we carve the statue ourselves.

This applies to the 'eternal' parts of reality as well: we shuffle our perceptions of intrinsic relation and arrange them just as freely. We read them in one serial order or another, class them in this way or in that, treat one or the other as more fundamental, until our beliefs about them form those bodies of truth known as logics, geometrics, or arithmetics, in each and all of which the form and order in which the whole is cast is flagrantly man-made.

Thus, to say nothing of the new *facts* which men add to the matter of reality by the acts of their own lives, they have already impressed their mental forms on that whole third of reality which I have called 'previous truths.' Every hour brings its new percepts, its own facts of sensation and relation, to be truly taken account of; but the whole of our *past* dealings with such facts is already funded in the previous truths. It is therefore only the smallest and recentest fraction of the first two parts of reality that comes to us without the human touch, and that fraction has immediately to become humanized in the sense of being squared, assimilated, or in some way adapted, to the humanized mass already there. As a matter of fact we can hardly take in an impression at all, in the absence of a preconception of what impressions there may possibly be.

When we talk of reality 'independent' of human thinking, then, it seems a thing very hard to find. It reduces to the notion of what is just entering into experience and yet to be named, or else to some imagined aboriginal presence in experience, before any belief about the presence had arisen, before any human conception had been applied. It is what is absolutely dumb and evanescent, the merely ideal limit of our minds. We may glimpse it, but we never grasp it; what we grasp is always some substitute for it which previous human thinking has peptonized and cooked for our consumption. If so vulgar an expression were allowed us, we might say that wherever we find it, it has been already *faked*. This is what Mr. Schiller has in mind when he calls independent reality a mere unresisting ὕλη, which *is* only to be made over by us.

That is Mr. Schiller's belief about the sensible core of reality. We 'encounter' it (in Mr. Bradley's words) but don't possess it. Superficially this sounds like Kant's view; but between categories fulminated before nature began, and categories gradually forming themselves in nature's presence, the whole chasm between rationalism and empiricism yawns. To the genuine 'Kantianer' Schiller will always be to Kant as a satyr to Hyperion.

Other pragmatists may reach more positive beliefs about the sensible core of reality. They may think to get at it in its independent nature, by peeling off the successive man-made wrappings. They may make theories that tell us where it comes from and all about it; and *if these theories work satisfactorily they will be true*. The transcendental idealists say there is no core, the finally completed wrapping being reality and truth in one. Scholasticism still teaches that the core is 'matter.' Professor Bergson, Heymans, Strong, and others believe in the core and bravely try to define it. Messrs. Dewey and Schiller treat it as a 'limit.' Which is the truer of all these diverse accounts, or of others comparable with them, unless it be the one that finally proves the most satisfactory? On the one hand there will stand reality, on the other an account of it which it proves impossible to better or to alter. If the impossibility prove permanent, the truth of the account will be absolute. Other content of truth than this I can find nowhere. If the anti-pragmatists have any other meaning, let them for heaven's sake reveal it, let them grant us access to it!

Not *being* reality, but only our belief *about* reality, it will contain human elements, but these will *know* the non-human element, in the only sense in which there can be knowledge of anything. Does the river make its banks, or do the banks make the river? Does a man walk with his right leg or with his left leg more essentially? Just as impossible may it be to separate the real from the human factors in the growth of our cognitive experience.

Let this stand as a first brief indication of the humanistic position. Does it seem paradoxical? If so, I will try to make it plausible by a few illustrations, which will lead to a fuller acquaintance with the subject.

In many familiar objects every one will recognize the human element. We conceive a given reality in this way or in that, to suit our purpose, and the reality passively submits to the conception. You can take the number 27 as the cube of 3, or as the product of 3 and 9, or as 26 *plus* 1, or 100 *minus* 73, or in countless other ways, of which one will be just as true as another. You can take a chessboard as black squares on a white ground, or as white squares on a black ground, and neither conception is a false one.

You can treat the adjoined figure as a star, as two big triangles crossing each other, as a hexagon with legs set up on its angles, as six equal triangles hanging together by their tips, etc. All these

treatments are true treatments – the sensible *that* upon the paper resists no one of them. You can say of a line that it runs east, or you can say that it runs west, and the line *per se* accepts both descriptions without rebelling at the inconsistency.

We carve out groups of stars in the heavens, and call them constellations, and the stars patiently suffer us to do so, – though if they knew what we were doing, some of them might feel much surprised at the partners we had given them. We name the same constellation diversely, as Charles's Wain, the Great Bear, or the Dipper. None of the names will be false, and one will be as true as another, for all are applicable.

In all these cases we humanly make an *addition* to some sensible reality, and that reality tolerates the addition. All the additions 'agree' with the reality; they fit it, while they build it out. No one of them is false. Which may be treated as the *more* true, depends altogether on the human use of it. If the 27 is a number of dollars which I find in a drawer where I had left 28, it is 28 minus 1. If it is the number of inches in a board which I wish to insert as a shelf into a cupboard 26 inches wide, it is 26 plus 1. If I wish to ennoble the heavens by the constellations I see there, 'Charles's Wain' would be more true than 'Dipper.' My friend Frederick Myers was humorously indignant that that prodigious star-group should remind us Americans of nothing but a culinary utensil.

What shall we call a *thing* anyhow? It seems quite arbitrary, for we carve out everything, just as we carve out constellations, to suit our human purposes. For me, this whole 'audience' is one thing, which grows now restless, now attentive. I have no use at present for its individual units, so I don't consider them. So of an 'army,' of a 'nation.' But in your own eyes, ladies and gentlemen, to call you 'audience' is an accidental way of taking you. The permanently real things for you are your individual persons. To an anatomist, again, those persons are but organisms, and the real things are the organs. Not the organs, so much as their constituent cells, say the histologists; not the cells, but their molecules, say in turn the chemists.

We break the flux of sensible reality into things, then, at our will. We create the subjects of our true as well as of our false propositions.

We create the predicates also. Many of the predicates of things express only the relations of the things to us and to our feelings. Such predicates of course are human additions. Caesar crossed the Rubicon, and was a menace to Rome's freedom. He is also an American schoolroom pest, made into one by the reaction of our schoolboys on his writings. The added predicate is as true of him as the earlier ones.

You see how naturally one comes to the humanistic principle: you can't weed out the human contribution. Our nouns and adjectives are all humanized heirlooms, and in the theories we build them into, the inner order and arrangement is wholly dictated by human considerations, intellectual consistency being one of them. Mathematics and logic themselves are fermenting with human rearrangements; physics, astronomy and biology follow massive cues of preference. We plunge forward into the field of fresh experience with the beliefs our ancestors and we have made already; these determine what we notice; what we notice determines what we do; what we do again determines what we experience; so from one thing to another, altho the stubborn fact remains that there *is* a sensible flux, what is *true of it* seems from first to last to be largely a matter of our own creation.

We build the flux out inevitably. The great question is: does it, with our additions, *rise or fall in value*? Are the additions *worthy* or *unworthy*? Suppose a universe composed of seven stars, and nothing else but three human witnesses and their critic. One witness names the stars 'Great Bear'; one calls them 'Charles's Wain'; one calls them the 'Dipper.' Which human addition has made the best universe of the given stellar material? If Frederick Myers were the critic, he would have no hesitation in 'turning down' the American witness.

Lotze has in several places made a deep suggestion. We naïvely assume, he says, a relation between reality and our minds which may be just the opposite of the true one. Reality, we naturally think, stands ready-made and complete, and our intellects supervene with the one simple duty of describing it as it is already. But may not our descriptions, Lotze asks, be themselves important additions to reality? And may not previous reality itself be there, far less for the purpose of reappearing unaltered in our knowledge, than for the very purpose of stimulating our minds to such additions as shall enhance the universe's total value. 'Die erhöhung des vorgefundenen daseins' is a phrase used by Professor Eucken somewhere, which reminds one of this suggestion by the great Lotze.

It is identically our pragmatistic conception. In our cognitive as well as in our active life we are creative. We *add*, both to the subject and to the predicate part of reality. The world stands really malleable, waiting to receive its final touches at our hands. Like the kingdom of heaven, it suffers human violence willingly. Man *engenders* truths upon it.

No one can deny that such a rôle would add both to our dignity and to our responsibility as thinkers. To some of us it proves a most inspiring notion. Signore Papini, the leader of Italian pragmatism, grows fairly dithyrambic over the view that it opens of man's divinely creative functions.

The import of the difference between pragmatism and rationalism is now in sight throughout its whole extent. The essential contrast is that *for rationalism reality is ready-made and complete from all eternity, while for pragmatism it is still in the making, and awaits part of its complexion from the future*. On the one side the universe is absolutely secure, on the other it is still pursuing its adventures.

We have got into rather deep water with this humanistic view, and it is no wonder that misunderstanding gathers round it. It is accused of being a doctrine of caprice. Mr. Bradley, for example, says that a humanist, if he understood his own doctrine, would have to 'hold any end, however perverted, to be rational, if I insist on it personally, and any idea, however mad, to be the truth if only

123

some one is resolved that he will have it so.' The humanist view of 'reality,' as something resisting, yet malleable, which controls our thinking as an energy that must be taken 'account' of incessantly (tho not necessarily merely *copied*) is evidently a difficult one to introduce to novices. The situation reminds me of one that I have personally gone through. I once wrote an essay on our right to believe, which I unluckily called the *Will* to Believe. All the critics, neglecting the essay, pounced upon the title. Psychologically it was impossible, morally it was iniquitous. The 'will to deceive,' the 'will to make-believe,' were wittily proposed as substitutes for it.

The alternative between pragmatism and rationalism, in the shape in which we now have it before us, is no longer a question in the theory of knowledge, it concerns the structure of the universe itself.

On the pragmatist side we have only one edition of the universe, unfinished, growing in all sorts of places, especially in the places where thinking beings are at work.

On the rationalist side we have a universe in many editions, one real one, the infinite folio, or *édition de Luxe*, eternally complete; and then the various finite editions, full of false readings, distorted and mutilated each in its own way.

So the rival metaphysical hypotheses of pluralism and monism here come back upon us. I will develope their differences during the remainder of our hour.

And first let me say that it is impossible not to see a temperamental difference at work in the choice of sides. The rationalist mind, radically taken, is of a doctrinaire and authoritative complexion: the phrase '*must* be' is ever on its lips. The bellyband of its universe must be tight. A radical pragmatist on the other hand is a happy-go-lucky anarchistic sort of creature. If he had to live in a tub like Diogenes he wouldn't mind at all if the hoops were loose and the staves let in the sun.

Now the idea of this loose universe affects your typical rationalists in much the same way as 'freedom of the press' might affect a veteran official in the Russian bureau of censorship; or as 'simplified spelling' might affect an elderly schoolmistress. It affects him as the swarm of protestant sects affects a papist onlooker. It appears as backboneless and devoid of principle as 'opportunism' in politics appears to an old-fashioned French legitimist, or to a fanatical believer in the divine right of the people.

For pluralistic pragmatism, truth grows up inside of all the finite experiences. They lean on each other, but the whole of them, if such a whole there be, leans on nothing. All 'homes' are in finite experience; finite experience as such is homeless. Nothing outside of the flux secures the issue of it. It can hope salvation only from its own intrinsic promises and potencies.

To rationalists this describes a tramp and vagrant world, adrift in space, with neither elephant nor tortoise to plant the sole of its foot upon. It is a set of stars hurled into heaven without even a centre of gravity to pull against. In other spheres of life it is true that we have got used to living in a state of relative insecurity. The authority of 'the State,' and that of an absolute 'moral law,' have resolved themselves into expediencies, and holy church has resolved itself into 'meeting-houses.' Not so as yet within the philosophic class-rooms. A universe with such as *us* contributing to create its truth, a world delivered to *our* opportunisms and our private judgments! Home-rule for Ireland would be a millennium in comparison. We're no more fit for such a part than the Filipinos are 'fit for self-government.' Such a world would not be *respectable* philosophically. It is a trunk without a tag, a dog without a collar in the eyes of most professors of philosophy.

What then would tighten this loose universe, according to the professors?

Something to support the finite many, to tie it to, to unify and anchor it. Something *un*exposed to accident, something eternal and unalterable. The mutable in experience must be founded on immutability. Behind our *de facto* world, our world in act, there must be a *de jure* duplicate fixed and previous, with all that can happen here already there *in posse*, every drop of blood, every smallest item, appointed and provided, stamped and branded, without chance of variation. The negatives that haunt our ideals here below must be themselves negated in the absolutely Real. This alone makes the universe solid. This is the resting deep. We live upon the stormy surface; but with this our anchor holds, for it grapples rocky bottom. This is Wordsworth's 'eternal peace abiding at the heart of endless agitation.' This is Vivekanda's mystical One of which I read to you. This is Reality with the big R, reality that makes the timeless claim, reality to which defeat can't happen. This is what the men of principles, and in general all the men whom I called tender-minded in my first lecture, think themselves obliged to postulate.

And this, exactly this, is what the tough-minded of that lecture find themselves moved to call a piece of perverse abstraction-worship.

The tough-minded are the men whose alpha and omega are *facts*. Behind the bare phenomenal facts, as my tough-minded old friend Chauncey Wright, the great Harvard empiricist of my youth, used to say, there is *nothing*. When a rationalist insists that behind the facts there is the *ground* of the facts, the *possibility* of the facts, the tougher empiricists accuse him of taking the mere name and nature of a fact and clapping it behind the fact as a duplicate entity to make it possible. That such sham grounds are often invoked is notorious. At a surgical operation I once heard a bystander ask a doctor why the patient breathed so deeply. 'Because ether is a respiratory stimulant,' the doctor answered. 'Ah!' said the questioner, as if that were a good explanation. But this is like saying that cyanide of potassium kills because it is a 'poison,' or that it is so cold to-night because it is 'winter,' or that we have five fingers because we are 'pentadactyls.' These are but names for the facts, taken from the facts, and then treated as previous and explanatory. The tender-minded notion of an absolute reality is, according to the radically tough-minded, framed on just this pattern. It is but our summarizing name for the whole spread-out and strung-along mass of phenomena, treated as if it were a different entity, both one and previous.

You see how differently people take things. The world we live in exists diffused and distributed, in the form of an indefinitely numerous lot of *eaches*, coherent in all sorts of ways and degrees; and the tough-minded are perfectly willing to keep them at that valuation. They can *stand* that kind of world, their temper being well adapted to its insecurity. Not so the tender-minded party. They must back the world we find ourselves born into by 'another and a better' world in which the eaches form an All and the All a One that logically presupposes, co-implicates, and secures each *each* without exception.

Must we as pragmatists be radically tough-minded? or can we treat the absolute edition of the world as a legitimate hypothesis? It is certainly legitimate, for it is thinkable, whether we take it in its abstract or in its concrete shape.

By taking it abstractly I mean placing it behind our finite life as we place the word 'winter' behind to-night's cold weather. 'Winter' is only the name for a certain number of days which we find generally characterized by cold weather, but it guarantees nothing in that line, for our thermometer to-morrow may soar into the 70's. Nevertheless the word is a useful one to plunge forward with into

126

the stream of our experience. It cuts off certain probabilities and sets up others. You can put away your straw hats; you can unpack your arctics. It is a summary of things to look for. It names a part of nature's habits, and gets you ready for their continuation. It is a definite instrument abstracted from experience, a conceptual reality that you must take account of, and which reflects you totally back into sensible realities. The pragmatist is the last person to deny the reality of such abstractions. They are so much past experience funded.

But taking the absolute edition of the world concretely means a different hypothesis. Rationalists take it concretely and *oppose* it to the world's finite editions. They give it a particular nature. It is perfect, finished. Everything known there is known along with everything else; here, where ignorance reigns, far otherwise. If there is want there, there also is the satisfaction provided. Here all is process; that world is timeless. Possibilities obtain in our world; in the absolute world, where all that is *not* is from eternity impossible, and all that *is* is necessary, the category of possibility has no application. In this world crimes and horrors are regretable. In that totalized world regret obtains not, for 'the existence of ill in the temporal order is the very condition of the perfection of the eternal order.'

Once more, either hypothesis is legitimate in pragmatist eyes, for either has its uses. Abstractly, or taken like the word winter, as a memorandum of past experience that orients us towards the future, the notion of the absolute world is indispensable. Concretely taken, it is also indispensable, at least to certain minds, for it determines them religiously, being often a thing to change their lives by, and by changing their lives, to change whatever in the outer order depends on them.

We can not therefore methodically join the tough minds in their rejection of the whole notion of a world beyond our finite experience. One misunderstanding of pragmatism is to identify it with positivistic tough-mindedness, to suppose that it scorns every rationalistic notion as so much jabber and gesticulation, that it loves intellectual anarchy as such and prefers a sort of wolf-world absolutely unpent and wild and without a master or a collar to any philosophic classroom product whatsoever. I have said so much in these lectures against the over-tender forms of rationalism, that I am prepared for some misunderstanding here, but I confess that the amount of it that I have found in this very audience surprises me, for I have simultaneously defended rationalistic hypotheses, so far as these re-direct you fruitfully into experience.

For instance I receive this morning this question on a post-card: 'Is a pragmatist necessarily a complete materialist and agnostic?' One of my oldest friends, who ought to know me better, writes me a letter that accuses the pragmatism I am recommending of shutting out all wider metaphysical views and condemning us to the most *terre-à-terre* naturalism. Let me read you some extracts from it.

"It seems to me," my friend writes, "that the pragmatic objection to pragmatism lies in the fact that it might accentuate the narrowness of narrow minds.

"Your call to the rejection of the namby-pamby and the wishy-washy is of course inspiring. But altho it is salutary and stimulating to be told that one should be responsible for the immediate issues and bearings of his words and thoughts, I decline to be deprived of the pleasure and profit of dwelling also on remoter bearings and issues, and it is the *tendency* of pragmatism to refuse this privilege.

"In short, it seems to me that the limitations, or rather the dangers, of the pragmatic tendency, are analogous to those which beset the unwary followers of the 'natural sciences.' Chemistry and physics are eminently pragmatic; and many of their devotees, smugly content with the data that their weights and measures furnish, feel an infinite pity and disdain for all students of philosophy and metaphysics whomsoever. And of course everything can be expressed, – after a fashion, and 'theoretically,' – in terms of chemistry and physics, that is, *everything except the vital principle of the whole*, and that, they say, there is no pragmatic use in trying to express; it has no bearings – for *them*. I for my part refuse to be persuaded that we can not look beyond the obvious pluralism of the naturalist and the pragmatist to a logical unity in which they take no interest."

How is such a conception of the pragmatism I am advocating possible, after my first and second lectures? I have all along been offering it expressly as a mediator between tough-mindedness and tender-mindedness. If the notion of a world *ante rem*, whether taken abstractly like the word winter, or concretely as the hypothesis of an Absolute, can be shown to have any consequences whatever for our life, it has a meaning. If the meaning works, it will have *some* truth that ought to be held to through all possible reformulations, for pragmatism.

The absolutistic hypothesis, that perfection is eternal, aboriginal, and most real, has a perfectly definite meaning, and it works religiously. To examine how, will be the subject of my next and final lecture.

LECTURE VIII
PRAGMATISM AND RELIGION

At the close of the last lecture I reminded you of the first one, in which I had opposed tough-mindedness to tender-mindedness and recommended pragmatism as their mediator. Tough-mindedness positively rejects tender-mindedness's hypothesis of an eternal perfect edition of the universe coexisting with our finite experience.

On pragmatic principles we can not reject any hypothesis if consequences useful to life flow from it. Universal conceptions, as things to take account of, may be as real for pragmatism as particular sensations are. They have, indeed, no meaning and no reality if they have no use. But if they have any use they have that amount of meaning. And the meaning will be true if the use squares well with life's other uses.

Well, the use of the Absolute is proved by the whole course of men's religious history. The eternal arms are then beneath. Remember Vivekanda's use of the Atman: it is indeed not a scientific use, for we can make no particular deductions from it. It is emotional and spiritual altogether.

It is always best to discuss things by the help of concrete examples. Let me read therefore some of those verses entitled 'To You' by Walt Whitman – 'You' of course meaning the reader or hearer of the poem whosoever he or she may be.

Whoever you are, now I place my hand upon you that you be my
    poem;
I whisper with my lips close to your ear,
I have loved many men and women and men, but I love none better
    than you.

O I have been dilatory and dumb;
I should have made my way to you long ago;
I should have blabbed nothing but you, I should have chanted
    nothing but you.

I will leave all and come and make the hymns of you;
None have understood you, but I understand you;
None have done justice to you – you have not done justice to
    yourself;

None but have found you imperfect – I only find no imperfection in
   you.

O I could sing such glories and grandeurs about you;
You have not known what you are – you have slumbered upon
   yourself all your life;
What you have done returns already in mockeries.

But the mockeries are not you;
Underneath them and within them, I see you lurk;
I pursue you where none else has pursued you.
Silence, the desk, the flippant expression, the night, the accus-
   tomed routine, if these conceal you from others, or from your-
   self, they do not conceal you from me;
The shaved face, the unsteady eye, the impure complexion, if these
   balk others, they do not balk me;
The pert apparel, the deformed attitude, drunkenness, greed,
   premature death, all these I part aside.

There is no endowment in man or woman that is not tallied in
   you;
There is no virtue, no beauty, in man or woman, but as good is in
   you;
No pluck nor endurance in others, but as good is in you;
No pleasure waiting for others, but an equal pleasure waits for you.

Whoever you are! claim your own at any hazard!
These shows of the east and west are tame, compared with you;
These immense meadows – these interminable rivers – you are
   immense and interminable as they;
You are he or she who is master or mistress over them,
Master or mistress in your own right over Nature, elements, pain,
   passion, dissolution.

The hopples fall from your ankles – you find an unfailing
   sufficiency;
Old or young, male or female, rude, low, rejected by the rest
   whatever you are promulges itself;

Through birth, life, death, burial, the means are provided, nothing
  is scanted;
Through angers, losses, ambition, ignorance, ennui, what you are
  picks its way.

Verily a fine and moving poem, in any case, but there are two
ways of taking it, both useful.

One is the monistic way, the mystical way of pure cosmic
emotion. The glories and grandeurs, they are yours absolutely,
even in the midst of your defacements. Whatever may happen to
you, whatever you may appear to be, inwardly you are safe. Look
back, *lie* back, on your true principle of being! This is the famous
way of quietism, of indifferentism. Its enemies compare it to a
spiritual opium. Yet pragmatism must respect this way, for it has
massive historic vindication.

But pragmatism sees another way to be respected also, the
pluralistic way of interpreting the poem. The you so glorified, to
which the hymn is sung, may mean your better possibilities pheno-
menally taken, or the specific redemptive effects even of your
failures, upon yourself or others. It may mean your loyalty to the
possibilities of others whom you admire and love so that you are
willing to accept your own poor life, for it is that glory's partner.
You can at least appreciate, applaud, furnish the audience, of so
brave a total world. Forget the low in yourself, then, think only of
the high. Identify your life therewith; then, through angers, losses,
ignorance, ennui, whatever you thus make yourself, whatever you
thus most deeply are, picks its way.

In either way of taking the poem, it encourages fidelity to
ourselves. Both ways satisfy; both sanctify the human flux. Both
paint the portrait of the *you* on a gold background. But the background of the first way is the static One, while in the second way it
means possibles in the plural, genuine possibles, and it has all the
restlessness of that conception.

Noble enough is either way of reading the poem; but plainly the
pluralistic way agrees with the pragmatic temper best, for it immediately suggests an infinitely larger number of the details of
future experience to our mind. It sets definite activities in us at
work. Altho this second way seems prosaic and earth-born in
comparison with the first way, yet no one can accuse it of tough-
mindedness in any brutal sense of the term. Yet if, as pragmatists,
you should positively set up the second way *against* the first way,

you would very likely be misunderstood. You would be accused of denying nobler conceptions, and of being an ally of tough-mindedness in the worst sense.

You remember the letter from a member of this audience from which I read some extracts at our previous meeting. Let me read you an additional extract now. It shows a vagueness in realizing the alternatives before us which I think is very widespread.

"I believe," writes my friend and correspondent, "in pluralism; I believe that in our search for truth we leap from one floating cake of ice to another, on an infinite sea, and that by each of our acts we make new truths possible and old ones impossible; I believe that each man is responsible for making the universe better, and that if he does not do this it will be in so far left undone.

"Yet at the same time I am willing to endure that my children should be incurably sick and suffering (as they are not) and I myself stupid and yet with brains enough to see my stupidity, only on one condition, namely, that through the construction, in imagination and by reasoning, of a *rational unity of all things*, I can conceive my acts and my thoughts and my troubles as *supplemented by all the other phenomena of the world, and as forming – when thus supplemented – a scheme which I approve and adopt as my own*; and for my part I refuse to be persuaded that we can not look beyond the obvious pluralism of the naturalist and pragmatist to a logical unity in which they take no interest or stock."

Such a fine expression of personal faith warms the heart of the hearer. But how much does it clear his philosophic head? Does the writer consistently favor the monistic, or the pluralistic, interpretation of the world's poem? His troubles become atoned for *when thus supplemented*, he says, supplemented, that is, by all the remedies that *the other phenomena* may supply. Obviously here the writer faces forward into the particulars of experience, which he interprets in a pluralistic-melioristic way.

But he believes himself to face backward. He speaks of what he calls the rational *unity* of things, when all the while he really means their possible empirical *unification*. He supposes at the same time that the pragmatist, because he criticises rationalism's abstract One, is cut off from the consolation of believing in the saving possibilities of the concrete many. He fails in short to distinguish

133

between taking the world's perfection as a necessary principle, and taking it only as a possible *terminus ad quem*.

I regard the writer of the letter as a genuine pragmatist, but as a pragmatist *sans le savoir*. He appears to me as one of that numerous class of philosophic amateurs whom I spoke of in my first lecture, as wishing to have all the good things going, without being too careful as to how they agree or disagree. 'Rational unity of all things' is so inspiring a formula, that he brandishes it off-hand, and abstractly accuses pluralism of conflicting with it (for the bare names do conflict), altho concretely he means by it just the pragmatistically unified and ameliorated world. Most of us remain in this essential vagueness, and it is well that we should; but in the interest of clearheadedness it is well that some of us should go farther, so I will try now to focus a little more discriminatingly on this particular religious point.

Is then this you of yous, this absolutely real world, this unity that yields the moral inspiration and has the religious value, to be taken monistically or pluralistically? Is it *ante rem* or *in rebus*? Is it a principle or an end, an absolute or an ultimate, a first or a last? Does it make you look forward or lie back? It is certainly worth while not to clump the two things together, for if discriminated, they have decidedly diverse meanings for life.

Please observe that the whole dilemma revolves pragmatically about the notion of the world's possibilities. Intellectually, rationalism invokes its absolute principle of unity, as a ground of possibility for the many facts. Emotionally, it sees it as a container and limiter of possibilities, a guarantee that the upshot shall be good. Taken in this way, the absolute makes all good things certain, and all bad things impossible (in the eternal, namely), and may be said to transmute the entire category of possibility into categories more secure. One sees at this point that the great religious difference lies between the men who insist that the world *must and shall be*, and those who are contented with believing that the world *may be*, saved. The whole clash of rationalistic and empiricist religion is thus over the validity of possibility. It is necessary therefore to begin by focusing upon that word. What may the word 'possible' definitely mean? To unreflecting men it means a sort of third estate of being, less real than existence, more real than non-existence, a twilight realm, a hybrid status, a limbo into which and out of which realities ever and anon are made to pass.

Such a conception is of course too vague and nondescript to

satisfy us. Here, as elsewhere, the only way to extract a term's meaning is to use the pragmatic method on it. When you say that a thing is possible, what difference does it make? It makes at least this difference that if any one calls it impossible you can contradict him, if any one calls it actual you can contradict *him*, and if anyone calls it necessary you can contradict him too.

But these privileges of contradiction don't amount to much. When you say a thing is possible, does not that make some farther difference in terms of actual fact?

It makes at least this negative difference that if the statement be true, it follows that *there is nothing extant capable of preventing* the possible thing. The absence of real grounds of interference may thus be said to make things *not impossible*, possible therefore in the *bare* or *abstract* sense.

But most possibles are not bare, they are concretely grounded, or well-grounded, as we say. What does this mean pragmatically? It means not only that there are no preventive conditions present, but that some of the conditions of production of the possible thing actually are here. Thus a concretely possible chicken means: (1) that the idea of chicken contains no essential self-contradiction; (2) that no boys, skunks, or other enemies are about; and (3) that at least an actual egg exists. Possible chicken means actual egg – plus actual sitting hen, or incubator, or what not. As the actual conditions approach completeness the chicken becomes a better-and-better-grounded possibility. When the conditions are entirely complete, it ceases to be a possibility, and turns into an actual fact.

Let us apply this notion to the salvation of the world. What does it pragmatically mean to say that this is possible? It means that some of the conditions of the world's deliverance do actually exist. The more of them there are existent, the fewer preventing conditions you can find, the better-grounded is the salvation's possibility, the more *probable* does the fact of the deliverance become.

So much for our preliminary look at possibility.

Now it would contradict the very spirit of life to say that our minds must be indifferent and neutral in questions like that of the world's salvation. Any one who pretends to be neutral writes himself down here as a fool and a sham. We all do wish to minimize the insecurity of the universe; we are and ought to be unhappy when we regard it as exposed to every enemy and open to every life-destroying draft. Nevertheless there are unhappy men who think the salvation of the world impossible. Theirs is the doctrine known as pessimism.

Optimism in turn would be the doctrine that thinks the world's salvation necessary.

Midway between the two there stands what may be called the doctrine of meliorism, tho it has hitherto figured less as a doctrine than as an attitude in human affairs. Optimism has always been the regnant *doctrine* in European philosophy. Pessimism was only recently introduced by Schopenhauer and counts few systematic defenders as yet. Meliorism treats salvation as neither necessary nor impossible. It treats it as a possibility, which becomes more and more of a probability the more numerous the actual conditions of salvation become.

It is clear that pragmatism must incline towards meliorism. Some conditions of the world's salvation are actually extant, and she can not possibly close her eyes to this fact: and should the residual conditions come, salvation would become an accomplished reality. Naturally the terms I use here are exceedingly summary. You may interpret the word 'salvation' in any way you like, and make it as diffuse and distributive, or as climacteric and integral a phenomenon as you please.

Take, for example, any one of us in this room with the ideals which he cherishes and is willing to live and work for. Every such ideal realized will be one moment in the world's salvation. But these particular ideals are not bare abstract possibilities. They are grounded, they are *live* possibilities, for we are their live champions and pledges, and if the complementary conditions come and add themselves, our ideals will become actual things. What now are the complementary conditions? They are first such a mixture of things as will in the fulness of time give us a chance, a gap that we can spring into, and, finally, *our act*.

Does our act then *create* the world's salvation so far as it makes room for itself, so far as it leaps into the gap? Does it create, not the whole world's salvation of course, but just so much of this as itself covers of the world's extent?

Here I take the bull by the horns, and in spite of the whole crew of rationalists and monists, of whatever brand they be, I ask *why not?* Our acts, our turning-places, where we seem to ourselves to make ourselves and grow, are the parts of the world to which we are closest, the parts of which our knowledge is the most intimate and complete. Why should we not take them at their face-value?

Why may they not be the actual turning-places and growing-places which they seem to be, of the world – why not the workshop of being, where we catch fact in the making, so that nowhere may the world grow in any other kind of way than this?

Irrational! we are told. How can new being come in local spots and patches which add themselves or stay away at random, independently of the rest? There must be a reason for our acts, and where in the last resort can any reason be looked for save in the material pressure or the logical compulsion of the total nature of the world? There can be but one real agent of growth, or seeming growth, anywhere, and that agent is the integral world itself. It may grow all-over, if growth there be, but that single parts should grow *per se* is irrational.

But if one talks of rationality – and of reasons for things, and insists that they can't just come in spots, what *kind* of a reason can there ultimately be why anything should come at all? Talk of logic and necessity and categories and the absolute and the contents of the whole philosophical machine-shop as you will, the only *real* reason I can think of why anything should ever come is that *some one wishes it to be here*. It is *demanded*, – demanded, it may be, to give relief to no matter how small a fraction of the world's mass. This is *living reason*, and compared with it material causes and logical necessities are spectral things.

In short the only fully rational world would be the world of wishing-caps, the world of telepathy, where every desire is fulfilled instanter, without having to consider or placate surrounding or intermediate powers. This is the Absolute's own world. He calls upon the phenomenal world to be, and it *is*, exactly as he calls for it, no other condition being required. In our world, the wishes of the individual are only one condition. Other individuals are there with other wishes and they must be propitiated first. So Being grows under all sorts of resistances in this world of the many, and, from compromise to compromise, only gets organized gradually into what may be called secondarily rational shape. We approach the wishing-cap type of organization only in a few departments of life. We want water and we turn a faucet. We want a kodak-picture and we press a button. We want information and we telephone. We want to travel and we buy a ticket. In these and similar cases, we hardly need to do more than the wishing – the world is rationally organized to do the rest.

But this talk of rationality is a parenthesis and a digression. What we were discussing was the idea of a world growing not integrally but piecemeal by the contributions of its several parts. Take the hypothesis seriously and as a live one. Suppose that the world's author put the case to you before creation, saying: "I am going to make a world not certain to be saved, a world the perfection of which shall be conditional merely, the condition being that each several agent does its own 'level best.' I offer you the chance of taking part in such a world. Its safety, you see, is unwarranted. It is a real adventure, with real danger, yet it may win through. It is a social scheme of co-operative work genuinely to be done. Will you join the procession? Will you trust yourself and trust the other agents enough to face the risk?"

Should you in all seriousness, if participation in such a world were proposed to you, feel bound to reject it as not safe enough? Would you say that, rather than be part and parcel of so fundamentally pluralistic and irrational a universe, you preferred to relapse into the slumber of nonentity from which you had been momentarily aroused by the tempter's voice?

Of course if you are normally constituted, you would do nothing of the sort. There is a healthy-minded buoyancy in most of us which such a universe would exactly fit. We would therefore accept the offer – "Top! und schlag auf schlag!" It would be just like the world we practically live in; and loyalty to our old nurse Nature would forbid us to say no. The world proposed would seem 'rational' to us in the most living way.

Most of us, I say, would therefore welcome the proposition and add our *fiat* to the *fiat* of the creator. Yet perhaps some would not; for there are morbid minds in every human collection, and to them the prospect of a universe with only a fighting chance of safety would probably make no appeal. There are moments of discouragement in us all, when we are sick of self and tired of vainly striving. Our own life breaks down, and we fall into the attitude of the prodigal son. We mistrust the chances of things. We want a universe where we can just give up, fall on our father's neck, and be absorbed into the absolute life as a drop of water melts into the river or the sea.

The peace and rest, the security desiderated at such moments is security against the bewildering accidents of so much finite experience. Nirvana means safety from this everlasting round of adventures of which the world of sense consists. The hindoo and the buddhist, for this is essentially their attitude, are simply afraid, afraid of more experience, afraid of life.

And to men of this complexion, religious monism comes with its consoling words: "All is needed and essential – even you with your sick soul and heart. All are one with God, and with God all is well. The everlasting arms are beneath, whether in the world of finite appearance you seem to fail or to succeed." There can be no doubt that when men are reduced to their last sick extremity absolutism is the only saving scheme. Pluralistic moralism simply makes their teeth chatter, it refrigerates the very heart within their breast.

So we see concretely two types of religion in sharp contrast. Using our old terms of comparison, we may say that the absolutistic scheme appeals to the tender-minded while the pluralistic scheme appeals to the tough. Many persons would refuse to call the pluralistic scheme religious at all. They would call it moralistic, and would apply the word religious to the monistic scheme alone. Religion in the sense of self-surrender, and moralism in the sense of self-sufficingness, have been pitted against each other as incompatibles frequently enough in the history of human thought.

We stand here before the final question of philosophy. I said in my fourth lecture that I believed the monistic–pluralistic alternative to be the deepest and most pregnant question that our minds can frame. Can it be that the disjunction is a final one? that only one side can be true? Are a pluralism and monism genuine incompatibles? So that, if the world were really pluralistically constituted, if it really existed distributively and were made up of a lot of eaches, it could only be saved piecemeal and *de facto* as the result of their behavior, and its epic history in no wise short-circuited by some essential oneness in which the severalness were already 'taken up' beforehand and eternally 'overcome'? If this were so, we should have to choose one philosophy or the other. We could not say 'yes, yes' to both alternatives. There would have to be a 'no' in our relations with the possible. We should confess an ultimate disappointment: we could not remain healthy-minded and sick-minded in one indivisible act.

Of course as human beings we can be healthy minds on one day and sick souls on the next; and as amateur dabblers in philosophy we may perhaps be allowed to call ourselves monistic pluralists, or free-will determinists, or whatever else may occur to us of a reconciling kind. But as philosophers aiming at clearness and consistency, and feeling the pragmatistic need of squaring truth with truth, the question is forced upon us of frankly adopting either the tender or the robustious type of thought. In particular *this* query has always come home to me: May not the claims of tender-mindedness go too far? May not the notion of a world already saved *in toto* anyhow, be too saccharine to stand? May not religious optimism be too idyllic? Must *all* be saved? Is *no* price to be paid in the work of salvation? Is the last word sweet? Is all 'yes, yes' in the universe? Does n't the fact of 'no' stand at the very core of life? Does n't the very 'seriousness' that we attribute to life mean that ineluctable noes and losses form a part of it, that there are genuine sacrifices somewhere, and that something permanently drastic and bitter always remains at the bottom of its cup?

I can not speak officially as a pragmatist here; all I can say is that my own pragmatism offers no objection to my taking sides with this more moralistic view, and giving up the claim of total reconciliation. The possibility of this is involved in the pragmatistic willingness to treat pluralism as a serious hypothesis. In the end it is our faith and not our logic that decides such questions, and I deny the right of any pretended logic to veto my own faith. I find myself willing to take the universe to be really dangerous and adventurous, without therefore backing out and crying 'no play.' I am willing to think that the prodigal-son attitude, open to us as it is in many vicissitudes, is not the right and final attitude towards the whole of life. I am willing that there should be real losses and real losers, and no total preservation of all that is. I can believe in the ideal as an ultimate, not as an origin, and as an extract, not the whole. When the cup is poured off, the dregs are left behind for ever, but the possibility of what is poured off is sweet enough to accept.

As a matter of fact countless human imaginations live in this moralistic and epic kind of a universe, and find its disseminated and strung-along successes sufficient for their rational needs. There is a finely translated epigram in the Greek anthology which admirably expresses this state of mind, this acceptance of loss as unatoned for, even though the lost element might be one's self:

"A shipwrecked sailor, buried on this coast,
    Bids you set sail.
Full many a gallant bark, when we were lost,
    Weathered the gale."

Those puritans who answered 'yes' to the question: Are you willing to be damned for God's glory? were in this objective and magnanimous condition of mind. The way of escape from evil on this system is *not* by getting it *'aufgehoben,'* or preserved in the whole as an element essential but 'overcome.' *It is by dropping it out altogether, throwing it overboard and getting beyond it, helping to make a universe that shall forget its very place and name.*

It is then perfectly possible to accept sincerely a drastic kind of a universe from which the element of 'seriousness' is not to be expelled. Whoso does so is, it seems to me, a genuine pragmatist. He is willing to live on a scheme of uncertified possibilities which he trusts; willing to pay with his own person, if need be, for the realization of the ideals which he frames.

What now actually *are* the other forces which he trusts to co-operate with him, in a universe of such a type? They are at least his fellow men, in the stage of being which our actual universe has reached. But are there not superhuman forces also, such as religious men of the pluralistic type we have been considering have always believed in? Their words may have sounded monistic when they said "there is no God but God"; but the original polytheism of mankind has only imperfectly and vaguely sublimated itself into monotheism, and monotheism itself, so far as it was religious and not a scheme of classroom instruction for the metaphysicians, has always viewed God as but one helper, *primus inter pares*, in the midst of all the shapers of the great world's fate.

I fear that my previous lectures, confined as they have been to human and humanistic aspects, may have left the impression on many of you that pragmatism means methodically to leave the superhuman out. I have shown small respect indeed for the Absolute, and I have until this moment spoken of no other super-human hypothesis but that. But I trust that you see sufficiently that the Absolute has nothing but its superhumanness in common with the theistic God. On pragmatistic principles, if the hypothesis of God works satisfactorily in the widest sense of the word, it is true. Now whatever its residual difficulties may be, experience shows that it certainly does work, and that the problem is to build it out and determine it so that it will combine satisfactorily with all the other working truths. I can not start upon a whole theology at the end of this last lecture; but when I tell you that I have written a book on men's religious experience, which on the whole has been regarded as making for the reality of God, you will perhaps exempt my own pragmatism from the charge of being an atheistic system. I firmly disbelieve, myself, that our human experience is the highest form of experience extant in the universe. I believe rather that we stand in much the same relation to the whole of the universe as our canine and feline pets do to the whole of human life. They inhabit our drawing-rooms and libraries. They take part in scenes of whose significance they have no inkling. They are merely tangent to curves of history the beginnings and ends and forms of which pass wholly beyond their ken. So we are tangent to the wider life of things. But, just as many of the dog's and cat's ideals coincide with our ideals, and the dogs and cats have daily living proof of the fact, so we may well believe, on the proofs that religious experience affords, that higher powers exist and are at work to save the world on ideal lines similar to our own.

You see that pragmatism can be called religious, if you allow that religion can be pluralistic or merely melioristic in type. But whether you will finally put up with that type of religion or not is a question that only you yourself can decide. Pragmatism has to postpone dogmatic answer, for we do not yet know certainly which type of religion is going to work best in the long run. The various overbeliefs of men, their several faith-ventures, are in fact what are needed to bring the evidence in. You will probably make your own ventures severally. If radically tough, the hurly-burly of the sensible facts of nature will be enough for you, and you will need no religion at all. If radically tender, you will take up with the more monistic form of religion: the pluralistic form, with its reliance on possibilities that are not necessities, will not seem to afford you security enough.

But if you are neither tough nor tender in an extreme and radical sense, but mixed as most of us are, it may seem to you that the type of pluralistic and moralistic religion that I have offered is as good a religious synthesis as you are likely to find. Between the two extremes of crude naturalism on the one hand and transcendental absolutism on the other, you may find that what I take the liberty of calling the pragmatistic or melioristic type of theism is exactly what you require.

MEANING AND
METAPHYSICS IN JAMES

Robert G. Meyers

William James's writings on meaning have long presented an enigma. On the one hand, his view that the meaning of a proposition or statement is its experiential consequences seems very close to a modern positivistic theory. Yet, on the other hand, he clearly considers traditional metaphysical propositions such as 'The world is One' and 'God created the universe' as meaningful even though they seem to imply no experiential effects.

Turning to the commentators on James, one finds a most plausible explanation in the work of A.O. Lovejoy and Paul Henle.[1] According to them, James holds that a statement is meaningful, not only if it has experiential consequences, but also if belief in the statement does. Although Lovejoy holds that these criteria are dissimilar and incongruous while Henle says they 'fit as neatly as the white and yolk of an egg', their interpretation explains how James agrees with positivism while accepting metaphysics. For, even though metaphysical statements have no sensible consequences, believing in them can affect our lives. Hence, although they fail to pass one test for meaningfulness, they pass the other.

In this paper, I will try to show that the Lovejoy–Henle interpretation is mistaken. In broad outline, the view I will defend is in the spirit of Ralph Barton Perry's interpretation of James. According to Perry, James's pragmatism and fideism must not be confused. 'Pragmatism', he says, 'is the application of practical principles to the theoretic process itself; fideism is the justification, on practical grounds, of overbelief – that is, of belief which lacks conclusive theoretic support.'[2] Perry's view thus denies that effects of beliefs are part of the meanings of the propositions believed as both Lovejoy and Henle hold. I will attempt to extend this view by showing how James can hold an apparently antimetaphysical theory of meaning while accepting metaphysics. Specifically I will argue that James does not use pragmatism as a criterion of meaningfulness that will rule out metaphysical doctrines, but rather that he assumes on common-sense grounds that they are meaningful and uses pragmatism to clarify their meaning. In section I, I will briefly explain Lovejoy's and Henle's interpretations, then point out certain textual and conceptual difficulties connected with them. In section II, I will attempt to show how James applies his pragmatic method and how I think effects of beliefs figure in James's general position, although not in his theory of meaning.

I

In *Pragmatism*, James explains what he means by the pragmatic method:

> To attain perfect clearness in our thoughts of an object . . . we need only consider what conceivable effects of a practical kind the object may involve – what sensations we are to expect from it, and what reactions we must prepare. Our conception of these effects, whether immediate or remote, is then for us the whole of our conception of the object, so far as that conception has positive significance at all.[3]

In 1908 in 'The thirteen pragmatisms', Lovejoy argued on the basis of James's discussion of the One and the many that James holds absolutism to be meaningful because believing that the world is One has desirable consequences, even though the doctrine of absolutism alone has no sensible effects. This means, Lovejoy said, that James's doctrine of meaning involves a radical ambiguity in that James sometimes interprets 'effects of a practical kind' as (a) sensible consequences of the proposition itself, whether believed or not, and sometimes as (b) 'future experiences which will occur *only upon condition that the proposition be believed*'.[4] According to Lovejoy, no two doctrines could be more dissimilar. Interpreted in sense (a), for instance, James's pragmatic maxim 'very narrowly' limits the range of meaningful propositions. When used in sense (b), however, the criterion is 'the mildest of truisms', since it is then so 'blandly catholic, tolerant and inclusive a doctrine that it can deny real meaning to no proposition whatever which any human being has ever cared enough about to believe'.[5]

The seriousness of Lovejoy's criticism can be seen if we take an example. Suppose that believing that gremlins exist gives A a feeling of comfort and ease. Then, even though 'Gremlins exist' has no verifiable consequences, A's belief that gremlins exist would still be meaningful for A's belief has consequences. Hence, according to sense (a) of James's doctrine of meaningfulness, 'Gremlins exist' is meaningless, while according to sense (b), 'Gremlins exist' is meaningful. Thus, it seems that, on James's account, 'Gremlins exist' is both meaningful and meaningless at the same time.

Although Paul Henle does not specifically consider Lovejoy's criticism that James's two criteria are incongruous, his interpretation does seem to offer an alternative, more sympathetic reading of James. Henle follows Lovejoy in distinguishing between effects of p and of belief in p in James, yet holds that 'James uses the two standards of meaning in a complementary fashion, being willing to make use of any statement which is meaningful by either criterion'.[6] According to Henle, if belief in p has sensible effects while p alone does not, it follows that p is meaningful and not, as Lovejoy suggests, that p is meaningful in one sense and meaningless in the other. That is, Henle denies that James uses the criteria incompatibly. Rather p is meaningless for James, Henle holds, only if p has no consequences and belief in p has no consequences. Hence, if p alone has no effects while belief in p does, it follows that p is meaningful and not that p is both meaningful and meaningless at the same time. More exactly, Henle attributes the following doctrine to James: p is meaningful, if, and only if, either p has sensible consequences or, if p has no sensible consequences, belief in p does.

Henle adds one important qualification. He holds that, in the case of the consequences of belief in p, James gives 'no explanation of what constitutes the meaning and we are left with the bare criterion of meaningfulness'.[7] That is, according to Henle, James never claims the effects of belief in p form part of the meaning of p, but rather only show that p is meaningful.

Although Henle's defence of James shows some promise, it will not do. In the first place, on Henle's account, James still cannot avoid Lovejoy's charge that his doctrine is an inadequate criterion of significance. For, even if the two senses of 'practical bearings' are not compatible, James's doctrine, by allowing effects of beliefs to have a part in determining meaningfulness, still admits as meaningful any proposition which anyone has ever cared enough about to believe.

Furthermore – and more important – Henle's qualification that effects of belief in p do not constitute the meaning of p leads to a very paradoxical, if not contradictory, result. Suppose p has no experiential consequences, but belief in p does. Then, on Henle's view, p is meaningful. Yet the fact that belief in p has consequences only shows that p is meaningful, according to Henle. The effects of belief in p do not form part of the meaning of p; rather the meaning of p is the sum of experiential effects of p alone. But, by hypothesis, p has no experiential effects, and, hence, no meaning. Thus, it appears that p is a meaningful proposition which has no meaning – a very strange consequence indeed. Consider the previous example of 'Gremlins exist'.[8] This proposition has no sensible effects, but let us suppose that belief in it does. Hence, it is meaningful according to Henle's interpretation of James's doctrine of meaning. Yet, since Henle holds that the consequences of 'Gremlins exist' alone constitute the meaning of the proposition, it follows that 'Gremlins exist' has no meaning, for it has no sensible effects unless believed. Hence, 'Gremlins exist' has meaning and no meaning at the same time. Since this is a contradiction, James – or Henle – has made a serious blunder. As a result, Henle's interpretation of James can hardly be a defence of James. If anything, the fact that Henle's view of James is untenable seems to lead back to Lovejoy's original thesis that James's doctrine was basically confused and, hence, itself in need of clarification. What are we to make of this situation? Is Lovejoy's reading of James correct?

Lovejoy's main support for his thesis is a remark by James in lecture VIII, 'Pragmatism and religion', in *Pragmatism*. There James writes:

> the use of the Absolute is proved by the whole course of man's religious history. The eternal arms are then beneath. Remember Vivekanda's use of the Atman: it is indeed not a scientific use, for we can make no particular deductions from it. It is emotional and spiritual altogether.[9]

Here James clearly denies that the doctrine of the Absolute has sensible consequences, although, as the rest of lecture VIII reveals, James still considers absolutism as a tenable though philosophically inadequate doctrine. That is, James considers absolutism as meaningful even though he says that absolutism implies no sensible consequences. On the basis of lecture VIII, the apparent reason for the meaningfulness of absolutism is that it has 'emotional and spiritual' consequences, or, as Lovejoy puts it, the Absolute is meaningful because believing in it has important consequences. This is strong textual evidence for Lovejoy's interpretation. Indeed James admitted that he had confused effects of propositions with effects of beliefs in them. Replying to some comments by Lovejoy in 1907 before the publication of 'The thirteen pragmatisms', James said:

> when it comes to your distinction between two meanings in the first meaning of pragmatism, I have to frankly cry *peccavi* – you convict me of real sin. Consequences of true ideas *per se*, and consequences of true ideas *qua believed by us*, are logically different consequences, and the whole 'will to believe' business has got to be re-edited with explicit uses made of the distinction. I have been careless here, and I hope that you, in your article, will spread out that matter at the length it deserves. Failure to do it on my part has been misdemeanor.[10]

However, although there can be no question that James has been careless, I do not think it follows that, according to James, the Absolute has meaning *only because* of the effects which follow from believing in the doctrine. Lecture IV, 'The One and the Many', for instance, where James considers the problem of monism vs pluralism in detail, reveals that, according to James, absolutism has experiential effects independently of belief in the doctrine and not, as Lovejoy holds, that the Absolute is meaningful only because belief in it has pleasant effects. Seen in this light, the passage in lecture VIII appears not as the main doctrine, but rather as an imprecise formulation of James's view toward the Absolute.

Let us look more carefully at the argument of lecture IV of *Pragmatism*. James begins by asking what practical value the oneness has for us if we grant that the world is One. What facts will be different if monism is true? What will the oneness of the world be known as? 'Asking such questions, we pass from the vague to the definite, from the abstract to the concrete. Many distinct ways in which a oneness predicated of the universe might make a difference, come to view.'[11] James then lists a number of different interpretations that might be given to monism: one subject of discourse, continuity, causal unity, generic unity, unity of purpose, aesthetic unity and the one Knower. James points out a number of practical, i.e. experiential, consequences for each of these possibilities, then tries to evaluate the oneness of the universe as an empirical hypothesis. In each case, he finds the evidence for monism wanting. For instance, of the 'one Knower' interpretation, James says:

> I must therefore treat the notion of an All-Knower simply as an hypothesis, exactly on a par logically with the pluralist notion that there is no point of view, no focus of information extant, from which the entire content of the universe is visible at once.[12]

When James says monism and pluralism are on a par logically, he means that the evidence is even and not that there is no practical difference between the doctrines. Monism argues for the unity of the universe; pluralism for the independence of the various parts of the universe. Yet, when brought down to concrete experiences which would support monism, James finds that the doctrine runs beyond the evidence. His conclusion is that, although monism and pluralism differ in practical consequences, and, hence, in meaning, the evidence for each is equal; the experienced universe exhibits both unity and independence. James makes this point clearly in lecture IV. Applying pragmatism, he says, we find that

> she must equally abjure absolute monism and absolute plural-ism. The world is One just so far as its parts hang together by any definite connection. It is many just so far as any definite connection fails to obtain.[13]

Hence, close reading of lecture IV shows that Lovejoy is mistaken in interpreting James as holding that the Absolute is meaningful only because belief in it has useful consequences. Although James holds that both the One and the Many go beyond the evidence, he clearly holds that the hypothesis of the One has practical conse-quences and not, as Lovejoy says, that only *belief* in the doctrine has them.[14]

II

If this is correct and the evidence that James uses two distinct criteria is inconclusive, we are still left with the problem of explain-ing how James could consider as meaningful so many doctrines which seem to have no sensible effects. Despite our wishes, I do not think we can find a clear and consistent explanation which is in line with everything James says on the subject. Still, by examining the way in which James applies his doctrine, I think it is possible to give an interpretation which is more plausible and, at the same time, more sympathetic than Lovejoy's. Let me begin by looking more closely at James's doctrine of meaning.

James's theory of meaning proper states:

(1) The meaning of a statement is the sum of experiential consequences.

From this we may derive:

(2) A statement has meaning, if, and only if, it has at least one experiential consequence.

The most obvious way of interpreting (2) is to say, as Lovejoy does, that it provides a rule for eliminating metaphysical nonsense and unresolvable disputes. That is, we apply the rule to specific doctrines in an attempt to determine whether they are meaningful or not. If they have experiential consequences, they are meaningful; if they have none, they are meaningless and, hence, not worthy of consideration. Although this is a reasonable way of looking at principles such as (2), it is really an oversimplification. Something else is required to make (2) a weapon for undermining the sense of metaphysics: the philosopher must consider it a live possibility that the metaphysician is uttering nonsense. Without this suspicion, the philosopher may hold (1) and, thus, (2) also, and yet still consider metaphysical disputes as meaningful. He may argue, for instance, that the truth of (2) only means that metaphysical propositions clearly have experiential consequences, since metaphysical propositions clearly have meaning. That is, he may start out from the assumption that metaphysical propositions are meaningful and conclude that, because of this, they must have sensible consequences. Such a view is clearly consistent with the truth of (2). It simply involves a refusal to treat the meaninglessness of metaphysics as a live issue.

This, I think, is James's attitude toward (2). Although he clearly believes that (2) is true, he does not consider metaphysics as basically nonsensical; rather he assumes along with common sense that metaphysicians defend meaningful positions even though their writings are difficult to understand. Hence, since there is no real question about the meaningfulness of metaphysics, James uses pragmatism, not to eliminate metaphysics, but rather to clarify the meaning of metaphysical doctrine so they can be evaluated more easily.[15] In accomplishing this clarification, the important doctrine becomes (1), since it tells us what to look for in clarifying propositions. Principle (2), although implied by (1), becomes relatively unimportant, for, without the live possibility that the metaphysician is making meaningless utterances, (2) has no real job to perform.[16]

Examples of this tolerance toward metaphysics are present throughout James's writings on meaning. We have already seen one in connection with his treatment of absolutism. When James considers the meaning of the doctrine that the world is One, he does not even entertain the possibility that the doctrine has no sensible consequences. Instead, he assumes that the absolutist intends to say something meaningful. Pragmatism's job is not to decide whether the doctrine is really meaningful, but to clarify the meaning by pointing out the kinds of unity one would expect to find if the world were One. Far from arguing that absolutism is meaningless, he proceeds to list seven different kinds of unity we could expect to obtain if absolutism were true. The same magnanimous attitude is reflected in James's treatment of the dispute between materialism and spiritualism. According to James, materialism is the doctrine that the universe is the result of blind physical forces while spiritualism is the view that God made and guides the universe. Viewed in terms of the past and present, James says, these doctrines have the same meaning because, on either hypothesis, the sensible universe would be the same in all its details. That is, from the standpoint of the past and present, no deductions can be made from either hypothesis which will distinguish it from the other.[17] When we look to what each doctrine predicts about the future, however, we find the real difference in meaning between them. Whereas materialism implies the ultimate decay and dissolution of the universe and man, spiritualism asserts ultimate salvation. Although James makes the point in *Pragmatism*, it is most clearly stated in the early paper 'Philosophical conceptions and practical results':

> A world with a God in it to say the last word, may indeed burn up or freeze, but we then think of Him as still mindful of the old ideals and sure to bring them elsewhere to fruition; so that, where He is, tragedy is only provisional and partial, and shipwreck and dissolution not the absolutely final things.[18]

Hence, materialism and spiritualism differ in practical consequences in that they imply different sensible experiences about the future. The point to be noticed here is that, as with the dispute between monism and pluralism, James starts from the assumption of the meaningfulness of the question, then uses pragmatism in order to clarify the issue by pin-pointing the different predictions which follow from the doctrines. The pragmatic maxim is not used to eliminate metaphysics, but rather to sharpen our common-sense awareness that there is a genuine dispute by showing us the heart of the controversy. The emphasis, in other words, is on pragmatism as a tool of clarification and not on pragmatism as a weapon for undermining metaphysics.[19]

If this approach to James is correct and he is more anxious to clarify obviously meaningful doctrines than to decide on their meaningfulness, some of the difficulties found in James appear in a new light. For one, the vagueness of 'practical consequences' in James becomes more understandable. Instead of giving clear criteria for sensible effects, James gives flourishes such as this:

Pragmatism is willing to take anything, to follow either logic or the senses and to count the humblest and most personal experiences. She will count mystical experiences if they have practical consequences. She will take a God who lives in the very dirt of private fact – if that should seem a likely place to find him.[20]

Such vagueness is unfortunate, especially since James seems to revel in it. Yet, once we understand James's attitude toward metaphysics, we can see why he is vague. For if pragmatism is to be a method independent of specific doctrines and a mediator between the tough-minded and tender-minded approaches, it must be open to any and all experiential consequences. If the criteria for such consequences are construed too narrowly, doctrines such as absolutism and spiritualism may be ruled out as meaningless; and such a result hardly seems fitting for a doctrine which is supposed to mediate between religion and science. Indeed, James suggests that too narrow a view of experiential effects is a main defect of British empiricism: 'The shortcomings and negations and baldnesses of the English philosophers in question come, not from their eye to merely practical results, but solely from their failure to track the practical results completely enough to see how far they extend.'[21] Thus, although James is ready to see Locke, Berkeley and Hume as important precursors of his pragmatism, he is also aware that experience cannot be construed narrowly without seriously under-mining the main aim of pragmatism, namely, the clarification of metaphysics.

In short, if the approach presented here is correct, the fact that James holds a tough-minded theory of meaning while admitting tender-minded doctrines as meaningful is not really puzzling at all. Although James holds that meaningful statements must have sen-sible consequences, he does not suspect that metaphysics is mean-ingless. Rather he believes that metaphysics, though meaningful, is unclear. Hence, he uses his pragmatism to elucidate metaphysical questions so they can be decided. This interpretation has a number of advantages over Lovejoy's. For one, it gives James the benefit of a doubt and, thus, is more sympathetic. Moreover, it is more in line with James's general approach to metaphysics – more in the spirit of James, if you wish – and, hence, more plausible.

Although my main thesis is that effects of beliefs do not deter-mine meaningfulness for James, it must not be thought that effects of beliefs are unimportant for James. In fact, I think nothing is more characteristic of him than the heavy emphasis he puts on the consequences of believing propositions. Effects of beliefs, how-ever, relate not to meaningfulness, but rather to the question whether we ought to believe when the evidence is insufficient. On this question, James holds that, even though the evidence for p is insufficient, there are certain conditions under which we have the right to believe. Although this famous doctrine is usually called 'the will to believe', I prefer to follow James's later wishes and call it 'the right to believe'.[22] According to this doctrine, it is permissible for A to believe p on the basis of insufficient evidence, if A desires X and believing p will help to bring about X. Here, clearly, effects of beliefs rather than effects of propositions move into the spot-light. This does not mean, however, that effects of beliefs guaran-tee cognitive meaningfulness, for the right to believe in James is not concerned with meaning but rather with quite a different question, namely, the ethics of belief.

Although the right to believe is a many-sided and involved doctrine, in closing let me sketch its role in James's overall treat-ment of the Absolute. In this way perhaps we can gain a proper perspective on effects of beliefs in James.

One fundamental function of the right to believe in James is to 'justify' the metaphysician's intense conviction in doctrines for which the evidence is insufficient. According to the pragmatic

maxim, the sensory consequences implied by a proposition constitute the meaning of the proposition. Hence, in order to support a
proposition, we deduce sensible consequences from it, then check
the consequences against experience. When we apply this procedure to doctrines such as the view that the universe is One, we
find that, although some observations support absolutism, other
observations are incompatible with it. Hence, intense belief in
absolutism is not justified by the evidence. For James, however,
this does not mean that absolutism is completely unjustified, for, in
another sense, the absolutist can 'justify' his belief. If, for instance,
the absolutist's temperament is such that he desires and needs a
feeling of security and believing that the world is One gives him
this feeling, he does have a reason for his belief, although not a
rational one in the usual sense. Hence, according to James, the
absolutist has a right to believe his doctrine even though it goes
beyond the evidence. On this level, the right to believe may be said
to be a plea for metaphysical tolerance.

James's application of the right to believe does not stop here,
however. Although James believes that the absolutist is free to
believe his doctrine even though the senses give it only a very low
probability, James also believes that the absolutist is morally wrong
in believing as he does. For, according to James, one should believe
that which helps to bring about the greatest social good.[23] That is,
in deciding whether to believe opposing doctrines where the evidence is indecisive, we ought to choose the belief whose effects
contribute to our accomplishing the greatest social good. Now,
since the absolutist holds that progress and social improvement are
inevitable, James feels that believing in absolutism will lead to
quietism. What we should believe, according to James, is a doctrine
which prompts us to make the world better. This doctrine James
calls melioristic pluralism. Although the evidence for it is as
tenuous as the evidence for absolutism, it is the 'better' belief to
hold, for, by believing it, we can help make the universe a better
place in which to live. That is, the desirable consequences which
will follow from believing in meliorism outweigh those which
follow from holding to absolutism.

The essential point to recognize is that effects of beliefs and the
right to believe do not confer meaningfulness on metaphysical
doctrines. Rather the right to believe provides a means of establish-
ing belief in doctrines for which *some* evidence is available but not
enough to show the truth of the doctrine decisively. In short, the

right to believe is not related to James's doctrine of cognitive meaning; instead James presupposes that the statements to which the right to believe applies have some sensible consequences and, hence, meaning. Of course, one might argue that James is too tender and that the right to believe itself has undesirable consequences. But this is quite different from arguing, as Lovejoy does, that James's theory of meaning is fundamentally confused.[24]

NOTES

1 A.O. Lovejoy, 'The thirteen pragmatisms', *The Journal of Philosophy* 5 (1908), 5–12 and 29–39, and Paul Henle, Introduction on William James, in *Classic American Philosophers*, ed. M.H. Fisch (New York, Appleton–Century–Crofts, 1951), 115–27.
2 R.B. Perry, *In the Spirit of William James* (Bloomington, Ind., Indiana University Press, 1958), 71.
3 William James, *Pragmatism* (New York, Meridian Books, New American Library, 1955), 39; all page numbers in the text refer to the present volume.
4 Lovejoy, op. cit., 8; Lovejoy's italics.
5 ibid., 9.
6 Fisch, op. cit., 126.
7 ibid.
8 Henle uses the example of 'God exists', ibid., 117. This, however, is problematic, for James seems to have felt that mystical experiences verify the existence of God. See James's 'Philosophical conceptions and practical results', reprinted in *Philosophy in America*, ed. P.R. Anderson and M.H. Fisch (New York, Appleton–Century, 1939), 536: 'These direct experiences of a wider spiritual life with which our superficial consciousness is continuous, and with which it keeps up an intense commerce, form the primary mass of direct religious experience on which all hearsay religion rests, and which furnishes that notion of an ever-present God, out of which systematic theology thereupon proceeds to make capital in its own unreal pedantic way.' See also James, *Pragmatism*, 141–2. Although it is open to question whether such experiences in fact justify God's existence, I think it is fair to say that James believed 'God exists' has sensible consequences and not that only belief in the doctrine has pleasant effects as Henle suggests.
9 James, *Pragmatism*, 130.
10 Quoted in R.B. Perry, *The Thought and Character of William James* (Boston, Mass., Little, Brown, 1936), vol. II, 481; James's italics.
11 James, *Pragmatism*, 73.
12 ibid., 78.
13 ibid., 83.
14 That the Absolute has consequences independently of belief in absolutism is clear also in James, 'Philosophical conceptions and practical results', in Anderson and Fisch, op. cit., 538–9.

15 One finds the same approach in C.S. Peirce. Consider, for example, his question: 'Where would such an idea, say as that of God, come from, if not from direct experience?', in *Collected Papers*, ed. Charles Hartshorne, Paul Weiss and A.W. Burks (Cambridge, Mass., Belknap Press, 1934–58), vol. VI, para. 493. Here Peirce, like James, assumes the meaningfulness of 'God' and looks for its origin.

16 I say that (2) becomes 'relatively unimportant' because, no matter how hard one tries to be tolerant, some metaphysicians will insist on cutting off their doctrines from any sensory verification whatsoever, and, thus, turn their doctrines into meaningless nonsense. In these cases, as James recognizes, (2) *does* become important. A case in point is the Lockian conception of matter. See James's 'Philosophical conceptions and practical results', in Anderson and Fisch, op. cit., 540, where James agrees with Berkeley that 'the cash-value of matter is our physical sensations. That is what it is known as, all that we concretely verify of its conception. That therefore is the whole meaning of the word "matter" – any other pretended meaning is mere wind of words.' See also James, *Pragmatism*, 55–6.

17 James later modified this view on the grounds that, even though no differing future consequences are deducible from the hypotheses, the concepts of God and matter would still differ in the same way that an 'automatic sweetheart' would differ from a spiritually animated maiden. Despite this change, however, James left the passage unaltered 'because the flaw did not destroy its illustrative value'. See *The Meaning of Truth* (New York, Longmans, Green, 1927), 189–90 note.

18 Anderson and Fisch, op. cit., 533.

19 Peter Hare has pointed out to me that James uses the same technique in dealing with the problem of the infinite in *Some Problems of Philosophy* (New York, Longmans, Green, 1916), chapters X and XI.

20 James, *Pragmatism*, 53.

21 Anderson and Fisch, op. cit., 540–1.

22 Perry, *Thought and Character*, vol. II, 243–8.

23 For this aspect of the right to believe, see James, *Pragmatism*, lecture VIII, 'Pragmatism and religion'.

24 I am indebted to Edward H. Madden and Peter Hare who read early versions of this paper and contributed greatly to sharpening the argument.

TRUTH AND ITS VERIFICATION

James Bissett Pratt

After all the discussions of pragmatism that have appeared in this journal and elsewhere during the last three years it would seem that one ought no longer to have any doubt as to what the pragmatist means by truth. I, at any rate, had supposed it pretty well settled that pragmatism identified the truth of an idea with its successful working, with its verification; that it held truth to be quite as much an experienced process as saying the multiplication table or watching a chemical experiment. Recently, however, there has appeared in the writings of some leading pragmatists a quite different point of view, a tendency, namely, to identify the truth of an idea not only with the process of its verification, but also with its *verifiability*.[1] A true idea would thus be either one that has actually been verified or one that could be verified, and the truth of it would consist either in its concretely experienced leading to a satisfactory issue or in the possibility of such a leading.

Now it seems to me of great importance, if we are to keep the issue between pragmatism and intellectualism perfectly clear-cut, to note exactly what position such a view must hold in the present controversy over the nature of truth. And I will say at once that to my mind, at least, the conception of truth as *verifiability* seems by its very nature essentially non-pragmatic. It is inconsistent with nearly all the characteristics which distinguish the ordinarily accepted pragmatic view of truth. For verifiability is not a process, it is not included within anyone's experience, but is a general condition or set of conditions which transcends every single finite experience. It is not a felt 'leading', it is not a 'form of the good', nor a 'satisfactory working', nor any other kind of experience or experience-process. It is a totality of relations which are not within any finite experience. It is a present condition of the idea, not something that 'happens' to it. It is not 'made'; it is already there. Verification is one thing; verifiability is quite another. They are *toto coelo* apart. Verifiability is transcendent of experience in exactly the same sense in which the intellectualist makes truth transcendent. The intellectualist, indeed, might not be willing to accept it as a complete account of truth; he might still want to ask, How comes it that the idea can be verified? Just what sort of condition is verifiability? Still the identification of truth with verifiability comes immeasurably nearer to the intellectualist's view of truth than to the ordinary pragmatic view. In short, it is quite as impossible to identify truth with both verification *and* verifiability as it is to be both a pragmatist and an intellectualist at the same time. The pragmatist cannot hold them both; he cannot say, truth is altogether within experience and truth transcends experience. He must choose between them.

That being the case, there can be no doubt, after all, as to the fundamental pragmatic view of truth. *Truth for the pragmatist does not mean verifiability*; it means the process of verification. It is wholly within experience. It is to be identified with 'the psychological or biological processes by which it is pursued and attained'.[2] It is either a 'function of our intellectual activity' or a 'manipulation of our objects which turns out to be useful'.[3] Or, in Professor James's clear statement, it is 'eventual verification', the 'function of a leading that is worth-while'. 'Truth *happens* to an idea. It *becomes* true, is *made* true by events. Its verity *is* in fact an event, a process, the process, namely, of its verifying itself, its verification.'[4]

These are certainly plain statements, and the pragmatic meaning of truth cannot be mistaken. But one feels tempted, incidentally, to ask, If truth be nothing but the process of its verification, or the processes by which it is pursued and attained, what is it that is verified, what is it that is pursued and attained? Are we verifying verification and pursuing pursuit? This, indeed, sounds like logomachy, and I ask the question only to show that the use of such a word as verification by a theory which seeks to reduce everything to psychology results naturally in strange twistings of language. Pragmatism may very properly speak of successful and satisfactory experiences, but it is hard to see how it can consistently use the term *verification* at all. However, I do not press this point, but shall merely remark in passing that to me, at least, it would seem as hard to lift oneself by one's boot-straps as to comprehend how truth can consist in the process of its own verification, or how it (or anything else, for that matter) can *be* 'the processes by which it is pursued and attained'.

Having satisfied ourselves as to the exact meaning which the pragmatist gives to truth, let us turn to the intellectualist. His account of the matter is, as everyone knows, that truth means the correspondence of an idea with its object. But, asks the pragmatist, is not *correspondence* about as meaningless as any term can be? Does it mean that the idea *copies* reality? And is it not apparent that at best the number of cases in which the idea can be said in any sense to copy its object is extremely small? Or is truth some more mysterious – or mythological – quality in which the idea *participates* – a sort of metaphysical entity to which we must all bow down in worship? – The fact is, the pragmatist is here making his own difficulties for himself. The intellectualist's meaning of truth is so simple, so commonplace, so close at hand, that the pragmatist has quite overlooked it. By the truth of an idea the intellectualist means merely this simple thing, *that the object of which one is thinking is as one thinks it.* Is there anything hard about this, anything meaningless, anything 'metaphysical' or abstract?

But to make the whole matter perfectly clear, let us take a concrete situation and apply to it the rival views of truth; thus we shall see exactly how they compare with each other. There will indeed, be nothing new in this, for concrete test cases have abounded in many of the discussions of this subject. Yet most of these cases have seemed to me a little unfortunate in involving, indirectly, other questions than the one at issue and getting confused through realistic or subjectivistic interpretations. What we want is a case in which the meaning of the object as well as that of the idea shall be clear and shall be the same for all schools. I think the following rather puerile case will satisfy these conditions: John thinks Peter has a toothache; the object of John's thought is Peter's present experience; and, as a fact, Peter *has* a toothache. Now the intellectualist's notion of truth is this: that John's thought is true *because its object is as he thinks it.*

Now let us apply the pragmatic meaning of truth to the same situation – remembering that truth here means 'a form of the good',[5] 'the useful, efficient, workable', 'the satisfactory', the process of verification'. The truth of John's idea about Peter's experience, therefore, according to the pragmatist, *consists in* its satisfactoriness to John, in its successful leading, in its verifying itself. If it works, if it harmonizes with John's later experiences of

Peter's actions, if it leads in a direction that is worth-while, it is true (a statement to which, indeed, all might assent), and its truth *consists in* this working, this harmony, this verification process. John's thought, the pragmatist insists, *becomes* true only when it has worked out successfully, only when his later experience confirms it by being consistent with it – for remember, truth is not verifiability, but the process of verification. 'Truth happens to an idea. It *becomes* true, is *made* true by events.' At the time when John had the thought about Peter, the thought was *neither true nor false*, for the process of verification had not yet begun, nothing had as yet happened to the idea. To be sure, Peter had a toothache, just as John thought, but, all the same, John's thought was not true. It did not become true till several hours afterward – in fact, we may suppose, not until Peter, having cured his toothache, told John about it. The thought, 'Peter has a toothache', thus, as it happens, turns out not to have been true while Peter actually had the toothache, and to have become true only after he had ceased to have a toothache. It became true only by being proved true, and its truth consisted in the process of its proof. One might, perhaps, be tempted to ask what it was that was proved, and say to the pragmatist, Either this satisfactoriness, this successful leading, is a proof of something outside of John's immediate experience, something by which his idea is to be judged and justified (in which case truth ceases to be mere verification process and becomes at least verifiability); or else it is merely John's subjective feeling of satisfaction and of successful leading and consistency, with no reference to anything else to justify it – in which case it may indeed be pleasant and 'good', but it is hard to see why it should be called *true*. For suppose that at the same time with John's thought, Tom thinks Peter has *not* a toothache. Suppose that, being a little stupid and perhaps a little hard of hearing, he misinterprets John's actions and expressions, and that later on he is assured by someone equally misinformed that Peter certainly had no toothache. His thought thus works out, is successful, harmonizes with his later experience, is to him genuinely verified. The whole matter ends here and he drops the question completely, never investigating farther. Were the thoughts of John and Tom true?

Now it will not do to respond, 'No; Tom's thought was not *genuinely* verified. Only that thought was really verified and therefore true which *would have* worked out had both been investigated sufficiently.' For what do you mean by '*sufficiently*'? Sufficiently for what? To argue thus would be to presuppose a criterion (apart from the leading of the thought) to which the thought must correspond if it is to be true. If you distinguish between a 'genuine' verification and one that is only subjectively satisfactory, you appeal to some other criterion than the process of verification – in other words, you go over to the intellectualist's point of view. If, on the other hand, you stick to your pragmatic criterion and say that the truth of the thought consists in its *actual* satisfactoriness, then the question becomes pertinent: Were the thoughts of both boys true? Obviously they were, for both worked, both were satisfactory, both were verified. Hence it was true at the same time and in the same sense that Peter had a toothache and that Peter had not a toothache. Nor is there anything surprising in this, if truth is nothing but a particular kind of satisfactory experience. The principle of contradiction has no meaning and can no longer hold if truth be altogether within one's experience.

The usefulness of an hypothesis is indeed an excellent test of its truth. This is a practical method for the verification of an idea on which pragmatism has done well to insist. But to identify the truth of a thought with the process of its own verification can hardly lead to anything but intellectual confusion.

NOTES

1 I seem to find such a tendency, for example, in certain passages in Professor James's article 'Pragmatism's conception of truth', *The Journal of Philosophy* 4 (1907), 141. See especially pp. 144, 145, 149 – e.g. 'Truth *ante rem* means only verifiability', etc.
2 Professor Montague, *The Journal of Philosophy* 4 (1907), 100.
3 Mr Schiller, 'Humanism', 61.
4 James, 'Pragmatism's conception of truth', 144 and 142.
5 Mr Schiller's expression, in 'The ambiguity of truth', *Mind* (April 1906).

PROFESSOR JAMES'S 'PRAGMATISM'

G.E. Moore

My object in this paper is to discuss some of the things which Prof. William James says about truth in the recent book, to which he has given the above name.[1] In lecture VI he professes to give an account of a theory, which he calls 'the pragmatist theory of truth'; and he professes to give a briefer preliminary account of the same theory in lecture II. Moreover, in lecture VII, he goes on to make some further remarks about truth. In all these lectures he seems to me to make statements to which there are very obvious objections; and my main object is to point out, as clearly and simply as I can, what seem to me to be the principal objections to some of these statements.

We may, I think, distinguish three different things which he seems particularly anxious to assert about truth.

(I) In the first place, he is plainly anxious to assert some connection between truth and 'verification' or 'utility'. Our true ideas, he seems to say, are those that 'work', in the sense that they are or can be 'verified' or are 'useful'.

(II) In the second place, he seems to object to the view that truth is something 'static' or 'immutable'. He is anxious to assert that truths are in some sense 'mutable'.

(III) In the third place, he asserts that 'to an unascertainable extent our truths are man-made products' (117).

To what he asserts under each of these three heads there are, I think, serious objections; and I now propose to point out what seem to me to be the principal ones, under each head separately.

161

I

Professor James is plainly anxious to assert *some* connection between truth and 'verification' or 'utility'. And that there is *some* connection between them everybody will admit. That *many* of our true ideas are verified; that *many* of them can be verified; and that *many* of them are useful, is, I take it, quite indisputable. But Professor James seems plainly to wish to assert something more than this. And one more thing which he wishes to assert is, I think, pretty plain. He suggests, at the beginning of lecture VI, that he is going to tell us in what sense it is that our true ideas 'agree with reality'. Truth, he says, certainly *means* their agreement with reality; the only question is as to what we are to understand by the words 'agreement' and 'reality' in this proposition. And he first briefly considers the theory, that the sense in which our true ideas agree with reality, is that they 'copy' some reality. And he affirms that some of our true ideas really do do this. But he rejects the theory, as a theory of what truth means, on the ground that they do not *all* do so. Plainly, therefore, he implies that no theory of what truth *means* will be correct, unless it tells us of some property which belongs to *all* our true ideas without exception. But his own theory is a theory of what truth means. Apparently, therefore, he wishes to assert that not only many but *all* our true ideas are or can be verified; that *all* of them are useful. And it is, I think, pretty plain that this is *one* of the things which he wishes to assert.

Apparently, therefore, Professor James wishes to assert that *all* our true ideas are or can be verified – that *all* are useful. And certainly this is not a truism like the proposition that *many* of them are so. Even if this were all that he meant, it would be worth discussing. But even this, I think, is not all. The very first proposition in which he expresses his theory is the following. '*True ideas*', he says (100), '*are those that we can assimilate, validate, corroborate and verify. False ideas are those that we cannot.*' And what does this mean? Let us, for brevity's sake, substitute the word 'verify' alone for the four words which Professor James uses, as he himself subsequently seems to do. He asserts, then, that true ideas are *those which* we can verify. And plainly he does not mean by this merely that *some* of the ideas which we can verify are true, while plenty of others, which we can verify, are not true. The plain meaning of his words is that *all* the ideas which we can verify are true. No one would use them who did not mean this. Apparently, therefore,

Professor James means to assert not merely that we can verify all our true ideas; but also that all the ideas, which we can verify, are true. And so, too, with utility or usefulness. He seems to mean not merely that all our true ideas are useful; but that all those which are useful are true. This would follow, for one thing, from the fact that he seems to use the words 'verification' or 'verifiability' and 'usefulness' as if they came to the same thing. But, in this case too, he asserts it in words that have but one plain meaning. 'The true' he says (109), 'is only the expedient in the way of our thinking.' 'The true' is *the* expedient: that is, *all* expedient thinking is true. Or again: 'An idea is "true" so long as to believe it is profitable to our lives' (51). That is to say, *every* idea, which is profitable to our lives, is, while it is so, true. These words certainly have a plain enough meaning. Apparently, therefore, Professor James means to assert not merely that all true ideas are useful, but also that all useful ideas are true.

Professor James's words, then, do at least suggest that he wishes to assert all four of the following propositions. He wishes to assert, it would seem –

(1) That we can verify all those of our ideas, which are true.
(2) That all those among our ideas, which we can verify, are true.
(3) That all our true ideas are useful.
(4) That all those of our ideas, which are useful, are true.

These four propositions are what I propose first to consider. He does mean to assert them, at least. Very likely he wishes to assert something more even than these. He does, in fact, suggest that he means to assert, in addition, that these properties of 'verifiability' and 'utility' are the *only* properties (beside that of being properly *called* 'true') which belong to all our true ideas and to none but true ideas. But this obviously cannot be true, unless all these four propositions are true. And therefore we may as well consider them first.

First, then, can we verify all our true ideas?

I wish only to point out the plainest and most obvious reasons why I think it is doubtful whether we can.

We are very often in doubt as to whether we did or did not do a certain thing in the past. We may have the idea that we did, and also the idea that we did not; and we may wish to find out which idea is the true one. Very often, indeed, I may believe very strongly, that I did do a certain thing; and somebody else, who has equally good

163

reason to know, may believe equally strongly that I did not. For instance, I may have written a letter, and may believe that I used certain words in it. But my correspondent may believe that I did not. Can we always verify either of these ideas? Certainly sometimes we can. The letter may be produced, and prove that I did use the words in question. And I shall then have verified my idea. Or it may prove that I did not use them. And then we shall have verified my correspondent's idea. But, suppose the letter has been destroyed; suppose there is no copy of it, nor any trustworthy record of what was said in it; suppose there is no other witness as to what I said in it, beside myself and my correspondent? Can we then always verify which of our ideas is the true one? I think it is very doubtful whether we can *nearly* always. Certainly we may often try to discover any possible means of verification, and be quite unable, for a time at least, to discover any. Such cases, in which we are unable, for a time at least, to verify either of two contradictory ideas, occur very commonly indeed. Let us take an even more trivial instance than the last. Bad whist-players often do not notice at all carefully which cards they have among the lower cards in a suit. At the end of a hand they cannot be certain whether they had or had not the seven of diamonds, or the five of spades. And, after the cards have been shuffled, a dispute will sometimes arise as to whether a particular player had the seven of diamonds or not. His partner may think that he had, and he himself may think that he had not. Both may be uncertain, and the memory of both, on such a point, may be well known to be untrustworthy. And, moreover, neither of the other players may be able to remember any better. Is it always possible to verify which of these ideas is the true one? Either the player did or did not have the seven of diamonds. This much is certain. One person thinks that he did, and another thinks he did not; and both, so soon as the question is raised, have before their minds both of these ideas – the idea that he did, and the idea that he did not. This also is certain. And it is certain that one or other of these two ideas is true. But can they always verify either of them? Sometimes, no doubt, they can, even after the cards have been shuffled. There may have been a fifth person present, overlooking the play, whose memory is perfectly trustworthy, and whose word may be taken as settling the point. Or the players may themselves be able, by recalling other incidents of play, to arrive at such a certainty as may be said to verify the one hypothesis or the other. But very often neither of these two things will occur. And, in such a case, is it always possible to verify the true idea? Perhaps, theoretically, it may be still possible. Theoretically, I suppose, the fact that one player, and not any of the other three, had the card in his hand, may have made some difference to the card, which *might* be discovered by some possible method of scientific investigation. Perhaps some such difference may remain even after the same card has been repeatedly used in many subsequent games. But suppose the same question arises again, a week after the original game was played. Did you, or did you not, last week have the seven of diamonds in that particular hand? The question has not been settled in the meantime; and now, perhaps, the original pack of cards has been destroyed. Is it still possible to verify either idea? Theoretically, I suppose, it may be still possible. But even this, I think, is very doubtful. And surely it is plain that, humanly and practically speaking, it will often have become quite impossible to verify either idea. In all probability it never will be possible for any man to verify whether I had the card or not on this particular occasion. No doubt we are here speaking of an idea, which some man *could have* verified at one time. But the hypothesis I am considering is the hypothesis that we never have a true idea, which we *can* not verify; that is to say, which we cannot verify *after* the idea has occurred. And with regard to this hypothesis, it seems to me quite plain that *very often indeed* we have two ideas, one or other of which is certainly true; and yet that, in all probability, it is no longer possible and never will be possible for any man to verify either.

It seems to me, then, that we very often have true ideas which we cannot verify; true ideas, which, in all probability, no man ever will be able to verify. And, so far, I have given only comparatively trivial instances. But it is plain that, in the same sense, historians are very frequently occupied with true ideas, which it is doubtful whether they can verify. One historian thinks that a certain event took place, and another that it did not; and both may admit that they cannot verify their idea. Subsequent historians may, no doubt, sometimes be able to verify one or the other. New evidence may be discovered or men may learn to make a better use of evidence already in existence. But is it certain that this will *always* happen? Is it certain that *every* question, about which historians have doubted, will some day be able to be settled by verification of one or the other hypothesis? Surely the probability is that in the case of an immense number of events, with regard to which we should like to know whether they happened or not, it never will be possible for any man to verify either the one hypothesis or the other. Yet it may be certain that either the events in question did happen or did not. Here, therefore, again, we have a large number of ideas – cases where many men doubt whether a thing did happen or did not, and have therefore the idea both of its having happened and of its not having happened – with regard to which it is certain that half of them are true, but where it seems highly doubtful whether any single one of them will ever be able to be verified. No doubt it is just possible that men will some day be able to verify every one of them. But surely it is very doubtful whether they will. And the theory against which I am protesting is the positive assertion that we *can* verify all our true ideas – that someone some day certainly will be able to verify every one of them. This theory, I urge, has all probability against it.

And so far I have been dealing only with ideas with regard to what happened in the past. These seem to me to be the cases which offer the most numerous and most certain exceptions to the rule that we can verify our true ideas. With regard to particular past events, either in their own lives or in those of other people, men very frequently have ideas, which it seems highly improbable that any man will ever be able to verify. And yet it is certain that a great many of these ideas are true, because in a great many cases we have both the idea that the event did happen and also the idea that it did not, when it is certain that one or other of these ideas is true. And these ideas with regard to past events would by themselves be sufficient for my purpose. If, as seems certain, there are many true ideas with regard to the past, which it is highly improbable that anyone will ever be able to verify, then, obviously, there is nothing in a true idea which makes it certain that we can verify it. But it is, I think, certainly not only in the case of ideas, with regard to the past, that it is doubtful whether we can verify all the true ideas we have. In the case of many generalizations dealing not only with the past but with the future, it is, I think, obviously doubtful whether we shall ever be able to verify all those which are true; although here, perhaps, in most cases, the probability that we shall not is not so great. But is it quite certain, that in all cases where scientific men have considered hypotheses, one or other of which must be true, either will ever be verified? It seems to be obviously doubtful. Take, for instance, the question whether our actual space is Euclidean or not. This is a case where the alternative has been considered; and where it is certain that, whatever be meant by 'our actual space', it either is Euclidean or is not. It has been held, too, that the hypothesis that it is not Euclidean might, conceivably, be verified by observations. But it is doubtful whether it ever will be. And though it would be rash to say that no man ever will be able to verify either hypothesis; it is also rash to assert positively that we shall – that we certainly can verify the true hypotheses. There are, I believe, ever so many similar cases, where alternative hypotheses, one or other of which must be true, have occurred to men of science, and where yet it is very doubtful whether either ever will be verified. Or take, again, such ideas as the idea that there is a God, or the idea that we are immortal. Many men have had not only contradictory ideas, but contradictory beliefs, about these matters. And here we have cases where it is disputed whether these ideas have not actually been verified. But it seems to me doubtful whether they have been. And there is a view, which seems to me to deserve respect, that, in these matters, we never shall be able to verify the true hypothesis. Is it perfectly certain that this view is a false one? I do not say that it is true. I think it is quite possible that we shall some day be able to verify either the belief that we are immortal or the belief that we are not. But it seems to me doubtful whether we shall. And for this reason alone I should refuse to assent to the positive assertion that we certainly can verify all our true ideas.

When, therefore, Professor James tells us that '*True ideas are those that we can assimilate, validate, corroborate and verify. False ideas are those that we cannot*', there seems to be a serious objection to part of what these words imply. They imply that no idea of ours is true, unless we can verify it. They imply, therefore, that whenever a man wonders whether or not he had the seven of diamonds in the third hand at whist last night, neither of these ideas is true unless he can verify it. But it seems certain that in this, and an immense number of similar cases, one or other of the two ideas is true. Either, he did have the card in his hand or he did not. If anything is a fact, this is one. Either, therefore, Professor James's words imply the denial of this obvious fact, or else he implies that in *all* such cases we *can* verify one or other of the two ideas. But to this the objection is that, in any obvious sense of the words, it seems very doubtful whether we can. On the contrary it seems extremely probable that in a *very large* number of such cases no man ever will be able to verify either of the two ideas. There is, therefore, a serious objection to what Professor James's words imply. Whether he himself really means to assert these things which his words imply I do not know. Perhaps he would admit that, in this sense, we probably cannot verify nearly all our true ideas. All that I have wished to make plain is that there is, at least, an objection to what he says, whether to what he means or not. There is ample reason why we should refuse assent to the statement that none of our ideas are true, except those which we can verify.

But to another part of what he implies by the words quoted above, there is, I think, no serious objection. There is reason to object to the statement that we can verify all our true ideas; but to the statement that all ideas, which we can 'assimilate, validate, corroborate and verify', are true, I see no serious objection. Here, I think, we might say simply that all ideas which we can verify are true. To this, which is the second of the four propositions, which I distinguished above (163) as what Professor James seems to wish to assert, there is, I think, no serious objection, if we understand the word 'verify' in its proper and natural sense. We may, no doubt, sometimes say that we have verified an idea or an hypothesis, when we have only obtained evidence which proves it to be probable, and does not prove it to be certain. And, if we use the word in this loose sense for incomplete verification, it is obviously the case that we may verify an idea which is not true. But it seems scarcely necessary to point this out. And where we really can *completely* verify an idea or an hypothesis, there, undoubtedly, the idea which we can verify is always true. The very meaning of the word 'verify' is to find evidence which does really prove an idea to be true; and where an idea can be really proved to be true, it is of course, always true.

This is all I wish to say about Professor James's first two propositions, namely: –

(1) That no ideas of ours are true, except those which we can verify.
(2) That all those ideas, which we can verify, are true.

The first seems to me extremely doubtful – in fact, almost certainly untrue; the second on the other hand, certainly true, in its most obvious meaning. And I shall say no more about them. The fact is, I doubt whether either of them expresses anything which Professor James is really anxious to assert. I have mentioned them, only because his words do, in fact, imply them and because he gives those words a very prominent place. But I have already had occasion to notice that he seems to speak as if to say that we can verify an idea came to the same thing as saying it is useful to us. And it is the connection of truth with usefulness, not its connection with 'verification', that he is, I think, really anxious to assert. He talks about 'verification' only, I believe, because he thinks that what he says about it will support his main view that truth is what 'works', is 'useful', is 'expedient', 'pays'. It is this main view we have now to consider. We have to consider the two propositions: –

(3) That all our true ideas are useful.
(4) That all ideas, which are useful, are true.

First, then: is it the case that all our true ideas are useful? Is it the case that none of our ideas are true, except those which are useful?

I wish to introduce my discussion of this question by quoting a passage in which Professor James seems to me to say something which is indisputably true. Towards the end of lecture VI, he attacks the view that truths 'have an unconditional claim to be recognized'. And in the course of his attack the following passage occurs: –

> Must I [he says] constantly be repeating the truth 'twice two are four' because of its eternal claim on recognition? or is it sometimes irrelevant? Must my thoughts dwell night and day on my personal sins and blemishes, because I truly have them? – or may I sink and ignore them in order to be a decent social unit, and not a mass of morbid melancholy and apology?
>
> It is quite evident [he goes on] that our obligation to acknowledge truth, so far from being unconditional, is tremendously conditional. Truth with a big T, and in the singular, claims abstractly to be recognized, of course; but concrete truths in the plural need be recognized only when their recognition is expedient. (113)

What Professor James says in this passage seems to me so indisputably true as fully to justify the vigour of his language. It is as clear as anything can be that it would not be useful for any man's mind to be *always* occupied with the true idea that he had certain faults and blemishes; or to be *always* occupied with the idea that twice two are four. It is clear, that is, that, if there are times at which a particular true idea is useful, there certainly are other times at which it would *not* be useful, but positively in the way. This is plainly true of nearly all, if not quite all, our true ideas. It is plainly true with regard to nearly all of them that, even if the occasions on which their occurrence is useful are many, the occasions on which their occurrence would *not* be useful are many more. With regard to most of them it is true that on most occasions they will, as Professor James says elsewhere, 'be practically irrelevant, and had better remain latent'.

It is, then, quite clear that almost any particular true idea *would* not be useful at all times and that the times at which it would *not* be useful, are many more than the times at which it would. And what we have to consider is whether, in just this sense in which it is so clear that most true ideas would *not* be useful at most times, it is nevertheless true that all our true ideas *are* useful. Is this so? Are all our true ideas useful?

Professor James, we see, has just told us that there are ever so many occasions upon which a particular true idea, such as that $2+2=4$, *would* not be useful – when, on the contrary, it would be positively in the way. And this seems to be indisputably clear. But is not something else almost equally clear? Is it not almost equally clear that cases, such as he says *would* not be useful, do sometimes actually happen? Is it not clear that we do actually sometimes have true ideas, at times when they are not useful, but are positively in the way? It seems to me to be perfectly clear that this does sometimes occur; and not sometimes only, but very commonly. The cases in which true ideas occur at times when they are useful, are, perhaps, far *more* numerous; but, if we look at men in general, the cases in which true ideas occur, at times when they are not useful, do surely make up positively a very large number. Is it not the case that men do sometimes dwell on their faults and blemishes, when it is *not* useful for them to do so? when they would much better be thinking of something else? Is it not the case that they are often unable to get their minds away from a true idea, when it is harmful for them to dwell on it? Still more commonly, does it not happen that they waste their time in acquiring pieces of information which are no use to them, though perhaps very useful to other people? All this seems to me to be undeniable – just as undeniable as what Professor James himself has said; and, if this is so, then, in one sense of the words, it is plainly not true that all, or nearly all, our true ideas are useful. *In one sense of the words.* For if I have the idea that $2+2=4$ on one day, and then have it again the next, I may certainly, in a sense, call the idea I have on one day *one* idea, and the idea I have on the next *another*. I have had two ideas that 2+2=4, and not one only. Or if two different persons both think that I have faults, there have been two ideas of this truth and not one only. And in asking whether *all* our true ideas are useful, we might mean to ask whether *both* of these ideas were useful and not merely whether one of them was. In this sense, then, it is plainly not true that *all* our true ideas are useful. It is not true, that is, that every true idea is useful, *whenever it occurs*.

In one sense, then, it is plainly not true that our true ideas are useful. But there still remains a perfectly legitimate sense in which it might be true. It might be meant, that is, not that every *occurrence* of a true idea is useful, but that every true idea is useful on at least one of the occasions when it occurs. But is this, in fact, the case? It seems to me almost as plain that it is not, as that the other was not. We have seen that true ideas are not by any means always useful on every occasion when they occur; though most that do occur many times over and to many different people are, no doubt, useful on some of these occasions. But there seems to be an immense number of true ideas, which occur but once and to one person, and never again either to him or to anyone else. I may, for instance, idly count the number of dots on the back of a card, and arrive at a true idea of their number; and yet perhaps, I may never think of their number again, nor anybody else ever know it. We are all, it seems to me, constantly noticing trivial details, and getting true ideas about them, of which we never think again, and which nobody else ever gets. And is it quite certain that all these true ideas are useful? It seems to me perfectly clear, on the contrary, that many of them are not. Just as it is clear that many men sometimes waste their time in acquiring information which is useful to others but not to them, surely it is clear that they sometimes waste their time in acquiring information, which is useful to nobody at all, because nobody else ever acquires it. I do not say that it is never useful idly to count the number of dots on the back of a card. Plainly it is sometimes useful to be idle, and one idle employment may often be as good as another. But surely it is true that men *sometimes* do these things, when their time would have been better employed otherwise? Surely they sometimes get into the habit of attending to trivial truths, which it is as great a disadvantage that they should attend to as that they should constantly be thinking of their own thoughts and blemishes? I cannot see my way to deny that this is so; and therefore I cannot see my way to assert positively that all our true ideas are useful, even so much as on *one occasion*. It seems to me that there are many true ideas which occur but once, and which are not useful when they do occur. And if this be so, then it is plainly not true that *all* our true ideas are useful in any sense at all.

These seem to me to be the most obvious objections to the assertion that all our true ideas are useful. It is clear, we saw to begin with, that true ideas, which are sometimes useful, *would* not be useful at all times. And it seemed almost equally clear that they do sometimes occur at times when they are not useful. Our true ideas, therefore, are not useful at every time when they actually occur. But in just this sense in which it is so clear that true ideas which are sometimes useful, nevertheless sometimes occur at times when they are not, it seems pretty plain that true ideas, which occur but once, are, some of them, not useful. If an idea, which is sometimes useful, does sometimes occur to a man at a time when it is irrelevant and in the way, why should not an idea, which occurs but once, occur at a time when it is irrelevant and in the way? It seems hardly possible to doubt that this does sometimes happen. But, if this be so, then it is not true that all our true ideas are useful, even so much as on one occasion. It is not true that none of our ideas are true, except those which are useful.

But now, what are we to say of the converse proposition – the proposition that all those among our ideas, which are useful, are true? That we never have a useful idea, which is not true?

I confess the matter seems to me equally clear here. The assertion should mean that every idea, which is at any time useful, is true; that no idea, which is not true, is ever useful. And it seems hardly possible to doubt that this assertion is false. It is, in the first place, commonly held that it is sometimes right positively to deceive another person. In war, for instance it is held that one army is justified in trying to give the enemy a false idea as to where it will be at a given time. Such a false idea is sometimes given, and it seems to me quite clear that it is sometimes useful. In such a case, no doubt, it may be said that the false idea is useful to the party who have given it, but not useful to those who actually believe in it. And the question whether it is useful on the whole will depend upon the question which side it is desirable should win. But it seems to me unquestionable that the false idea is sometimes useful on the whole. Take, for instance, the case of a party of savages, who wish to make a night attack and massacre a party of Europeans but are deceived as to the position in which the Europeans are encamped. It is surely plain that such a false idea is sometimes useful on the whole. But quite apart from the question whether deception is ever justifiable, it is not very difficult to think of cases where a false idea, not produced by deception, is plainly useful – and useful, not merely on the whole, but to the person who has it as well. A man often thinks that his watch is right, when, in fact, it is slow, and his false idea may cause him to miss his train. And in such cases, no doubt, his false idea is *generally* disadvantageous. But, in a particular case, the train which he would have caught but for his false idea may be destroyed in a railway accident, or something may suddenly occur at home, which renders it much more useful that he should be there, than it would have been for him to catch his train. Do such cases never occur? And is not the false idea sometimes useful in some of them? It seems to me perfectly clear that it is *sometimes* useful for a man to think his watch is right when it is wrong. And such instances would be sufficient to show that it is not the case that every idea of ours, which is ever useful, is a true idea. But let us take cases, not, like these, of an idea, which occurs but a few times or to one man, but of ideas which have occurred to many men at many times. It seems to me very difficult to be sure that the belief in an eternal hell has not been often useful to many men, and yet it may be doubted whether this idea is true. And so, too, with the belief in a happy life after death, or the belief in the existence of a God; it is, I think, very difficult to be sure that these beliefs have not been, and are not still, often useful, and yet it may be doubted whether they are true. These beliefs, of course, are matters of controversy. Some men believe that they are both useful and true; and others, again, that they are neither. And I do not think we are justified in giving them as certain instances of beliefs, which are not true, but, nevertheless, have often been useful. But there is a view that these beliefs, though not true, have, nevertheless, been often useful; and this view seems to me to deserve respect, especially since, as we have seen, some beliefs, which are not true, certainly are sometimes useful. Are we justified in asserting positively that it is false? Is it perfectly certain that beliefs, which have often been useful to many men, may not, nevertheless, be untrue? Is it perfectly certain that beliefs, which are not true, have not often been useful to many men? The certainty may at least be doubted, and in any case it seems certain that some beliefs, which are not true, are, nevertheless, sometimes useful.

For these reasons, it seems to me almost certain that *both* the assertions which I have been considering are false. It is almost certainly false that all our true ideas are useful, and almost certainly false that all our useful ideas are true. But I have only urged what seem to me to be the most obvious objections to these two statements; I have not tried to sustain these objections by elaborate arguments, and I have omitted elaborate argument, partly because of a reason which I now wish to state. The fact is, I am not at all sure that Professor James would not himself admit that both these statements are false. I think it is quite possible he would admit that they are, and would say that he never meant either to assert or to imply the contrary. He complains that some of the critics of Pragmatism are unwilling to read any but the silliest of possible meanings into the statements of Pragmatism; and, perhaps, he would say that this is the case here. I certainly hope that he would. I certainly hope he would say that these statements, to which I have objected, are silly. For it does seem to me intensely silly to say that we can verify all our true ideas; intensely silly to say that every one of our true ideas is at some time useful; intensely silly to say that every idea which is ever useful is true. I hope Professor James would admit all these things to be silly, for if he and other pragmatists would admit even as much as this, I think a good deal would be gained. But it by no means follows that because a philosopher would admit a view to be silly, when it is definitely put before him, he has not himself been constantly holding and implying that very view. He may quite sincerely protest that he never has either held or implied it, and yet he may all the time have been not only implying it but holding it – vaguely, perhaps, but really. A man may assure us, quite sincerely that he is not angry; he may really think that he is not, and yet we may be able to judge quite certainly from what he says that he really is angry. He may assure us quite sincerely that he never meant anything to our discredit by what he said – that he was not thinking of anything in the least discreditable to us, and yet it may be plain from his words that he was actually condemning us very severely. And so with a philosopher. He may protest, quite angrily, when a view is put before him in other words than his own, that he never either meant or implied any such thing, and yet it may be possible to judge, from what he says, that this very view, wrapped up in other words, was not only held by him but was precisely what made his thoughts seem to him to be interesting and important. Certainly he may quite often imply a given thing which, at another time, he denies. Unless it were possible for a philosopher to do this, there would be very little inconsistency in philosophy, and surely everyone will admit that *other* philosophers are very often inconsistent. And so in this case, even if Professor James would say that he never meant to imply the things to which I have been objecting, yet in the case of two of these things, I cannot help thinking that he does actually imply them – nay more, that he is frequently actually vaguely thinking of them, and that his theory of truth owes its interest, in very great part, to the fact that he is implying them. In the case of the two views that all our true ideas are useful, and that all our useful ideas are true, I think this is so, and I do not mean merely that his *words* imply them. A man's *words* may often imply a thing, when he himself is in no way, however vaguely, thinking either of that thing or of anything which implies it; he may simply have expressed himself unfortunately. But in the case of the two views that all our true ideas are useful, and all our useful ideas true, I do not think this is so with Professor James. I think that his thoughts seem interesting to him and others, largely because he is thinking, not merely of words, but of things which imply these two views, in the very form in which I have objected to them. And I wish now to give some reasons for thinking this.

Professor James certainly wishes to assert that there is *some* connection between truth and utility. And the connection which I have suggested that he has vaguely before his mind is this: that every true idea is, at some time or other, useful, and conversely that every idea, which is ever useful, is true. And I have urged that there are obvious objections to both these views. But now, supposing Professor James does not mean to assert either of these two things, what else can he mean to assert? What else can he mean, that would account for the interest and importance he seems to attach to his assertion of connection between truth and utility? Let us consider the alternatives.

And, first of all, he might mean that *most* of our true ideas are useful, and *most* of our useful ideas true. He might mean that most of our true ideas are useful at some time or other; and even that most of them are useful, whenever they actually occur. And he might mean, moreover, that if we consider the whole range of ideas, which are useful to us, we shall find that by far the greater number of them are true ones; that true ideas are far more often useful to us, than those which are not true. And all this, I think, may be readily admitted to be true. If this were all that he meant, I do not think that anyone would be very anxious to dispute it. But is it conceivable that this is *all* that he means? Is it conceivable that he should have been so anxious to insist upon this admitted common-place? Is it conceivable that he should have been offering us this, and nothing more, as a theory of what truth means, and a theory worth making a fuss about, and being proud of? It seems to me quite inconceivable that this should have been *all* that he meant. He must have had something more than this in his mind. But, if so, what more?

In the passage which I quoted at the beginning, as showing that he does mean to assert that *all* useful ideas are true, he immediately goes on to assert a qualification, which must now be noticed. '*The true*', he says, '. . . *is only the expedient in the way of our thinking*' (109). But he immediately adds: 'Expedient in the long run, and on the whole, of course; for what meets expediently all the experience in sight won't necessarily meet all farther experiences equally satisfactorily.' Here, therefore, we have something else that he might mean. What is expedient *in the long run*, he means to say, is true. And what exactly does this mean? It seems to mean that an idea, which is not true, may be expedient *for some time*. That is to say, it may occur *once*, and be expedient then; and again, and be expedient then; and so on, over a considerable period. But (Professor James seems to prophesy) if it is not true, there will come a time, when it will cease to be expedient. If it occurs again and again over a long *enough* period, there will at last, if it is not true, come a time when it will (for once at least) fail to be useful, and will (perhaps he means) *never* be useful again. This is, I think, what Professor James means in this passage. He means, I think, that though an idea, which is not true, may for some time be repeatedly expedient, there will at last come a time when its occurrence will, perhaps, *never* be expedient again, and certainly will, for a time, not be *generally* expedient. And this is a view which, it seems to me, may possibly be true. It is certainly possible that a time may come, in the far future, when ideas, which are not true, will hardly ever, if ever, be expedient. And this is all that Professor James seems here positively to mean. He seems to mean that, if you take time *enough*, false ideas will some day cease to be expedient. And it is very difficult to be sure that this is not true; since it is very difficult to prophesy as to what may happen in the far future. I am sure I hope that this prophecy will come true. But in the meantime (Professor James seems to admit) ideas, which are not true, may, for an indefinitely long time, again and again be expedient. And is it conceivable that a theory, which admits this, is *all* that he has meant to assert? Is it conceivable that what interests him, in his theory of truth, is merely the belief that, some day or other, false ideas will cease to be expedient? 'In the long run, *of course*', he says, as if this were what he had meant all along. But I think it is quite plain that this is *not* all that he has meant. This may be one thing which he is anxious to assert, but it certainly does not explain the whole of his interest in his theory of truth.

And, in fact, there is quite a different theory which he seems plainly to have in his mind in other places. When Professor James says, 'in the long run, *of course*', he implies that ideas which are expedient only for a *short* run, are very often not true. But in what he says elsewhere he asserts the very opposite of this. He says elsewhere that a belief is true '*so long as* to believe it is profitable to our lives' (51). That is to say, a belief will be true, *so long as* it is useful, even if it is *not* useful in the long run! This is certainly quite a different theory; and, strictly speaking, it implies that an idea, which is useful even *on one occasion*, will be true. But perhaps this is only a verbal implication. I think very likely that here Professor James was only thinking of ideas, which can be said *to have a run*, though only a comparatively short one – of ideas, that is, which are expedient, not merely on one occasion, but *for some time*. That is to say, the theory which he now suggests, is that ideas, which occur again and again, perhaps to one man only, perhaps to several different people, over some space of time are, if they are expedient on most occasions within that space of time, true. This is a view which he is, I think, really anxious to assert; and if it were true, it would, I think, be important. And it is difficult to find instances which show, with certainty, that it is false. I believe that it is false; but it is difficult to prove it, because, in the case of some ideas it is so difficult to be certain that they ever were useful, and in the case of others so difficult to be certain that they are not true. A belief such as I spoke of before – the belief in eternal hell – is an instance. I think this belief has been, for a long time, useful, and that yet it is false. But it is, perhaps, arguable that it never has been useful; and many people on the other hand, would still assert that it is true. It cannot, therefore, perhaps, fairly be used as an instance of a belief, which is certainly not true, and yet has for some time been useful. But whether this view that all beliefs, which are expedient for some time, are true, be true or false; can it be all that Professor James means to assert? Can it constitute the whole of what interests him in his theory of truth?

I do not think it can. I think it is plain that he has in his mind something more than *any* of these alternatives, or than all of them taken together. And I think so partly for the following reason. He speaks from the outset as if he intended to tell us what *distinguishes* true ideas from those which are not true; to tell us, that is to say, not merely of some property which belongs to all our true ideas; nor yet merely of some property, which belongs to none but true ideas; but of some property which satisfies *both* these requirements at once – which both belongs to all our true ideas, and *also* belongs to none but true ones. Truth, he says to begin with, means the agreement of our ideas with reality; and he adds 'as falsity their disagreement'. And he explains that he is going to tell us what property it is that is meant by these words 'agreement with reality'. So again in the next passage which I quoted: '*True ideas*', he says, '*are those that we can assimilate, validate, corroborate and verify.*' But, he also adds: '*False ideas are those that we cannot.*' And no one, I think, could possibly speak in this way, who had not in his head the intention of telling us what property it is which *distinguishes* true ideas from those which are not true, and which, therefore, not only belongs to all ideas which are true, but also to none that are not. And that he has this idea in his head and thinks that the property of being 'useful' or 'paying' is such a property, is again clearly shown by a later passage. 'Our account of truth', he says (107), 'is an account of truths in the plural, of processes of leading, realized *in rebus*, and having only this quality in common, that they *pay.*' *Only* this quality in common! If this be so, the quality must obviously be one, which is *not* shared by any ideas which are *not* true. Plainly, therefore, Professor James is intending to tell us of a property which belongs both to *all* true ideas and *only* to true ideas. And this property, he says, is that of 'paying'. But now let us suppose that he means by 'paying', not 'paying *once* at least', but, according to the alternative he suggests, 'paying in the long run' or 'paying for some time'. Can he possibly have supposed that these were properties which belonged *both* to all true ideas *and also* to none but true ones? They may, perhaps, be properties which belong to *none but* true ones. I doubt, as I have said, whether the latter does; but still it is difficult to prove the opposite. But even if we granted that they belong to *none but* true ones, surely it is only too obvious that they do *not* fulfil the other requirement – that they do *not* belong to

178

nearly all true ones. Can anyone suppose that *all* our true ideas pay 'in the long run' or repeatedly for some time? Surely it is plain that an enormous number do not for the simple reason that an enormous number of them *have no run at all*, either long or short, but occur but once, and never recur. I believe truly that a certain book is on a particular shelf about 10.15 p.m. on 21 December 1907; and this true belief serves me well and helps me to find it. But the belief that that book is there at that particular time occurs to no one else, and never again to me. Surely there are thousands of useful true beliefs which, like this, are useful but once, and never occur again; and it would, therefore, be preposterous to say that every true idea is useful 'in the long run' or repeatedly for some time. If, therefore, we supposed Professor James to mean that 'paying in the long run' or 'paying repeatedly over a considerable period' were properties which belonged to all true ideas aud to none but true ones, we should be supposing him to mean something still more monstrous than if we suppose him to mean that 'paying at least once' was such a property.

To sum up then:

I think there is no doubt that Professor James's interest in 'the pragmatist theory of truth' is largely due to the fact that he thinks it tells us what distinguishes true ideas from those which are not true. And he thinks the distinction is that true ideas 'pay', and false ones don't. The most natural interpretation of this view is: That every true idea pays at least once; and that every idea, which pays at least once, is true. These were the propositions I considered first, and I gave reasons for thinking that *both* are false. But Professor James suggested elsewhere that what he means by 'paying' is 'paying in the long run'. And here it seems possibly true that all ideas which 'pay in the long run' are true; but it is certainly false that all our true ideas 'pay in the long run', if by this be meant anything more than 'pay at least once'. Again, he suggested that what he meant by paying was 'paying for some time'. And here, again, even if it is true (and it seems very doubtful) that all ideas which pay for some time are true, it is certainly false that all our true ideas pay for some time, if by this be meant anything more than that they pay 'at least once'.

This, I think, is the simplest and most obvious objection to Professor James's 'instrumental' view of truth – the view that truth is what 'works', 'pays', is 'useful'. He seems certainly to have in his mind the idea that this theory tells us what distinguishes true ideas from false ones, and to be interested in it mainly for this reason. He has vaguely in his mind that he has told us of some property which belongs to all true ideas and to none but true ones; and that this property is that of 'paying'. And the objection is, that, whatever we understand by 'paying', whether 'paying at least once', or 'paying in the long run', or 'paying for some time', it seems certain that none of these properties will satisfy *both* requirements. As regards the first, that of 'paying at least once', it seems almost certain that it satisfies *neither*: it is neither true that all our true ideas 'pay at least once', nor yet that every idea which pays at least once, is true. On the contrary, many true ideas never pay at all; and many ideas, which are not true, do pay on at least one occasion. And as regards the others, 'paying in the long run' and 'paying for some time', even if these do belong to none but true ideas (and even this seems very doubtful), they certainly neither of them satisfy the *other* requirement – neither of them belong to *all* our true ideas. For, in order that either of them may belong to an idea, that idea must pay at least once; and, as we have seen, many true ideas do not pay even once, and cannot, therefore, pay either in the long run or for some time. And, moreover, many true ideas, which do pay on one occasion, seem to pay on one occasion and one only.

And, if Professor James does not mean to assert any of these things, what is there left for him to mean? There is left in the first place, the theory that *most* of our true ideas do pay; and that *most* of the ideas which pay are true. This seems to me to be true, and, indeed, to be all that is certainly true in what he says. But is it conceivable that this is all he has meant? Obviously, these assertions tell us of no property at all which belongs to all true ideas, and to none but true ones; and, moreover, it seems impossible that he should have been so anxious to assert this generally admitted commonplace. What a very different complexion his whole discussion would have worn, had he merely asserted this – this quite clearly, and nothing but this, while admitting openly that many true ideas do not pay, and that many, which do pay, are not true!

And, besides this commonplace, there is only left for him to mean two one-sided and doubtful assertions to the effect that certain properties belong to none but true ideas. There is the assertion that all ideas which pay in the long run are true, and the assertion that all ideas which pay for some considerable time are true. And as to the first, it *may* be true; but it may also be doubted, and Professor James gives us no reason at all for thinking that it is true. Assuming that religious ideas have been useful in the past, is it quite certain that they may not permanently continue to be useful, even though they are false? That, in short, even though they are not true, they nevertheless will be useful, not only for a time, but in the long run? And as for the assertion that all ideas, which pay for a considerable time, are true, this is obviously more doubtful still. Whether certain religious ideas will or will not be useful in the long run, it seems difficult to doubt that many of them have been useful for a considerable time. And why should we be told dogmatically that all of these are true? This, it seems to me, is by far the most interesting assertion, which is left for Professor James to make, when we have rejected the theory that the property of being useful belongs to *all* true ideas, as well as to none but true ones. But he has given no reason for asserting it. He seems, in fact, to base it merely upon the general untenable theory, that utility belongs to *all* true ideas, and to none but true ones; that this is what truth means.

These, then, seem to me the plainest and most obvious objections to what Professor James says about the connection between truth and utility. And there are only two further points, in what he says under this head, that I wish to notice.

In the first place, we have hitherto been considering only whether it is true, as a matter of empirical fact, that all our true ideas are useful, and those which are not true, never. Professor James seems, at least, to mean that, *as a matter of fact*, this is so; and I have only urged hitherto that *as a matter of fact*, it is not so. But as we have seen, he also asserts something more than this – he also asserts that this property of utility is the *only* one which belongs to all our true ideas. And this further assertion cannot possibly be true, if, as I have urged, there are many true ideas which do not possess this property; or if, as I have urged, many ideas, which do possess it, are nevertheless not true. The objections already considered are, then, sufficient to overthrow this further assertion also. If there are any true ideas, which are not useful, or if any, which are useful, are not true, it cannot be the case that utility is the *only* property which true ideas have in common. There must be some property, other than utility, which is common to all true ideas; and a correct theory as to what property it is that does belong to all true ideas, and to none but true ones, is still to seek. The empirical objections, hitherto given, are then sufficient objections to this further assertion also; but they are not the only objections to it. There is another and still more serious objection to the assertion that utility is the *only* property which all true ideas have in common. For this assertion does not *merely* imply that, as a matter of fact, all our true ideas and none but true ideas are useful. It does, indeed, imply this; and therefore the fact that these empirical assertions are not true is sufficient to refute it. But it also implies something more. If utility were the *only* property which all true ideas had in common, it would follow not merely that all true ideas are useful, but also that any idea, which was useful, *would* be true *no matter what other properties it might have or might fail to have*. There can, I think, be no doubt that Professor James does frequently speak as if this were the case; and there is an independent and still more serious objection to this implication. Even if it were true (as it is not) that all our true ideas and none but true ideas are, as a matter of fact, useful, we should still have a strong reason to object to the statement that any idea, which was useful, *would* be true. For it implies that if such an idea as mine, that Professor James exists, and has certain thoughts, *were* useful, this idea would be true, *even if* no such person as Professor James ever did exist. It implies that, if the idea that I had the seven of diamonds in my hand at cards last night, *were* useful, this idea would be true, even if, in fact, I did not have that card in my hand. And we can, I think, see quite plainly that this is not the case. With regard to some kinds of ideas, at all events – ideas with regard to the existence of other people, or with regard to past experiences of our own – it seems quite plain that they would not be true, unless they 'agreed with reality' in some other sense than that which Professor James declares to be the only one in which true ideas must agree with it. Even if my idea that Professor James exists were to 'agree with reality', in the sense that, owing to it, I handled *other* realities better than I should have done without it, it would, I think, plainly not be true, unless Professor James really did exist – unless *he* were a reality. And this, I think, is one of the two most serious objections to what he seems to hold about the connection of truth with utility. He seems to hold that any idea, which was useful, *would* be true, *no matter what other properties it might fail to have*. And with regard to some ideas, at all events, it seems plain that they cannot be true, *unless* they have the property that what they believe to exist, really does or did exist. Beliefs in the existence of other people might be useful to me, even if I alone existed; but, nevertheless, in such a case, they would not be true.

And there is only one other point, in what Professor James says in connection with the 'instrumental' view of truth, upon which I wish to remark. We have seen that he seems sometimes to hold that beliefs are true, *so long as* they are 'profitable to our lives'. And this implies, as we have seen, the doubtful proposition than any belief which is useful for some length of time, is true. But this is not all that it implies. It also implies that beliefs are true *only* so long as they are profitable. Nor does Professor James appear to mean by this that they *occur*, only so long as they are profitable. He seems to hold, on the contrary, that beliefs, which are profitable for some time, do sometimes finally occur at a time when they are not profitable. He implies, therefore, that a belief, which occurs at several different times, may be true at some of the times at which it occurs, and yet untrue at others. I think there is no doubt that this view is what he is sometimes thinking of. And this, we see, constitutes a quite new view as to the connection between truth and utility – a view quite different from any that we have hitherto considered. This view asserts not that every true idea is useful at some time, or in the long run, or for a considerable period; but that the truth of an idea may come and go, as its utility comes and goes. It admits that one and the same idea sometimes occurs at times when it is useful, and sometimes at times when it is not; but it maintains that this same idea is true, at those times when it is useful, and not true, at those when it is not. And the fact that Professor James seems to suggest this view, constitutes, I think, a second most serious objection to what he says about the connection of truth and utility. It seems so obvious that utility is a property which comes and goes – which belongs to a given idea at one time, and does not belong to it at another, that anyone who says that the true is the useful naturally seems not to be overlooking this obvious fact, but to be suggesting that truth is a property which comes and goes in the same way. It is in this way, I think, that the 'instrumental' view of truth is connected with the view that truth is 'mutable'. Professor James does, I think, imply that truth is mutable in just this sense – namely, that one and the same idea may be true at some of the times at which it occurs, and not true at others, and this is the view which I have next to consider.

II

Professor James seems to hold, generally, that 'truth' is mutable. And by this he seems sometimes to mean that an idea which, when it occurs at one time, is true, *may*, when it occurs at another time, not be true. He seems to hold that one and the same idea *may* be true at one time and false at another. That it *may* be, for I do not suppose he means that all ideas do actually undergo this change from true to false. Many true ideas seem to occur but once, and, if so, they, at least, will not actually be true at one time and false at another, though, even with regard to these, perhaps Professor James means to maintain that they *might* be false at another time, if they were to occur at it. But I am not sure that he even means to maintain this with regard to *all* our true ideas. Perhaps he does not mean to say, with regard to *all* of them, even that they *can* change from true to false. He speaks, generally, indeed, as if truth were mutable; but, in one passage, he seems to insist that there is a certain class of true ideas, none of which are mutable in this respect.

Relations among purely mental ideas [he says (104)] form another sphere where true and false beliefs obtain, and here the beliefs are absolute, or unconditional. When they are true they bear the name either of definitions or of principles. It is either a principle or a definition that 1 and 1 make 2, that 2 and 1 make 3, and so on; that white differs less from grey than it does from black; that when the cause begins to act the effect also commences. Such propositions hold of all possible 'ones', of all conceivable 'whites', 'greys', and 'causes.' The objects here are mental objects. Their relations are perceptually obvious at a glance, and no sense-verification is necessary. Moreover, once true, always true, of those same mental objects. Truth here has an 'eternal' character. If you can find a concrete thing anywhere that is 'one' or 'white' or 'grey' or an 'effect', then your principles will everlastingly apply to it.

Professor James does seem here to hold that there are true ideas, which once true, are always true. Perhaps, then, he does not hold that *all* true ideas are mutable. Perhaps he does not even hold that all true ideas, *except* ideas of this kind, are so. But he does seem to hold at least that *many* of our true ideas are mutable. And even this proposition seems to me to be disputable. It seems to me that there is a sense in which it is the case with *every* true idea that, if once true, it is always true. That is to say, that every idea, which is true once, *would* be true at any other time at which it were to occur; and that every idea which does occur more than once, if true once, *is* true at every time at which it does occur. There seems to me, I say, to be *a sense* in which this is so. And this seems to me to be the sense in which it is most commonly and most naturally maintained that all truths are 'immutable'. Professor James seems to mean to deny it, even in this sense. He seems to me constantly to speak as if there were *no* sense in which *all* truths are immutable. And I only wish to point out what seems to me to be the plainest and most obvious objection to such language.

And, first of all, there is one doctrine, which he seems to connect with this of his that 'truths are mutable', with regard to which I fully agree with him. He seems very anxious to insist that reality is mutable: that it does change, and that it is not irrational to hope that in the future it will be different from and much better than it is now. And this seems to me to be quite undeniable. It seems to me quite certain that I do have ideas at one time which I did not have at another; that change, therefore, does really occur. It seems to me quite certain that in the future many things will be different from what they are now; and I see no reason to think that they may not be much better. There is much misery in the world now; and I think it is quite possible that some day there will really be much less. This view that *reality* is mutable, that *facts* do change, that some things have properties at one time which they do not have at other times, seems to me certainly true. And so far, therefore, as Professor James merely means to assert this obvious fact, I have no objection to his view. Some philosophers, I think, have really implied the denial of this fact. All those who deny the reality of time do seem to me to imply that nothing really changes or can change – that, in fact, reality is wholly immutable. And so far as Professor James is merely protesting against this view, I should, therefore, agree with him.

But I think it is quite plain that he does not mean *merely* this, when he says that truth is mutable. No one would choose this way of expressing himself if he merely meant to say that *some* things are mutable. Truth, Professor James has told us, is a property of certain of our ideas. And those of our ideas, which are true or false, are certainly only a part of the Universe. Other things in the Universe might, therefore, change, even if our ideas never changed in respect of this property. And our ideas themselves do undoubtedly change in some respects. A given idea exists in my mind at one moment and does not exist in it at another. At one moment it is in my mind and not in somebody else's, and at another in somebody else's and not in mine. I sometimes think of the truth that twice two are four when I am in one mood, and sometimes when I am in another. I

sometimes think of it in connection with one set of ideas and sometimes in connection with another set. Ideas, then, are constantly
changing in some respects. They come and go; and at one time they
stand in a given relation to other things or ideas, to which at
another time they do not stand in that relation. In this sense, any
given idea may certainly have a property at one time which it has
not got at another time. All this seems obvious; and all this cannot
be admitted, without admitting that reality is mutable – that *some*
things change. But obviously it does not seem to follow from this
that there is *no* respect in which ideas are immutable. It does not
seem to follow that because ideas, and other things, change some of
their properties, they necessarily change that one which we are
considering – namely, 'truth'. It does not follow that a given idea,
which has the property of truth at one time, ever exists at any other
time without having that property. And yet that this *does* happen
seems to be part of what is meant by saying that truth is mutable.
Plainly, therefore, to say this is to say something quite different
from saying that *some* things are mutable. Even therefore, if we
admit that *some* things are mutable, it is still open to consider
whether truth is so. And this is what I want now to consider. Is it
the case that an idea which exists at one time, and is true then, ever
exists at any other time, without being true? Is it the case that any
idea ever changes from true to false? That it has the property of
being true on one of the occasions when it exists, and that it has *not*
this property, but that of being false instead, on some other occasion when it exists?

In order to answer this question clearly, it is, I think, necessary to
make still another distinction. It does certainly seem to be true *in a
sense*, that a given idea may be true on one occasion and false on
another. We constantly speak as if there were cases in which a given
thing was true on one occasion and false on another; and I think it
cannot be denied that, when we so speak, we are often expressing
in a perfectly proper and legitimate manner something which is
undeniably true. It is true now, I might say, that I am in this room;
but tomorrow this will not be true. It is true now that men are
often very miserable; but perhaps in some future state of society
this will not be true. These are perfectly natural forms of expression, and what they express is something which certainly may
be true. And yet what they do apparently assert is that something
or other, which is true at one time, will not, or *perhaps* will not, be
true at another. We constantly use such expressions, which imply

that what is true at one time is not true at another; and it is certainly legitimate to use them. And hence, I think, we must admit that, *in a sense* it is true that a thing may be true at one time which is not true at another; in that sense, namely, in which we use these expressions. And it is, I think, also plain that these things, which may be true at one time and false at another, may, *in a sense*, be ideas. We might even say: the idea that I am in this room, is true now; but tomorrow it will not be true. We might say this without any strain on language. In any ordinary book – indeed, in any philosophical book, where the subject we are at present discussing was not being expressly discussed – such expressions do, I think, constantly occur. And we should pass them, without any objection. We should at once understand what they meant, and treat them as perfectly natural expressions of things undeniably true. We must, then, I think, admit that, *in a sense*, an idea may be true at one time, and false at another. The question is: In what sense? What is the truth for which these perfectly legitimate expressions stand?

It seems to me that in all these cases, so far as we are not merely talking of *facts*, but of true *ideas*, that the 'idea' which we truly say to be true at one time and false at another, is merely the idea of a *sentence* – that is, of certain *words*. And we do undoubtedly call *words* 'true'. The words 'I am at a meeting of the Aristotelian Society' are true, if I use them now; but if I use the same words tomorrow, they would not be true. The words 'George III is king of England' were true in 1800, but they are not true now. That is to say, a given set of words may undoubtedly be true at one time, and false at another; and since we may have ideas of words as well as of other things, we may, in this sense, say the same of certain of our 'ideas'. We may say that some of our 'ideas' (namely those of words) are true at one time and not true at another.

But is it conceivable that Professor James *merely* meant to assert that the same *words* are sometimes true at one time and false at another? Can this be *all* he means by saying that truth is mutable? I do not think it can possibly be so. No one, I think, in definitely discussing the mutability of truth, could say that true ideas were mutable, and yet mean (although he did not say so) that this proposition applied *solely* to ideas of words. Professor James must, I think, have been sometimes thinking that *other* ideas, and not merely ideas of words, do sometimes change from true to false. And this is the proposition which I am concerned to dispute. It seems to me that if we mean by an idea, not merely the idea of

187

certain words, but the kind of idea which words express, it is very doubtful whether such an idea ever changes from true to false – whether any such idea is ever true at one time and false at another.

And plainly, in the first place, the mere fact that the same set of words, as in the instances I have given, really are true at one time and false at another, does not afford any presumption that anything which they stand for is true at one time and false at another. For the same words may obviously be used in different senses at different times; and hence though the same words, which formerly expressed a truth, may cease to express one, that may be because they now express a *different* idea, and not because the idea which they formerly expressed has ceased to be true. And that, in instances such as I have given, the words *do* change their meaning according to the time at which they are uttered or thought of, is, I think, evident. If I use now the words 'I am in this room', these words certainly express (among other things) the idea that my being in this room is contemporary with my present use of the words; and if I were to use the same words tomorrow, they would express the idea that my being in this room tomorrow, was contemporary with the use of them *then*. And since my use of them then would not be the same fact as my use of them now, they would certainly then express a different idea from that which they express now. And in general, whenever we use the present tense in its primary sense, it seems to me plain that we do mean something different by it each time we use it. We always mean (among other things) to express the idea that a given event is contemporary with our actual use of it; and since our actual use of it on one occasion is always a different fact from our actual use of it on another, we express by it a different idea each time we use it. And similarly with the past and future tenses. If anybody had said in 1807 'Napoleon is dead', he would certainly have meant by these words something different from what I mean by them when I use them now. He would have meant that Napoleon's death occurred at a time previous to *his* use of those words; and this would not have been true. But in this fact there is nothing to show that if he *had* meant by them what I mean now, his idea would not have been as true then as mine is now. And so, if I say 'it will rain tomorrow', these words have a different meaning today from what they would have if I used them tomorrow. What we mean by 'tomorrow' is obviously a different day, when we use the word on one day, from what we mean by it when we use it on another. But in this there is nothing to show that if the idea which I *now* mean by 'It will rain tomorrow', *were* to occur again tomorrow, it would not be true then, if it is true now. All this is surely very obvious. But, if we take account of it, and if we concentrate our attention not on the words but on what is meant by them, is it so certain that what we mean by them on any one occasion ever changes from true to false? If there were to occur to me tomorrow the very same idea which I now express by the words 'I am in this room', is it certain that this idea would not be as true then as it is now? It is perhaps true that the *whole* of what I mean by such a phrase as this never does recur. But part of it does, and that a part which is true. Part of what I mean is certainly identical with part of what I should mean tomorrow by saying 'I *was* in that room last night'. And this part would be as true then, as it is now. And is there *any* part, which, if it were to recur at any time, would *not* then be true, though it is true now? In the case of all ideas or parts of ideas, which ever do actually recur, can we find a single instance of one, which is plainly true at one of the times when it occurs, and yet not true at another? I cannot think of any such instance. And on the other hand this very proposition that any idea (other than mere words) which is true once, would be true at any time, seems to me to be one of those truths of which Professor James has spoken as having an 'eternal', 'absolute', 'unconditional' character – as being 'perceptually obvious at a glance' and needing 'no sense – verification'. Just as we know that, if a particular colour differs more from black than from grey at one time, the same colour would differ more from black than from grey at any time, so, it seems to me, we can see that, if a particular idea is true at one time, the same idea would be true at any time.

It seems to me, then, that if we mean by an idea, not mere words, but the kind of idea which words express, any idea, which is true at one time when it occurs, *would* be true at any time when it were to occur; and that this is so, even though it is an idea, which refers to facts which are mutable. My being in this room is a fact which is now, but which certainly has not been at every time and will not be at every time. And the words 'I *am* in this room', though they express a truth now, would not have expressed one if I had used them yesterday, and will not if I use them tomorrow. But if we consider the idea which these words *now* express – namely, the idea of the connection of my being in this room with this particular time – it seems to me evident that anybody who had thought of that connection at any time in the past, would have been thinking truly, and that anybody who were to think of it at any time in the future would be thinking truly. This seems to be the sense in which truths are immutable – in which no idea can change from true to false. And I think Professor James means to deny of truths generally, if not of all truths, that they are immutable even in this sense. If he does not mean this there seems nothing left for him to mean, when he says that truths are mutable, except (1) that some *facts* are mutable, and (2) that the same *words* may be true at one time and false at another. And it seems to me impossible that he could speak as he does, if he meant *nothing more* than these two things. I believe, therefore, that he is really thinking that ideas which have been once true (*ideas*, and not merely words) do sometimes afterwards become false: that the very same idea is at one time true and at another false. But he certainly gives no instance which shows that this does ever occur. And how far does he mean his principle to carry him? Does he hold that this idea that Julius Caesar was murdered in the Senate House, though true now, may, at some future time cease to be true, if it should be more profitable to the lives of future generations to believe that he died in his bed? Things like this are what his words seem to imply; and, even if he does hold that truths like this are *not* mutable, he never tries to tell us to what kinds of truths he would limit mutability, nor how they differ from such as this.

III

Finally, there remains the view that 'to an unascertainable extent our truths are man-made products'. And the only point I want to make about this view may be put very briefly.

It is noticeable that all the instances which Professor James gives of the ways in which, according to him, 'our truths' are 'made' are instances of ways in which our *beliefs* come into existence. In many of these ways, it would seem, false beliefs sometimes come into existence as well as true ones; and I take it Professor James does not always wish to deny this. False beliefs, I think he would say, are just as much 'man-made products' as true ones: it is sufficient for his purpose if true beliefs do come into existence in the ways he mentions. And the only point which seems to be illustrated by all these instances, is that in all of them the existence of a true belief does depend in some way or other upon the previous existence of something in some man's mind. They are all of them cases in which we may truly say: This man would not have had just that belief, had not some man previously had such and such experiences, or interests, or purposes. In some cases they are instances of ways in which the existence of a particular belief in a man depends upon *his own* previous experiences or interests or volitions. But this does not seem to be the case in all. Professor James seems also anxious to illustrate the point that one man's beliefs often depend upon the previous experiences or interests or volitions of *other* men. And, as I say, the only point which seems to be definitely illustrated in all cases is that the existence of a true belief does depend, *in some way or other*, upon something which has previously existed in some man's mind. Almost any kind of dependence, it would seem, is sufficient to illustrate Professor James's point.

And as regards this general thesis that almost all our beliefs, true as well as false, depend, in some way or other, upon what has previously been in some human mind, it will, I think, be readily admitted. It is a commonplace, which, so far as I know, hardly anyone would deny. If this is all that is to be meant by saying that our true beliefs are 'man-made', it must, I think, be admitted that almost all, if not quite all, really are man-made. And this is all that Professor James's instances seem to me, in fact, to show.

But is this all that Professor James means, when he says that *our truths* are man-made? Is it conceivable that he only means to insist upon this undeniable, and generally admitted, commonplace? It seems to me quite plain that this is not all that he means. I think he certainly means to suggest that, from the fact that we 'make' our true beliefs, something *else* follows. And I think it is not hard to see one thing more which he does mean. I think he certainly means to suggest that we not only make our true beliefs, but also that we *make them true*. At least as much as this is certainly naturally suggested by his words. No one would persistently say that we make *our truths*, unless he meant, at least, not merely that we make our true beliefs, but also that we make them true – unless he meant not merely that the existence of our true beliefs, but also that their *truth*, depended upon human conditions. This, it seems to me, is one consequence which Professor James means us to draw from the commonplace that the *existence* of our true beliefs depends upon human conditions. But does this consequence, in fact, follow from that commonplace? From the fact that we make our true beliefs, does it follow that we *make them true*?

In one sense, undoubtedly, even this does follow. If we say (as we may say) that no belief can be true, unless it exists, then it follows that, in a sense, the truth of a belief must always depend upon any conditions upon which its existence depends. If, therefore, the occurrence of a belief depends upon human conditions, so, too, must its truth. If the belief had never existed, it would never have been true; and therefore its truth must, in a sense, depend upon human conditions in exactly the same degree in which its existence depends upon them. This is obvious. But is this all that is meant? Is this all that would be suggested to us by telling us that we make our beliefs true?

It is easy to see that it is not. I may have the belief that it will rain tomorrow. And I may have 'made' myself have this belief. It may be the case that I should not have had it, but for peculiarities in my past experiences, in my interests and my volitions. It may be the case that I should not have had it, but for a deliberate attempt to consider the question whether it will rain or not. This may easily happen. And certainly this particular belief of mine would not have been true, unless it existed. Its truth, therefore, depends, in a sense, upon any conditions upon which its existence depends. And this belief may be true. It will be true, if it does rain tomorrow. But, in spite of all these reasons, would anyone think of saying that, in case it is true, I had *made* it true? Would anyone say that I had had any hand *at all* in making it true? Plainly no one would. We should say that I had a hand in making it true, if and only if I had a hand in *making the rain fall*. In every case in which we believe in the existence of anything, past or future, we should say that we had helped to make the belief true, if and only if we had helped to cause the existence of the fact which, in that belief, we believed did exist or would exist. Surely this is plain. I may believe that the sun will rise tomorrow. And I may have had a hand in 'making' this belief; certainly it often depends for its existence upon what has been previously in my mind. And if the sun does rise, my belief will have been true. I have, therefore, had a hand in making a true belief. But would anyone say that, therefore, I had a hand in *making this belief true*? Certainly no one would. No one would say that anything had contributed to make this belief true, except those conditions (whatever they may be) which contributed to making the sun actually rise.

It is plain, then, that by 'making a belief true', we mean something quite different from what Professor James means by 'making' that belief. Conditions which have a hand in making a given true belief, may (it appears) have no hand at all in making it true; and conditions which have a hand in making it true may have no hand at all in making *it*. Certainly this is how we use the words. We should never say that we had made a belief. But now, which of these two things does Professor James mean? Does he mean *merely* the accepted commonplace that we make our true beliefs, in the sense that almost all of them depend for their existence on what has been previously in some human mind? Or does he mean also that we *make them true* – that their truth also depends on what has been previously in some human mind?

I cannot help thinking that he has the latter, and not only the former in his mind. But, then, what does this involve? If his instances of 'truth-making' are to be anything to the purpose, it should mean that, whenever I have a hand in causing one of my own beliefs, I always have to that extent a hand in making it true. That, therefore, I have a hand in actually making the sun rise, the wind blow, and the rain fall, whenever I cause my beliefs in these things. Nay, more, it should mean that, whenever I 'make' a true belief about the past, I must have had a hand in making this true. And if so, then certainly I must have had a hand in causing the French Revolution, in causing my father's birth, in making Professor James write this book. Certainly he implies that some man or other must have helped in causing almost every event, in which any man ever truly believed. That it was we who made the planets revolve round the sun, who made the Alps rise, and the floor of the Pacific sink – all these things, and others like them, seem to be involved. And it is these consequences which seem to me to justify a doubt whether, in fact 'our truths are to an unascertainable extent man-made'. That some of our truths are man-made – indeed, a great many – I fully admit. We certainly do make some of our beliefs true. The Secretary probably had a belief that I should write this paper, and I have made his belief true by writing it. Men certainly have the power to alter the world to a certain extent; and, so far as they do this, they certainly 'make true' any beliefs, which are beliefs in the occurrence of these alterations. But I can see no reason for supposing that they 'make true' *nearly* all those of their beliefs which are true. And certainly the only reason which Professor James seems to give for believing this – namely, that the *existence* of almost all their beliefs depends on them – seems to be no reason for it at all. For unquestionably a man does not 'make true' nearly every belief whose *existence* depends on him; and if so, the question which of their beliefs and how many, men do 'make true' must be settled by quite other considerations.

In conclusion, I wish to sum up what seem to me to be the most important points about this 'pragmatist theory of truth', as Professor James represents it. It seems to me that, in what he says about it, he has in his mind some things which are true and others which are false; and I wish to tabulate separately the principal ones which I take to be true, and the principal ones which I take to be false. The true ones seem to me to be these: –

That *most* of our true beliefs are useful to us; and that *most* of the beliefs that are useful to us are true.

That the world really does change in some respects; that facts exist at one time, which didn't and won't exist at others; and that hence the world may be better at some future time than it is now or has been in the past.

That the very same words may be true at one time and false at another – that they may express a truth at one time and a falsehood at another.

That the existence of most, if not all, of our beliefs, true as well as false, does depend upon previous events in our mental history; that we should never have had the particular beliefs we do have, had not our previous mental history been such as it was.

That the truth, and not merely the existence, of *some* of our beliefs, does depend upon us. That we really do make some alterations in the world, and that hence we do help to 'make true' all those of our beliefs which are beliefs in the existence of these alterations.

To all of these propositions I have no objection to offer. And they seem to me to be generally admitted commonplaces. A certain class of philosophers do, indeed, imply the denial of every one of them – namely, those philosophers who deny the reality of time. And I think that part of Professor James's object is to protest against the views of these philosophers. All of these propositions do constitute a protest against such views; and so far they might be all that Professor James meant to assert. But I do not think that anyone, fairly reading through what he says, could get the impression that these things, and nothing more, were what he had in his mind. What gives colour and interest to what he says, seems to be obviously something quite different. And, if we try to find out what exactly the chief things are which give his discussion its colour and interest, it seems to me we may distinguish that what he has in his mind, wrapped up in more or less ambiguous language, are the following propositions, to all of which I have tried to urge what seem to me the most obvious objections: –

That utility is a property which distinguishes true beliefs from those which are not true; that, therefore, *all* true beliefs are useful, and *all* beliefs, which are useful, are true – by 'utility' being sometimes meant 'utility on at least one occasion', sometimes 'utility in the long run', sometimes 'utility for some length of time'.

That all beliefs which are useful for some length of time are true.

That utility is the *only* property which all true beliefs have in common: that, therefore, *if* it were useful to me to believe in Professor James's existence, this belief *would* be true, even if he didn't exist; and that, *if* it were not useful to me to believe this, the belief *would* be false, even if he did.

That the beliefs, which we express by words, and not merely the words themselves, may be true at one time and *not* true at another; and that this is a general rule, though perhaps there may be some exceptions.

That whenever the *existence* of a belief depends to some extent on us, then also the *truth* of that belief depends to some extent on us; in the sense in which this implies, that, when the existence of my belief that a shower will fall depends upon me, then, if this belief is true, I must have had a hand in making the shower fall: that, therefore, men must have had a hand in making to exist almost every fact which they ever believe to exist.

NOTES

1 William James, *Pragmatism: a new name for some old ways of thinking: popular lectures on philosophy* (New York, Longmans, Green, 1907); all page numbers in the text refer to the present volume.

WILLIAM JAMES'S
CONCEPTION OF TRUTH[1]

Bertrand Russell

'The history of philosophy', as William James observes, 'is to a great extent that of a certain clash of human temperaments.' In dealing with a temperament of such charm as his, it is not pleasant to think of a 'clash'; one does not willingly differ, or meet so much urbanity by churlish criticisms. Fortunately, a very large part of his book is concerned with the advocacy of positions which pragmatism shares with other forms of empiricism; with all this part of his book, I, as an empiricist, find myself, broadly speaking, in agreement. I might instance the lecture devoted to a problem which he considers 'the most central of all philosophic problems', namely, that of the One and the Many. In this lecture he declares himself on the whole a pluralist, after a discussion of the kinds and degrees of unity to be found in the world to which any empiricist may wholly assent. Throughout the book, the distinctive tenets of pragmatism only make their appearance now and again, after the ground has been carefully prepared. James speaks somewhere of Dr Schiller's 'butt–end–foremost statement of the humanist position'. His own statement is the very reverse of 'butt–end–foremost'; it is insinuating, gradual, imperceptible.

A good illustration of his insinuating method is afforded by his lecture on common sense. The categories of common sense, as he points out, and as we may all agree, embody discoveries of our remote ancestors; but these discoveries cannot be regarded as final, because science, and still more philosophy, finds common–sense notions inadequate in many ways. Common sense, science and philosophy, we are told, are all insufficiently true in some respect; and to this again we may agree. But he adds: 'It is evident that the conflict of these so widely differing systems obliges us to overhaul the very idea of truth, for at present we have no definite notion of what the word may mean' (97). Here, as I think, we have a mere *non sequitur*. A damson-tart, a plum-tart, and a gooseberry-tart may all be insufficiently sweet; but does that oblige us to overhaul the very notion of sweetness, or show that we have no definite notion of what the word 'sweetness' may mean? It seems to me, on the contrary, that if we perceive that they are insufficiently sweet, that shows that we do know what 'sweetness' is; and the same surely applies to truth. But this remark is merely by the way.

James, like most philosophers, represents his views as mediating between two opposing schools. He begins by distinguishing two philosophic types called respectively the 'tender-minded' and the 'tough-minded'. The 'tender-minded' are 'rationalistic, intellectualistic, idealistic, optimistic, religious, free-willist, monistic, dogmatical'. The 'tough-minded' are 'empiricist, sensationalistic, materialistic, pessimistic, irreligious, fatalistic, pluralistic, sceptical'. Traditionally, German philosophy was on the whole 'tender-minded', British philosophy was on the whole 'tough-minded'. It will clear the ground for me to confess at once that I belong, with some reserves, to the 'tough-minded' type. Pragmatism, William James avers, 'can satisfy both kinds of demand. It can remain religious like the rationalism, but at the same time, like the empiricisms, it can preserve the richest intimacy with facts'. This reconciliation, to my mind, is illusory; I find myself agreeing with the 'tough-minded' half of pragmatism and totally disagreeing with the 'tender-minded' half. But the disentangling of the two halves must be postponed till we have seen how the reconciliation professes to be effected. Pragmatism represents, on the one hand, a method and habit of mind, on the other, a certain theory as to what constitutes truth. The latter is more nearly what Dr Schiller calls humanism; but this name is not adopted by James. We must, therefore, distinguish the pragmatic *method* and the pragmatic *theory of truth*. The former, up to a point, is involved in all induction, and is certainly largely commendable. The latter is the essential novelty and the point of real importance. But let us first consider the pragmatic method.

Pragmatism [says James] represents a perfectly familiar attitude in philosophy, the empiricist attitude, but it represents it, as it seems to me, both in a more radical and in a less objectionable form than it has ever yet assumed. A pragmatist turns his back resolutely and once for all upon a lot of inveterate habits dear to professional philosophers. He turns away from abstraction and insufficiency, from verbal solutions, from bad *a priori* reasons, from fixed principles, closed systems and pretended absolutes and origins. He turns towards concreteness and adequacy, towards facts, towards action and towards power. That means the empiricist temper regnant and the rationalist temper sincerely given up. It means the open air and possibilities of nature, as against dogma, artificiality and the pretence of finality in truth. (41)

The temper of mind here described is one with which I, for my part, in the main cordially sympathize. But I think there is an impression in the mind of William James, as of some other pragmatists, that pragmatism involves a more open mind than its opposite. As regards scientific questions, or even the less important questions of philosophy, this is no doubt more or less the case. But as regards the fundamental questions of philosophy – especially as regards what I consider *the* fundamental question, namely, the nature of truth – pragmatism is absolutely dogmatic. The hypothesis that pragmatism is erroneous is not allowed to enter for the pragmatic competition; however well it may work, it is not to be entertained. To 'turn your back resolutely and once for all' upon the philosophy of others may be heroic or praiseworthy, but it is not undogmatic or open-minded. A modest shrinking from self-assertion, a sense that all our theories are provisional, a constant realization that after all the hypothesis of our opponents may be the right one – these characterize the truly empirical temper, but I do not observe that they invariably characterize the writings of pragmatists. Dogmatism in fundamentals is more or less unavoidable in philosophy, and I do not blame pragmatists for what could not be otherwise; but I demur to their claim to a greater open-mindedness than is or may be possessed by their critics.

William James, however, it must be admitted, is about as little pontifical as a philosopher well can be. And his complete absence of unction is most refreshing. 'In this real world of sweat and dirt', he says, 'it seems to me that when a view of things is "noble", that ought to count as a presumption against its truth, and as a philosophic disqualification' (50). Accordingly his contentions are never supported by 'fine writing'; he brings them into the market-place, and is not afraid to be homely, untechnical and slangy. All this makes his books refreshing to read, and shows that they contain what he really lives by, not merely what he holds in his professional capacity.

But it is time to return to the pragmatic method.

'The pragmatic method', we are told,

> is primarily a method of settling metaphysical disputes that otherwise might be interminable. Is the world one or many? – fated or free? – material or spiritual? – here are notions either of which may or may not hold good of the world; and disputes over such notions are unending. The pragmatic method in such cases is to try to interpret each notion by tracing its respective practical consequences. What difference would it practically make to anyone if this notion rather than that notion were true? If no practical difference whatever can be traced, then the alternatives mean practically the same thing, and all dispute is idle. Whenever a dispute is serious, we ought to be able to show some practical difference that must follow from one side or the other's being right. [And again:] To attain perfect clearness in our thoughts of an object, then, we need only consider what conceivable effects of a practical kind the object may involve – what sensations we are to expect from it, and what reactions we must prepare. Our conception of these effects, whether immediate or remote, is then for us the whole of our conception of the object so far as that conception has positive significance at all. (39)

To this method, applied within limits and to suitable topics, there is no ground for objecting. On the contrary, it is wholesome to keep in touch with concrete facts, as far as possible, by remembering to bring our theories constantly into connection with them. The method, however, involves more than is stated in the extract which I quoted just now. It involves also the suggestion of the pragmatic criterion of truth: a belief is to be judged true in so far as the practical consequences of its adoption are good. Some pragmatists, for example, Le Roy (who has lately suffered Papal condemnation), regard the pragmatic test as giving *only* a criterion;[2] others, notably Dr Schiller, regard it as giving the actual *meaning* of truth. William James agrees on this point with Dr Schiller, though, like him, he does not enter into the question of criterion versus meaning.

The pragmatic theory of truth is the central doctrine of pragmatism, and we must consider it at some length. William James states it in various ways, some of which I shall now quote. He says: '*Ideas (which themselves are but parts of our experience) become true just in so far as they help us to get into satisfactory relation with other parts of our experience'* (44). Again: 'Truth is *one species of good*, and not, as is usually supposed, a category distinct from good, and co-ordinate with it. *The true is the name of whatever proves itself to be good in the way of belief, and good, too, for definite, assignable reasons'* (51). That truth means 'agreement with reality' may be said by a pragmatist as well as by anyone else, but the pragmatist differs from others as to what is meant by *agreement*, and also (it would seem) as to what is meant by *reality*. William James gives the following definition of agreement: 'To "agree" in the widest sense with a reality *can only mean to be guided either straight up to it or into its surroundings, or to be put into such working touch with it as to handle either it or something connected with it better than if we disagreed'* (105). This language is rather metaphorical, and a little puzzling; it is plain, however, that 'agreement' is regarded as practical, not as merely intellectual. This emphasis on practice is, of course, one of the leading features of pragmatism.

In order to understand the pragmatic notion of truth, we have to be clear as to the basis of *fact* upon which truths are supposed to rest. Immediate sensible experience, for example, does not come under the alternative of *true* and *false*. 'Day follows day,' says James, 'and its contents are simply added. The new contents themselves are not true, they simply *come* and *are*. Truth is *what we say about* them' (46). Thus when we are merely aware of sensible objects, we are not to be regarded as knowing any truth, although we have a certain kind of contact with reality. It is important to realize that the *facts* which thus lie outside the scope of truth and falsehood supply the material which is presupposed by the pragmatic theory. Our beliefs have to agree with matters of fact: it is an essential part of their 'satisfactoriness' that they should do so. James also mentions what he calls 'relations among purely mental ideas' as part of our stock-in-trade with which pragmatism starts. He mentions as instances '1 and 1 make 2', 'white differs less from grey than it does from black', and so on. All such propositions as these, then, we are supposed to know for certain before we can get under way. As James puts it: 'Between the coercions of the sensible order and those of the ideal order, our mind is thus wedged tightly. Our ideas must agree with realities, be such realities concrete or abstract, be they facts or be they principles, under penalty of endless inconsistency and frustration' (104–5). Thus it is only when we pass beyond plain matters of fact and *a priori* truisms that the pragmatic notion of truth comes in. It is, in short, the notion to be applied to doubtful cases, but it is not the notion to be applied to cases about which there can be no doubt. And that there are cases about which there can be no doubt is presupposed in the very statement of the pragmatist position. 'Our account of truth', James tells us, 'is an account . . . of processes of leading, realized *in rebus*, and having only this quality in common, that they *pay*' (107). We may thus sum up the philosophy in the following definition: 'A truth is anything which it pays to believe.' Now, if this definition is to be useful, as pragmatism intends it to be, it must be possible to know that it pays to believe something without knowing anything that pragmatism would call a truth. Hence the knowledge that a certain belief pays must be classed as knowledge of a sensible fact or of a 'relation among purely mental ideas', or as some compound of the two, and must be so easy to discover as not to be worthy of having the pragmatic test applied to it. There is, however, some difficulty in this view. Let us consider for a moment what it means to say that a belief 'pays'. We must suppose that this means that the consequences of entertaining the belief are better than those of rejecting it. In order to know this, we must know what are the consequences of entertaining it, and what are the consequences of rejecting it; we must know also what consequences are good, what bad, what consequences are better, and what worse. Take, say, belief in the Roman Catholic faith. This, we may agree, causes a certain amount of happiness at the expense of a certain amount of stupidity and priestly domination. Such a view is disputable and disputed, but we will let that pass. But then comes the question whether, admitting the effects to be such, they are to be classed as on the whole good or on the whole bad; and this question is one which is so difficult that our test of truth becomes practically useless. It is far easier, it seems to me, to settle the plain question of fact: 'Have Popes been always infallible?' than to settle the question whether the effects of thinking them infallible are on the whole good. Yet this question, of the truth of Roman Catholicism, is just the sort of question that pragmatists consider specially suitable to their method.

The notion that it is quite easy to know when the consequences of a belief are good, so easy, in fact, that a theory of knowledge need take no account of anything so simple – this notion, I must say, seems to me one of the strangest assumptions for a theory of knowledge to make. Let us take another illustration. Many of the men of the French Revolution were disciples of Rousseau, and their belief in his doctrines had far-reaching effects, which make Europe at this day a different place from what it would have been without that belief. If, on the whole, the effects of their belief have been good, we shall have to say that their belief was true; if bad, that it was false. But how are we to strike the balance? It is almost impossible to disentangle what the effects have been; and even if we could ascertain them, our judgement as to whether they have been good or bad would depend upon our political opinions. It is surely far easier to discover by direct investigation that the *Contrat Social* is a myth than to decide whether belief in it has done harm or good on the whole.

Another difficulty which I feel in regard to the pragmatic meaning of 'truth' may be stated as follows: Suppose I accept the pragmatic criterion, and suppose you persuade me that a certain belief is useful. Suppose I thereupon conclude that the belief is true. Is it not obvious that there is a transition in my mind from seeing that the belief is useful to actually holding that the belief is true? Yet this could not be so if the pragmatic account of truth were valid. Take, say, the belief that other people exist. According to the pragmatists, to say 'it is true that other people exist' *means* 'it is useful to believe that other people exist'. But if so, then these two phrases are merely different words for the same proposition; therefore when I believe the one I believe the other. If this were so, there could be no transition from the one to the other, as plainly there is. This shows that the word 'true' represents for us a different idea from that represented by the phrase 'useful to believe', and that, therefore, the pragmatic definition of truth ignores, without destroying, the meaning commonly given to the word 'true', which meaning, in my opinion, is of fundamental importance, and can only be ignored at the cost of hopeless inadequacy.

This brings me to the difference between *criterion* and *meaning* – a point on which neither James nor Dr Schiller is very clear. I may best explain the difference, to begin with, by an instance. If you wish to know whether a certain book is in a library, you consult the catalogue: books mentioned in the catalogue are presumably in the library, books not mentioned in it are presumably not in the library. Thus the catalogue affords a *criterion* of whether a book is in the library or not. But even supposing the catalogue perfect, it is obvious that when you say the book is in the library you do not *mean* that it is mentioned in the catalogue. You mean that the actual book is to be found somewhere in the shelves. It therefore remains an intelligible hypothesis that there are books in the library which are not yet catalogued, or that there are books catalogued which have been lost and are no longer in the library. And it remains an inference from the discovery that a book is mentioned in the catalogue to the conclusion that the book is in the library. Speaking abstractly, we may say that a property A is a *criterion* of a property B when the same objects possess both; and A is a *useful* criterion of B if it is easier to discover whether an object possesses the property A than whether it possesses the property B. Thus being mentioned in the catalogue is a *useful* criterion of being in the library, because it is easier to consult the catalogue than to hunt through the shelves.

Now if pragmatists only affirmed that utility is a *criterion* of truth, there would be much less to be said against their view. For there certainly seem to be few cases, if any, in which it is clearly useful to believe what is false. The chief criticism one would then have to make of pragmatism would be to deny that utility is a *useful* criterion, because it is so often harder to determine whether a belief is useful than whether it is true. The arguments of pragmatists are almost wholly directed to proving that utility is a *criterion*; that utility is the *meaning* of truth is then supposed to follow. But, to return to our illustration of the library, suppose we had conceded that there are no mistakes in the British Museum catalogue: would it follow that the catalogue would do without the books? We can imagine some person long engaged in a comparative study of libraries, and having, in the process, naturally lost all taste for reading, declaring that the catalogue is the only important thing – as for the books, they are useless lumber; no one ever wants them, and the principle of economy should lead us to be content with the catalogue. Indeed, if you consider the matter with an open mind, you will see that the catalogue *is* the library, for it tells you everything you can possibly wish to know about the library. Let us, then, save the taxpayers' money by destroying the books: allow free access to the catalogue, but condemn the desire to read as involving an exploded dogmatic realism.

This analogy of the library is not, to my mind, fantastic or unjust, but as close and exact an analogy as I have been able to think of. The point I am trying to make clear is concealed from pragmatists, I think, by the fact that their theories start very often from such things as the general hypotheses of science – ether, atoms, and the like. In such cases, we take little interest in the hypotheses themselves, which, as we well know, are liable to rapid change. What we care about are the inferences as to sensible phenomena which the hypotheses enable us to make. All we ask of the hypotheses is that they should 'work' – though it should be observed that what constitutes 'working' is not the general agreeableness of their results, but the conformity of these results with observed phenomena. But in the case of these general scientific hypotheses, no sensible man believes that they are true as they stand. They are believed to be true in part, and to work because of the part that is true; but it is expected that in time some element of falsehood will be discovered, and some truer theory will be substituted. Thus pragmatism would seem to derive its notion of what constitutes belief from cases in which, properly speaking, belief is absent, and in which – what is pragmatically important – there is but a slender interest in truth or falsehood as compared to the interest in what 'works'.

But when this method is extended to cases in which the proposition in question has an emotional interest on its own account, apart from its working, the pragmatic account becomes less satisfactory. This point has been well brought out by Professor Stout in *Mind*,[3] and what I have to say is mostly contained in his remarks. Take the question whether other people exist. It seems perfectly possible to suppose that the hypothesis that they exist will always work, even if they do not in fact exist. It is plain, also, that it makes for happiness to believe that they exist – for even the greatest misanthropist would not wish to be deprived of the objects of his hate. Hence the belief that other people exist is, pragmatically, a true belief. But if I am troubled by solipsism, the discovery that a belief in the existence of others is 'true' in the pragmatist's sense is not enough to allay my sense of loneliness: the perception that I should profit by rejecting solipsism is not alone sufficient to make me reject it. For what I desire is not that the belief in solipsism should be false in the pragmatic sense, but that other people should in fact exist. And with the pragmatist's meaning of truth, these two do not necessarily go together. The belief in solipsism might be false even if I were the only person or thing in the universe.

This paradoxical consequence would, I presume, not be admitted by pragmatists. Yet it is an inevitable outcome of the divorce which they make between *fact* and *truth*. Returning to our illustration, we may say that 'facts' are represented by the books, and 'truths' by the entries in the catalogue. So long as you do not wish to read the books, the 'truths' will do in place of the 'facts', and the imperfections of your library can be remedied by simply making new entries in the catalogue. But as soon as you actually wish to read a book, the 'truths' become inadequate, and the 'facts' become all-important. The pragmatic account of truth assumes, so it seems to me, that no one takes any interest in facts, and that the truth of the proposition that your friend exists is an adequate substitute for the fact of his existence. 'Facts', they tell us, are neither true nor false, therefore truth cannot be concerned with them. But the truth 'A exists', if it is a truth, is concerned with A, who in that case is a fact; and to say that 'A exists' may be true even if A does not exist is to give a meaning to 'truth' which robs it of all interest. Dr Schiller is fond of attacking the view that truth must correspond with reality; we may conciliate him by agreeing that *his* truth, at any rate, need not correspond with reality. But we shall have to add that reality is to us more interesting than such truth.

I am, of course, aware that pragmatists minimize the basis of 'fact', and speak of the 'making of reality' as proceeding *pari passu* with the 'making of truth'. It is easy to criticize the claim to 'make reality' except within obvious limits. But when such criticisms are met by pointing to the pragmatist's admission that, after all, there must be a basis of 'fact' for our creative activity to work upon, then the opposite line of criticism comes into play. Dr Schiller, in his essay on 'the making of reality', minimizes the importance of the basis of 'fact', on the ground (it would seem) that 'facts' will not submit to pragmatic treatment, and that, if pragmatism is true, they are unknowable.[4] Hence, on pragmatistic principles, it is useless to think about facts. We therefore return to fictions with a sigh of relief, and soothe our scruples by calling them 'realities'. But it seems something of a *petitio principii* to condemn 'facts' because pragmatism, though it finds them necessary, is unable to deal with them. And William James, it should be said, makes less attempt than Dr Schiller does to minimize facts. In this essay, therefore, I have considered the difficulties which pragmatism has to face if it admits 'facts' rather than those (no less serious) which it has to face if it denies them.

It is chiefly in regard to religion that the pragmatist use of 'truth' seems to me misleading. Pragmatists boast much of their ability to reconcile religion and science, and William James, as we saw, professes to have discovered a position combining the merits of tender-mindedness and tough-mindedness. The combination is really effected, if I am not mistaken, in a way of which pragmatists are not themselves thoroughly aware. For their position, if they fully realized it, would, I think, be this: 'We cannot know whether, in fact, there is a God or a future life, but we can know that the belief in God and a future life is true.' This position, it is to be feared, would not afford much comfort to the religious if it were understood, and I cannot but feel some sympathy with the Pope in his condemnation of it.

'On pragmatic principles', James says, 'we cannot reject any hypothesis if consequences useful to life flow from it'(130). He proceeds to point out that consequences useful to life flow from the hypothesis of the Absolute, which is therefore so far a true hypothesis. But it should be observed that these useful consequences flow from the hypothesis that the Absolute is a fact, not from the hypothesis that useful consequences flow from belief in the Absolute. But we cannot believe the hypothesis that the Absolute is a fact merely because we perceive that useful consequences flow from this hypothesis. What we can believe on such grounds is that this hypothesis is what pragmatists call 'true', i.e. that it is useful; but it is not from this belief that the useful consequences flow, and the grounds alleged do not make us believe that the Absolute is a fact, which is the useful belief. In other words, the useful belief is that the Absolute is a fact, and pragmatism shows that this belief is what it calls 'true'. Thus pragmatism persuades us that belief in the Absolute is 'true', but does not persuade us that the Absolute is a fact. The belief which it persuades us to adopt is therefore not the one which is useful. In ordinary logic, if the belief in the Absolute is true, it follows that the Absolute is a fact. But with the pragmatist's meaning of 'true' this does not follow; hence the proposition which he proves is not, as he thinks, the one from which comforting consequences flow.

In another place James says: 'On pragmatistic principles, if the hypothesis of God works satisfactorily in the widest sense of the word, it is true'(130). This proposition is, in reality, a mere tautology. For we have laid down the definition: 'The word "true" means "working satisfactorily in the widest sense of the word".' Hence the proposition stated by James is merely a verbal variant on the following: 'On pragmatistic principles, if the hypothesis of God works satisfactorily in the widest sense of the word, then it works satisfactorily in the widest sense of the word.' This would hold even on other than pragmatistic principles; presumably what is peculiar to pragmatism is the belief that this is an important contribution to the philosophy of religion. The advantage of the pragmatic method is that it decides the question of the truth of the existence of God by purely mundane arguments, namely, by the effects of belief in His existence upon our life in this world. But unfortunately this gives a merely mundane conclusion, namely, that belief in God is true, i.e. useful, whereas what religion desires is the conclusion that God exists, which pragmatism never even approaches. I infer, therefore, that the pragmatic philosophy of religion, like most philosophies whose conclusions are interesting, turns on an unconscious play upon words. A common word – in this case, the word 'true' – is taken at the outset in an uncommon sense, but as the argument proceeds, the usual sense of the word gradually slips back, and the conclusions arrived at seem, therefore, quite different from what they would be seen to be if the initial definition had been remembered.

The point is, of course, that, so soon as it is admitted that there are things that exist, it is impossible to avoid recognizing a distinction, to which we may give what name we please, between believing in the existence of something that exists and believing in the existence of something that does not exist. It is common to call the one belief true, the other false. But if, with the pragmatists, we prefer to give a different meaning to the words 'true' and 'false', that does not prevent the distinction commonly called the distinction of 'true' and 'false' from persisting. The pragmatist attempt to ignore this distinction fails, as it seems to me, because a basis of fact cannot be avoided by pragmatism, and this basis of fact demands the *usual* antithesis of 'true' and 'false'. It is hardly to be supposed that pragmatists will admit this conclusion. But it may be hoped that they will tell us in more detail how they propose to avoid it.

Pragmatism, if I have not misunderstood it, is largely a generalization from the procedure of the inductive sciences. In so far as it lays stress upon the importances of induction, I find myself in agreement with it; and as to the nature of induction also, I think it is far more nearly right than are most of the traditional accounts. But on fundamental questions of philosophy I find myself wholly opposed to it, and unable to see that inductive procedure gives any warrant for its conclusions. To make this clear, I will very briefly explain how I conceive the nature and scope of induction.

When we survey our beliefs, we find that we hold different

beliefs with very different degrees of conviction. Some – such as the belief that I am sitting in a chair, or that 2+2=4 – can be doubted by few except those who have had a long training in philosophy. Such beliefs are held so firmly that non-philosophers who deny them are put into lunatic asylums. Other beliefs, such as the facts of history, are held rather less firmly, but still in the main without much doubt where they are well authenticated. Beliefs about the future, as that the sun will rise tomorrow and that the trains will run approximately as in Bradshaw, may be held with almost as great conviction as beliefs about the past. Scientific laws are generally believed less firmly, and there is a gradation among them from such as seem nearly certain to such as have only a slight probability in their favour. Philosophical beliefs, finally, will, with most people, take a still lower place, since the opposite beliefs of others can hardly fail to induce doubt. Belief, therefore, is a matter of degree. To speak of belief, disbelief, doubt, and suspense of judgement as the only possibilities is as if, from the writing on the thermometer, we were to suppose that blood heat, summer heat, temperate and freezing were the only temperatures. There is a continuous gradation in belief, and the more firmly we believe anything, the less willing we are to abandon it in case of conflict.

Besides the degree of our belief, there is another important respect in which a belief may vary, namely, in the extent to which it is *spontaneous* or *derivative*. A belief obtained by inference may be called *derivative*; one not so obtained, *spontaneous*. When we do not need any outside evidence to make us entertain a belief, we may say that what we believe is *obvious*. Our belief in the existence of sensible objects is of this nature: 'seeing is believing', and we demand no further evidence. The same applies to certain logical principles, e.g. that whatever follows from a true proposition must be true. A proposition may be obvious in very varying degrees. For example, in matters of aesthetic taste we have to judge immediately whether a work of art is beautiful or not, but the degree of obviousness involved is probably small, so that we feel no very great confidence in our judgement. Thus our spontaneous beliefs are not necessarily stronger than derivative beliefs. Moreover, few beliefs, if any, are *wholly* spontaneous in an educated man. The more a man has organized his knowledge, the more his beliefs will be interdependent, and the more will obvious truths be reinforced by their connection with other obvious truths. In spite of this fact, however, obviousness remains always the ultimate source of our beliefs; for what is called verification or deduction consists always in being brought into relation with one or more obvious propositions. This process of verification is necessary even for propositions which seem obvious, since it appears on examination that two apparently obvious propositions may be inconsistent, and hence that apparent obviousness is not a sufficient guarantee of truth. We therefore have to subject our beliefs to a process of organization, making groups of such as are mutually consistent, and when two such groups are not consistent with each other, selecting that group which seems to us to contain the most evidence, account being taken both of the degree of obviousness of the propositions it contains and of the number of such propositions. It is as the result of such a process, for example, that we are led, if we are led, to conclude that colours are not objective properties of things. Induction, in a broad sense, may be described as the process of selecting hypotheses which will organize our spontaneous beliefs, preserving as many of them as possible, and interconnecting them by general propositions which, as is said, 'explain' them, i.e. give a ground from which they can be deduced. In this sense, all knowledge is inductive as soon as it is reflective and organized. In any science, there is a greater or less degree of obviousness about many of its propositions: those that are obvious are called *data*; other propositions are only accepted because of their connection with the data. This connection itself may be of two kinds, either that the propositions in question can be deduced from the data, or that the data can be deduced from the propositions in question, and we know of no way of deducing the data without assuming the propositions in question. The latter is the case of working hypotheses, which covers all the general laws of science and all the metaphysics both of common sense and of professed philosophy. It is, apparently, by generalizing the conception of 'working hypothesis' that pragmatism has arisen. But three points seem to me to have been overlooked in this generalization. First, working hypotheses are only a small part of our beliefs, not the whole, as pragmatism seems to think. Secondly, prudent people give only a low degree of belief to working hypotheses; it is therefore a curious procedure to select them as the very types of beliefs in general. Thirdly, pragmatism seems to confound two very different conceptions of 'working'. When *science* says that a hypothesis works, it means that from this hypothesis we can deduce a number of propositions which are verifiable, i.e. obvious under suitable circumstances, and that we cannot deduce any propositions of which the contradictories are verifiable. But when *pragmatism* says that a hypothesis works, it means that the effects of believing it are good, including among the effects not only the beliefs which we deduce from it, but also the emotions entailed by it or its perceived consequences, and the actions to which we are prompted by it or its perceived consequences. This is a totally different conception of 'working', and one for which the authority of scientific procedure cannot be invoked. I infer, therefore, that induction, rightly ana-lysed, does not lead us to pragmatism, and that the inductive results which pragmatism takes as the very type of truth are precisely those among our beliefs which should be held with most caution and least conviction.

To sum up: while agreeing with the empirical temper of pragma-tism, with its readiness to treat all philosophical tenets as 'working hypotheses', we cannot agree that when we say a belief is true we mean that it is a hypothesis which 'works', especially if we mean by this to take account of the excellence of its effects, and not merely of the truth of its consequences. If, to avoid disputes about words, we agree to accept the pragmatic definition of the word 'truth', we find that the belief that A exists may be 'true' even when A does not exist. This shows that the conclusions arrived at by pragmatism in the sphere of religion do not have the meaning which they appear to have, and are incapable, when rightly understood, of yielding us the satisfaction which they promise. The attempt to get rid of 'fact' turns out to be a failure, and thus the old notion of truth reappears. And if the pragmatist states that utility is to be merely a *criterion* of truth, we shall reply first, that it is not a useful criterion, because it is usually harder to discover whether a belief is useful than whether it is true; secondly, that since no *a priori* reason is shown why truth and utility should always go together, utility can only be shown to be a criterion at all by showing inductively that it accompanies truth in all known instances, which requires that we should already know in many instances what things are true. Finally, therefore, the pragmatist theory of truth is to be condemned on the ground that it does not 'work'.

NOTES

1 William James, *Pragmatism: a new name for some old ways of thinking: popular lectures on philosophy* (New York, Longmans, Green, 1907); all

page numbers in the text refer to the present volume. The following article is reprinted from the *Albany Review* (January 1908), where it appeared under the title 'Transatlantic "truth" '. It has been criticized by William James in *The Meaning of Truth* (New York, Longmans, 1909), in the article called 'Two English critics'.

2 cf., e.g., Le Roy, 'Comment se pose le problème de Dieu', *Revue de Métaphysique et de Morale* 15, 4 (July 1907), 506, 507 note.

3 October 1907, 586–8. This criticism occurs in the course of a very sympathetic review of Dr Schiller's *Studies in Humanism*.

4 cf. *Studies in Humanism*, 434–6.

NOTES ON THE PRAGMATIC THEORY OF TRUTH

Moreland Perkins

Although pragmatism has been primarily an analysis of cognition and its validation, the largest portion of the criticisms of this philosophy have been aimed at its theory of truth. Critics have most often taken the pragmatists' conception of truth to be the core of the doctrine. For example, Russell, writing in 1908, remarks that:

> the cardinal point in the pragmatist philosophy, namely its theory of truth, is so new, and necessary to the rest of the philosophy . . . that its inventors cannot be regarded as merely developing the thoughts of . . . predecessors.[1]

And writing forty years later Russell again notes that:

> Pragmatism, as it appears in James, is primarily a new definition of 'truth'.[2] From the strictly philosophical point of view, the chief importance of Dewey's work lies in his criticism of the traditional notion of 'truth' which is embodied in the theory he calls instrumentalism.[3]

Similar emphasis upon the theory of truth in pragmatism can be found in many writers.[4]

I believe that it is a mistake to construe the conception of truth as the central notion in pragmatism. It is rather their conception of knowledge which deserves that position. However, I shall not argue that point. Instead I shall consider some of the misunderstandings of the pragmatic view of truth which are in part responsible for the critics' emphasis on this subject. I shall also try to indicate what seems to me to be the chief source of these misunderstandings.

It will be convenient to limit the discussion more or less to the writings of William James. For James possesses the double advantage of having written a great deal on the explicit subject of truth and of having expressed views susceptible to the kind of serious misinterpretation I wish to remove. Peirce lacks the latter advantage and Dewey the former.

In the first part of the paper I shall deal with the relation of truth to verification in James, and in the second part with the bearing of the semantic conception of truth upon James's treatment of the subject.

I

Criticisms of the pragmatic theory of truth (and, indeed, of their philosophy in general) have focused upon three assertions which have been credited to the pragmatists. They are the following:

(1) Truth is the same as verification.
(2) The true is the useful or satisfactory or successful (in beliefs).
(3) The truth or falsehood of a belief or statement is not fixed and eternal but is mutable.

But both (2) and (3) are, in so far as they are to be found in the pragmatic writings, corollaries of (1). If (1) is justifiably attributed to the pragmatist then (2) follows by a substitution of his definition of verification. And if (1) is justifiably attributed to the pragmatist then (3) follows in virtue of the mutability of the status of any belief or statement with respect to its degree of verification or falsification. The first proposition is, then, the strategic one. If it is not accepted by the pragmatist then the evidence for their acceptance of the second two becomes negligible, and much of the criticism of pragmatism is nullified.

Numerous writers have found this identification of truth and verification in pragmatism. For example, Pratt writes:

[the pragmatist] deduces the rather amazing conclusion that since its usefulness proves it true, its trueness consists in its usefulness. The test of truth and the meaning of truth are thus completely identified.[5]

And Russell argues:

At first sight it might seem a perfectly proper inductive proceeding to inquire what properties a belief must have in

order that we may call it *true*, and to infer that those properties constitute the meaning of 'truth'. There is, however, a
fallacy in this method of inquiry; and this fallacy, in our
opinion, is at the bottom of the whole pragmatic
philosophy.[6]

Not infrequently James has written accounts of truth which seem
to justify the belief that, for him, to be true is no more than to be
verified. Three examples are the following:[7]

> any idea that will carry us prosperously from any one part of
> our experience to any other part, linking things satisfactorily,
> working securely, simplifying, saving labour; is true for just
> so much . . . (P: 44)

> Our account of truth is an account of truths in the plural, of
> processes of leading, realized *in rebus*, and having only this
> quality in common, that they *pay*. They pay by guiding us
> into or towards some part of a system . . . with which at any
> rate we are now in the kind of commerce vaguely designated
> as verification. (P: 107)

> The truth of an idea is not a stagnant property inherent in it.
> Truth *happens* to an idea. It *becomes* true, is *made* true by
> events. Its verity *is* in fact an event, a process: the process
> namely of its verifying itself, its veri-*fication*. (P: 100)

Assuming, then, that James is committed to the belief that the
true is the same as the verified, serious difficulties are encountered,
as his critics have pointed out. There are undoubtedly many statements which never have been and never will be verified or falsified,
not because they cannot be but because no one has or will take the
trouble to test them. Such statements are, on James's theory,
neither true nor false. But this violates a basic rule of language, the
law of excluded middle, which requires that every statement be
either true or false. Also, since the verification–status of a statement
may vary at different times – it may be verified or confirmed at one
time and falsified or disconfirmed at another – a statement may be
true at one time and false at another. But again this violates a
fundamental rule concerning the use of the word 'true'. A statement cannot be both true and false, according to the law of
contradiction. The statement 'Caesar crossed the Rubicon' cannot

be true in 1500 and false in 1900. For Caesar could not have both crossed the Rubicon and not crossed it. A statement might be warranted, or reasonably well verified, in 1500 and not warranted in 1900; but warrant or credibility is quite different from truth. Truth, in short, is something which a statement either has or does not have once and for all and independently of whether or not it has been or ever will be actually confirmed or disconfirmed by any person. James may very well be explicating the notion of verification in an interesting way but his account is obviously inadequate if taken, as he takes it, as a theory of the nature of truth.

These difficulties would be fatal, I believe, if James's theory were as it appears to be in the remarks quoted – if he did identify the true and the confirmed. However, I do not believe that his critical theory is of such a naïve kind. To render this contention plausible it will be necessary both to show that he expressed some other conception of truth, and to give some explanation for this tendency to equate truth and verification.

The definition of truth to which James adheres when he is seeking formal rigour is one which identifies truth and verifi*ability*. To say that a belief is true is not to say that it is verifi*ed* – or even simply that it *will* be verified – but to say that it is verifi*able*. And 'verifiable' does not here mean theoretically capable of being either verified or falsified, confirmed or disconfirmed. It means rather something like this:

> p is verifiable = If p *were* carefully tested over an indefinitely long period it *would* be verified (confirmed) to an increasingly higher degree.

The truth of a belief is its disposition to be confirmed in the long run and under certain conditions, i.e. if it is carefully tested. It is a potentiality or tendency of the belief or statement to be confirmed eventually if tested; it is not a state of actual confirmation.

Some version of the verifiability view is frequently expressed by James. Thus as early as *Pragmatism* James writes:

> The quality of truth, obtaining *ante rem*, pragmatically means, then, the fact that in such a world innumerable ideas work better by their indirect or possible than by their direct and actual verification. Truth *ante rem* means only verifiability . . .
> (P: 108)

And later he writes:

What constitutes the relation known as truth, I now say, is just
the *existence in the empirical world of this fundamentum of circum-
stance surrounding object and idea* and ready to be either short-
circuited or traversed at full length. So long as it exists, and a
satisfactory passage through it between the object and the idea
is possible, that idea will both *be* true, and will *have been* true
of that object, whether fully developed verification has taken
place or not. (MT: 165)

I myself agree most cordially that for an idea to be true the
object must be 'as' the idea declares it, but I explicate the 'as'-
ness as meaning the idea's verifiability . . . (MT: 170)

Other expressions of this point of view will appear as the discussion
continues.

Now this conception of truth is free from the criticisms which
have been directed at his alleged identification of truth and verification. Verifiability is a property which every statement either
definitely has or definitely does not have, regardless of whether it
ever has been or will be actually verified. Furthermore it is a
property which a statement has once and for all. It is not capable of
being confirmed in the indefinitely long run in one year and incapable of such long-run confirmation in another year. The verifiability is a disposition of the statement which exists in the statement
initially and permanently, even though it may never manifest itself
in any particular verification if it is never actually tested. It is a
dispositional property which is such that the laws of contradiction
and excluded middle are valid when it is identified with truth.

Of course the present definition has its own difficulties. The
definiens is a counterfactual conditional and therefore poses problems in analysis. It also involves a reference to the 'long run' which
might be difficult to clarify. However, I am not concerned with
such problems of further explication. I wish only to point out that
the present conception is free from the formal difficulties which
have been urged against the pragmatic theory in virtue of its alleged
identification of truth and verification.

Possession of these merits by the 'verifiability' definition demon-
strates that it is inconsistent with the unqualified definition in terms
of verification alone, which James seems also to have advanced.
One naturally asks whether any motives or principles can be found
in James's writings which would conspire to produce expression of

two incompatible definitions of truth. If there are such they might provide clues for the solution of questions of priority. Further motives of this sort are clearly revealed in the writings of James.

The most important cause, in the opinion of this writer, for the failure of James to adhere consistently to expression of the 'verifiability' definition is the fact that James was usually trying to forward three different but related projects simultaneously. And two of these projects frequently interfered with the third. The three endeavours were (a) to explain truth in terms of a certain relation of an 'idea' to verification, that of ability to be verified; (b) to develop a new theory of actual verification and hence of knowledge, the 'utilitarian' theory; and (c) to champion aggressively an extreme nominalism, insisting upon the analysis of concepts in terms of the concreta which alone constitute their ultimate referents. His frequent preoccupation with (b) and (c) when ostensibly doing (a) has accounted for most of his defections from expression of the verifiability theory of truth.

In considering the effects of (b) upon (a) it is important to remember that James's conception of truth contains three elements which call for analysis: the conditional form, if p *were* . . . then it *would* be . . .; the notion of the 'long run'; and the notion of verification. A complete understanding of his idea of truth could not be conveyed without explication of all of these elements. The first two pose thorny problems. But it is not surprising that they were frequently neglected and even ignored in the interest of explaining the verification component. For it was the notion of verification as satisfactory functioning or successful working which was the most distinctively novel element in the whole philosophy expounded by James. Consequently he finds it difficult to deal with a problem whose solution requires essential reference to verification without allowing the analysis of the latter to become his preponderant concern. We find, then, such remarks as this:

> Any idea that helps us to *deal* . . . with either the reality or its belongings, that doesn't entangle our progress in frustrations, that *fits*, in fact, and adapts our life to the reality's whole setting, will . . . hold true of that reality. (P: 105)

Here no suggestion of the adequacy of mere potential confirmation and no considerations concerning the long run seem to be expressed. On the other hand when he is conscious of the need for meeting formal requirements he is able to deal with (a) and (b) at the same time:

> 'The true' . . . *is only the expedient in the way of our thinking.* . . . Expedient in almost any fashion; and expedient in the long run and on the whole of course; for what meets expediently all the experience in sight won't necessarily meet all farther experiences equally satisfactorily. Experience . . . has ways of *boiling over*, and making us correct our present formulas. (P: 109)

It seems, however, that the third motive suggested – the strong concern for the concrete – was the most important stimulus to James's characterizations of truth in terms of actual rather than potential verification. At the first level of analysis truth is, indeed, to be conceived as a kind of dispositional property of an 'idea':

> a healthy man need not always be sleeping, or always digesting, any more than a wealthy man need be always handling money. . . . All such qualitities sink to the status of 'habits' between their times of exercise; and similarly truth becomes a habit of certain of our ideas and beliefs in their intervals of rest from their verifying activities. (P: 109)

> just as a man may be called an heir and treated as one before the executor has divided the estate, so an idea may practically be credited with truth before the verification process has been exhaustively carried out – the existence of the mass of verifying circumstances is enough. Where potentiality counts for actuality in so many cases one does not see why it may not so count here. (MT: 164)

But, as even these remarks suggest, a reference to a disposition or a potentiality is always incomplete for James. The disposition–term must be analysed into the aggregate of concrete events which it denotes. Hence he continues the first remark above by pointing out that nevertheless 'those activities [the concrete verifications] are the root of the whole matter, and the conditions of there being any habit to exist in the intervals'. I am not here concerned with the adequacy of James's theory of the analysis of counterfactuals or disposition-terms. What is relevant is simply to notice that it is on the basis of such a theory that so many of his formulations of the definition of truth are made, and that therefore these formulations should not be taken so much as evidence of his theory of truth as evidence of his nominalism.

Perhaps nothing is more emphasized in the writing of James than the axiom that a concept is merely an abstraction of a class of concrete particulars and that these particulars exhaust the concept's reference. And the rule of exposition which is derived from this axiom and equally emphasized in practice is that each abstraction, and hence each concept which one is concerned to understand, should be broken down into its concrete denota. This holds for the concept of truth as well as for any other:

> The pragmatist clings to facts and concreteness, observes truth at its work in particular cases, and generalizes. Truth, for him, becomes a class-name for all sorts of definite working-values in experience. (P: 48)

> The full reality of a truth for him [the pragmatist] is always some process of verification, in which the abstract property of connecting ideas with the objects truly is workingly embodied. Meanwhile it is endlessly serviceable to be able to talk of properties abstractly and apart from their working. . . . We thus form whole universes of platonic ideas *ante rem*, universes *in posse*, though none of them exists effectively except *in rebus*. . . . Countless relations obtain there which nobody experiences as obtaining. . . . In the same way countless opinions 'fit' realities, and countless truths are valid, though no thinker thinks them. . . .
> For the anti-pragmatist these prior timeless relations are the presupposition of the concrete ones. . . . When intellectualists do this, pragmatism charges them with inverting the real relation. Truth *in posse means* only truth in act; and he insists that these latter take precedence in order of logic as well as in that of being. (MT: 203–6)

Truth is, in the first analysis, a rather abstract relation between ideas or statements and facts – a relation determining potential interaction of a certain sort. But there are no abstract relations in the final analysis, holds James. And since the only concrete relation which he can find for the prototype of the abstract one in question (the verifiability) is that of *actual* verification he reduces the verifiability to a class of concrete verifications. The result is undoubtedly an oversimplification, but it is a result of a general theory of abstractions rather than of a theory of truth. The initial concept of truth remains that of verifiability.

Finally we may note that James himself was quite conscious that his own emphasis on the concrete constituted not only the chief difference between him and the others, but also constituted a chief source of misunderstanding on the part of his critics. Referring to the 'antipragmatist' in general he writes:

> His trouble seems to me mainly to arise from his fixed inability to understand how a concrete statement can possibly mean as much, or be as valuable, as an abstract one. I said above that the main quarrel between us and our critics was that of concreteness *versus* abstractness. (MT: 201)

And contrasting his view with that of most epistemologists he says:

> . . . and the most general way of characterizing the two views is by saying that my view describes knowing as it exists concretely, while the other view only describes its results abstractly taken. (MT: 144)

Perhaps the best example of a passage in which all three of the motives which have been suggested operate in conjunction with an awareness of the importance of his own nominalism is the following:

> Of course if you take the satisfactoriness concretely, . . . and if, by truth, you mean truth taken abstractly and verified in the long run you cannot make them equate, for it is notorious that the temporarily satisfactory is often false. Yet at each and every concrete moment, truth for each man is what that man 'trowth' at that moment with the maximum of satisfaction to himself; and similarly abstract truth, truth verified by the long run, and abstract satisfactoriness, long-run satisfactoriness, coincide. If, in short, we compare concrete with concrete and abstract with abstract, the true and satisfactory do mean the same thing. I suspect that a certain muddling hereabouts is what makes the general public so impervious to humanism's claims. (MT: 88–9)[8]

II

The criticisms which we have discussed above appear as a part of a family quarrel in comparison with the implications which have been drawn for all philosophic theories of truth as a result of the work of Tarski on truth.[9] For according to many interpreters of the 'semantic conception' of truth, the pragmatic theory, along with all other philosophic theories of truth, is left in the humiliating position of a theory without a subject-matter.

I do not believe that the semantic conception of truth provides grounds for such a drastic conclusion. In fact, I should maintain that not only does the semantic conception itself suggest a subject-matter for a theory of truth but that it suggests a way of viewing the problem which is essentially the way of James and the pragmatists. Before testing this claim let us examine briefly the semantic conception and the misgivings it has aroused.

What Tarski has described as the 'semantic conception of truth' is to be distinguished from the semantic definition of truth developed by him. The former is not a definition but a criterion which, according to Tarski, every adequate definition should meet. It is employed by Tarski as a test of adequacy in the construction of a formal definition of truth for a particular language. In this discussion we may ignore the definition because the difficulties for philosophic theories of truth have been suggested chiefly by the semantic conception.

The semantic criterion for a definition of truth is the following: Allow the letter 'p' to be a substitute for some particular but unspecified sentence, and allow the letter 'X' to be the *name* of the sentence for which the letter 'p' stands. Then any definition of truth must be such that it implies all equivalences of the following form:

X is true if and only if p.

For example, it must imply the equivalence:

'Crows are black' is true if and only if crows are black.

It will be noticed that the statement which *occurs* on the right-hand side of the equivalence sign does not occur on the left-hand side but is named – in this case by surrounding the same words with single quotes. And the name appears as the subject of the sentence which does occur on the left-hand side – the sentence, ' "Crows are black" is true'.

Such a criterion does seem to express an equivalence which is universally valid. Clearly if crows are black then the sentence 'Crows are black' is true; and it is also clear that if the sentence 'Crows are black' is true, then crows are black. In general it would seem that such a mutual implication obtains between statements of the form specified. We can agree, then, that any definition of truth should involve a *definiens* which warrants all such equivalences.

What are the misgivings to which this conception has given rise? They can best be illustrated by quoting two writers whose interpretations are quite similar. Professor Black, after summarizing Tarski's work on truth, proposed tentatively a 'new philosophical theory' of truth:

> On this view, the locution 'that . . . is true' would be regarded as a linguistic device for converting an unasserted into an asserted sentence. Truth would then tend to lose some of its present dignity. One might be inclined to call the word redundant, and to baptize the theory, in the customary misleading fashion, as a 'No Truth' theory. [10]

However, Black is hesitant about going even that far towards a 'theory' and concludes on the same page that:

> any search for a direct answer to the 'philosophical problem of truth' can at best produce a formula that is platitudinous and tautologous or arbitrary and paradoxical; and that a more hopeful method for investigating the 'problem' is to dispel the confusions of thought which generate it.

A.J. Ayer is even more emphatic. His analysis does not seem to have been directed by Tarski's work, but the source of his conclusions is essentially the semantic conception as it is presented above. He writes:

> Reverting to the analysis of truth, we find that in all sentences of the form 'p is true', the phrase 'is true' is logically superfluous. When, for example, one says that the proposition 'Queen Anne is dead' is true, all that one is saying that Queen Anne is dead. . . . Thus to say that a proposition is true is just to assert it. . . . And this indicates that the terms 'true' and 'false' connote nothing, but function in the sentence simply as marks of assertion and denial. And in that case there can be no sense in asking us to analyse the concept of 'truth'.
>
> We conclude, then, that there is no problem of truth as it is ordinarily conceived. The traditional conception of truth as a 'real quality' or a 'real relation' is due like most philosophical mistakes to a failure to analyse sentences correctly. [11]

We may note that the first sentence of Ayer's remarks above is incorrect. The phrase 'is true' is certainly not superfluous in sentences of the form 'X is true'. To say that it is is to suggest that we start with a sentence, add the words 'is true' to it, and find that no new meaning has been added. But in fact we do not add 'is true' to a sentence at all. If we did we would get an expression like 'Crows are black is true'. But this is grammatical nonsense. What we do is add the words 'is true' to a *name* of a sentence; the *name* of one sentence functions as the subject of the sentence in which the phrase 'is true' occurs. For example, we write:

'Crows are black' is true.

If we removed the words 'is true' from this sentence we should have no sentence at all but merely a name standing by itself.

However, what we cannot deny is what Ayer goes on to assert and what Black suggests – that the phrase 'is true' functions merely to assert a sentence. Our qualification of Ayer's remarks in the previous paragraph indicates just that. It shows simply that there are at least two ways of asserting a sentence. On the one hand (restricting ourselves to written assertions) we may simply capitalize the first word and place a period at the end; or, on the other hand, we may take the same words and surround them with single quotation marks and add the words 'is true' and a period. Both operations achieve the same end, assertion of a given sentence. Of course the sentences may be named by some other method than the use of quotation marks, as in our analysis above where we let the letter 'X' be the name of a sentence. Also a sentence may be asserted, as the sentence on the right-hand side of the equivalence in the semantic conception is, by simply placing it properly in the context of a compound sentence. The essential point is that the semantic conception of truth puts in clear relief the fact that to say of a sentence that it is true is no more and no less than simply to assert that sentence.

The conclusion to be drawn is that a theory of truth must be in some sense a theory of assertion.

For Ayer and Black this is tantamount to saying that there is no longer any subject-matter for a theory of truth. If to predicate truth of a sentence is simply to assert the same sentence then there is no problem left for philosophical analysis.

I suggest, however, that this latter is an unwarranted addition to the justified and interesting conclusion that an analysis of truth is in some sense an analysis of the nature of assertion. Furthermore, I believe that the approach to the analysis of truth which has been advanced by the pragmatists is distinguished by an emphasis which is congruent with the implications of the semantic conception and which at least points the way towards the allaying of the misgivings which that conception has aroused.

The first point to notice is that James's conception of the nature of the inquiry into the meaning of truth is, broadly speaking, that which the semantic conception suggests – that of an inquiry into the nature of assertion. One of the salient emphases in the writings of James is on the need for conceiving the analysis of truth as an examination of the structure and workings of the *active attitude* which constitutes assertion or belief. Over and over he insists that theories of truth have too long settled for a mere reference to some sort of correspondence between the 'idea' and the reality without giving any hint of the nature of this correspondence. And with equal frequency he insists that the only way that such correspondence can be dissected is by examining the nature of the *act* of *cognitive intention* which, or some ingredient in which, is said to 'resemble' the reality. The analysis of truth must centre on the examination of the peculiar state of mind of the asserter or believer and the effects it promises for the rest of the world. James writes:

> The trueness of an idea must mean *something definite in it that determines its tendency to work,* and indeed towards this object rather than that. . . . What that something is in the case of truth psychology tell us: the idea has associates peculiar to itself, motor as well as ideational; it tends by its place and nature to call these into being, one after another; and the appearance of them in succession is what we mean by the 'workings' of the idea. According to what they are, does the trueness or falseness which the idea harbored come to light. (MT: 174)

> Truth meaning agreement with reality, the mode of the agreeing is a practical problem which the subjective term of the relation alone can solve. (MT: 224)

However, merely to show that James considered the analysis of truth to centre around the analysis of the cognitive act is not enough. It is necessary also to show how the particular conception of truth advocated by James – truth as verifiability – can be maintained while admitting the equivalence between assertion of a sentence and ascription of truth to a sentence. How can 'truth' mean verifiability when to predicate truth of a sentence is merely to assert that sentence? Since the problem has not been considered by James or the other pragmatists in just this form it will be necessary to suggest the lines which a defence of the pragmatic approach would take.

By way of an approach which might throw a different light on the semantic conception I propose that we reverse our orientation and – instead of looking to assertion for insight into truth – look to truth predication for insight into assertion. To assert a sentence is the same, according to the semantic conception, as to predicate truth of that sentence. This suggests then that the very act of assertion itself has the nature of a *claim* – a claim of truth. Now what could be a plausible content for this claim? James would suggest, initially, that the claim is that the sentence 'agrees with the facts'. But this, says James, requires further explication. What does it mean to claim that the sentence 'agrees with the facts'? This means, James concludes, that one claims that the sentence would be verified in the long run if tested carefully. By asserting a sentence one claims that the sentence is verifiable. One assumes responsibility for the positive results of an indefinitely extended sequence of tests.[12]

The first difficulty which occurs to this proposal is that it seems far-fetched to suppose that when one asserts a sentence one is talking about the sentence. But this is no more implausible than the semantic conception itself. For the latter implies precisely that. According to that conception to assert a sentence is logically equivalent to saying *of* the same sentence that it is true. In so far, then, as one assumes the semantic conception one cannot bring such an objection against the present hypothesis. However, we suggest that even if the two processes are truth-functionally equivalent there may still be a difference between the *explicit* contents of each. The assertion of a sentence refers only implicitly or indirectly to the sentence asserted, while such a reference becomes explicit when one *names* the sentence and says it 'is true'. When one asserts a sentence one is claiming that a correlation exists between an indefinitely extended series of *operations* – testing operations – and a similar series of positive *confirming results*. A correlation, such that if the first series comes to be, the second will eventually parallel it, is claimed. Directly, then, one is speaking only of certain potential organism–environment interactions. Indirectly, however, one is also claiming that the *sentence* is verifiable. For what we *mean* by saying that the *sentence* is verifiable is simply that a kind of connection between certain tests and positive results exists. We assume or take for granted a connection between the sentence as a physical object and the possible testing operations which are the meaning of the sentence. Hence, if we say that a sentence is verifiable, and if the sentence is meaningful, then we can, in theory, translate our remark into one about a connection between certain operations and certain confirming results; or if we originally claim the latter connection we can translate that into a claim about the verifiability of the sentence. The difference between the mere assertion of a sentence and the assertion of another sentence which predicates truth of the first (e.g. between asserting 'Snow is white' and asserting ' "Snow is white" is true') is the difference between speaking in the first case explicitly or directly about a correlation between tests and confirming results and only implicitly or indirectly about a sentence, and, in the second case, speaking explicitly about a sentence and only implicitly about a correlation between tests and confirming results. In both instances the explicit utterance implies the correlative implicit one in virtue of the presupposition concerning the correlation between the physical sentence itself and the testing operations – the presupposition of a connection between the sentence and its meaning.

The second and closely related objection is simply that it does not seem likely that one makes such a complex claim by merely asserting a sentence. And here it seems we have to choose between the plausibility of construing the equivalence of assertion and predication of truth as a reduction in the apparent meaning of 'true' or as an increase in the apparent significance of mere assertion. My proposal is that we at least give the latter alternative serious consideration rather than accept the former unquestioningly. I would suggest simply that since a sentence is supposed to have implications extending indefinitely into the future, and since a sentence has no implications independently of a context of assertion, or potential assertion, by someone, then the act of assertion itself must in some way have such indefinitely extended implications.[13]

Finally we may turn to the charge by Ayer that those philosophers who have considered truth to be a 'real' relation have been involved in a confusion of language. William James clearly fits into the category, for he considered truth to be such a relation. Can

James maintain plausibly that to say of something that it is true is to say of it that it has a certain relation to something else? According to our interpretation of pragmatism such language would seem to be meaningful and consistent. To say of a sentence that it is true is to say that it is verifiable. This in turn is to say that if the sentence were tested over an indefinitely long run it would be increasingly confirmed. And this is to say, first, that the sentence is related to certain possible operations and expectancies of results in the way we designate by saying the latter are the meaning of the former, and, second, that the possible operations are related to the expected results by a kind of correlation which will manifest itself fairly consistently over a long run.

But since assertion of a sentence is itself equivalent to ascribing truth to the sentence it must be legitimate to say that in the act of assertion itself a similar relation is claimed to exist. But, as we have seen, the act of assertion itself does not explicitly claim exactly the same relation as does the predication of truth. For it does not *explicitly* say anything about the sentence which it asserts. However, it does claim a relation – namely that relation of correlation between the testing responses and confirming results which has been mentioned earlier. And it is presupposed that the sentence which is asserted has its meaning in these testing responses. Therefore the mere assertion of the sentence implicitly claims the same relation between the sentence and the series of test-confirmation pairs as the explicit ascription of truth to the sentence claims.

NOTES

1 Bertrand Russell, *Philosophical Essays* (New York, Longmans, Green, 1910), 88.
2 Bertrand Russell, *A History of Western Philosophy* (New York, Simon & Schuster, 1945), 816.
3 ibid., 820.
4 See, for example, G.E. Moore's article on James in *Philosophical Studies*; W.P. Montague, *Ways of Knowing* (New York, Macmillan, 1925), 147, 162–4; and J.B. Pratt, *What Is Pragmatism?* (New York, Macmillan, 1909), especially 87, 113, 116–17.
5 ibid., 89.
6 Russell, *Philosophical Essays*, 137–8.
7 In quoting James I shall use 'P' to refer to *Pragmatism* (New York, Longmans, Green, 1947; all page numbers in the text refer to the present volume) and 'MT' to refer to *The Meaning of Truth* (New York,

Longmans, Green, 1909). In all cases the italics are those of the original author.

8 The conception of truth as potential verification in the long run seems to be what Peirce has in mind when he writes: 'That is to say, I hold that truth's independence of individual opinions is due . . . to its being the predestined result to which sufficient inquiry would eventually lead' (*Collected Papers of Charles Sanders Peirce*, vol. 5, 343–4) and 'The truth of the proposition that Caesar crossed the Rubicon consists in the fact that the further we push our archaeological and other studies, the more strongly will that conclusion force itself on our minds forever – or would do so, if study were to go on forever' (ibid., 395). And Dewey indicates his agreement with the conception of Peirce in his *Logic, the Theory of Inquiry* (New York, Henry Holt, 1938), 345 footnote.

9 Alfred Tarski, 'Der Wahrheitsbegriff in den formalisierten Sprachen', *Studia Philosophica* 1 (1935), 261–405. Also Alfred Tarski, 'The semantic conception of truth', *Philosophy and Phenomenological Research* 4 (1944), 341–75.

10 Max Black, *Language and Philosophy* (Ithaca, NY, Cornell University Press, 1949), 107.

11 A.J. Ayer, *Language, Truth and Logic* (London, Gollancz, 1949), 88–9.

12 Peirce stresses the 'assumption of responsibility' in the act of assertion. See especially op. cit., 386.

13 However, we do not wish to stretch our hypothesis too far. And it may be one of the results of such an analysis that certain attitudes for which the predicates 'true' and 'false' have generally been considered relevant are not within the scope of such predicates. Beliefs have generally been described as true or false, or as having contents which are true or false. And often included in the class of beliefs are those mechanical habits or dispositions to respond which are shared by humans with the lowest animals – adjustments to the environment which have an anticipatory character and which are modifiable through experience. But it would seem implausible indeed to suppose that such dispositions involve a claim concerning the indefinitely extended future career of a set of possible responses by many organisms. It may be necessary, then, to conclude that such dispositions or attitudes do not involve a claim of truth, thus marking off such attitudes from the peculiarly human acts of explicit assertion.

WAS WILLIAM JAMES
TELLING THE TRUTH
AFTER ALL?

D.C. Phillips

It is a truth of military history that major battles are not clearly understood by the rank-and-file who are embroiled in them. There is a flurry of activity, a 'blooming, buzzing confusion', and anything that moves in the surrounding terrain is likely to be identified as the enemy. Usually it is only after the 'tumult and the shouting dies' that a clear picture emerges, and a tally can be obtained of how many of one's friends were felled by mistake.

The same may well be true in philosophy. Consider the battle over relativism – which, having continued with fluctuating intensity for several millennia, is probably more aptly conceived as a war of attrition rather than as a one-time fray. In recent years there has been increased activity in no man's land, due to the reinforcements delivered to the relativist position by Kuhnian paradigms, Wittgensteinian games and forms of life, Hansonian (and Wittgensteinian) duck-rabbits, and Quinean ontological relativity and undetached rabbit parts. There have been pot-shots aplenty, but sometimes the target has not been clearly defined in the midst of all the excitement.

I

Consider relativism's fellow-traveller, instrumentalism. Most philosophers, when push comes to shove, are clear about the differences between the two, and they would offer an account along the following lines: relativists are not committed to the position that statements do not have truth-values, but rather it is held that their truth-values are relative to some theoretical frame; whereas instrumentalists do regard it as otiose to talk about truth (or rather, as

Rorty puts it, *Truth*), and advocate instead that statements be assessed in terms of their instrumental value (or fruitfulness or the like).

In the popular mind, however, the two views can easily merge together, as is illustrated in the following revealing passage written by an educational theorist:

> scientists themselves hold beliefs, even within science, that cannot be warranted by scientific methods. In the social sciences, this most clearly is the case. The differences in basic assumptions among Freudians, Rogerians, Skinnerians, Heiderians, Ericksonians, Piagetians, and the like are not resolvable through science. The fundamental theoretical structures through which each defines psychological reality differ, and there is no critical test that will resolve the truth or falsity of their respective belief systems. . . . My point here is simply this: objectivity is a function of intersubjective agreement among a community of believers. What we can productively ask of a set of ideas is not whether it is *really* true but whether it is useful, whether it allows one to do one's work more effectively.[1]

Here it is apparent that an instrumental criterion has been adopted (whether a theory is 'useful' rather than 'really true'), although the author also was toying with relativism (the view that what is true depends on the framework being adopted). And there is some justification for the two being run together; a prima-facie case can be made that the theoretical framework an individual adopts will help to determine what priorities and interests he or she will have, what problems will be seen and what type of solutions will be sought, what criteria will be used, and so forth.

It is significant, for the argument that follows, that the running-together of relativism and instrumentalism is not confined to the non-philosophical world. There is a tendency in Popper, for example, to see them as closely allied – in his view they both oppose the objectivist or correspondence theory of truth which, flushed with post-Tarskian vigour, he himself defends.[2] And evidently Russell saw 'epistemological relativism' and 'epistemological pragmatism' as being somewhat similar, for they both were closely linked with certain authoritarian and totalitarian ideas that he found odious.[3] Scheffler characterized William James's pragmatic or instrumentalist theory of truth as embodying a 'fundamental relativism'.[4] Furthermore, in Wittgenstein's *On Certainty* there are several passages which are relativistic[5] and others that are instrumentalistic.[6]

To add a final complexity, it is interesting to note that Wittgenstein's latter-day admirer, Richard Rorty, has wanted to *defend* pragmatism or instrumentalism from the charge of relativism; or, as he more picturesquely put it, he wanted to construct (from his own view of philosophy as 'edifying') a reply to the familiar charge of 'relativism' levelled at the subordination of truth to edification.[7] At the very least, it is clear that Rorty is implicitly agreeing that the two positions are often run together by members of the philosophical community.

Now, there is nothing surprising in showing that there are points of similarity between two doctrines (for of course points of similarity can be found between any two doctrines). And it is not necessarily a blemish on the reputations of good people that they see two doctrines as being rather similar when other good people see the same things as rather dissimilar. The real issues, and the genuine blemishes, have yet to emerge.

II

In current philosophical disputes most often it is relativism that is under attack, not instrumentalism. One of the reasons for this is the widely held belief that instrumentalism has already been refuted. Most contemporary philosophers have their own favourite critical arguments, but the *locus classicus*, the source of many of the knock-down moves, is G.E. Moore's 'no-holds-barred' paper on William James. But a careful rereading of this paper yields surprising results: none of Moore's arguments are convincing, and most are quite wide of the target; contemporary writers often advance facsimiles of Moore's points – with similar outcome; and some of the now-common arguments against modern relativism were used by Moore in his vain attempt to combat instrumentalism (although of course the attack was not recognized as vain, except perhaps by James himself).

In the discussion that follows, Moore's paper will be evaluated piece-by-piece, and it will be suggested (*contra* Scheffler) that Jamesian instrumentalism might still stand as a viable alternative to relativism – an alternative that should not be as shocking to the sensibilities of realists as it once was. And in the course of reasessing Moore's attack on James, some important distinctions will emerge, which will be shown to clarify some of the present debates over relativism.

III

On 6 January 1908, G.E. Moore read to the Aristotelian Society his lengthy polemic 'William James's "Pragmatism" '. Looking back at the paper more than three decades later he judged it 'to have been a good piece of work'.[8] Over the years most commentators have made a similar judgement; in recent decades the paper has been cited by such writers as John Passmore in *A Hundred Years of Philosophy*, Alan R. White in his text on *Truth*, and A.J. Ayer in his critical study *The Origins of Pragmatism*.

It generally has been agreed that Moore's arguments were both sound and devastating. Several of Moore's readers have even been moved to wonder how such an outstanding thinker as William James could possibly have held such an untenable theory of the nature of truth; as Ayer put it,

These objections are so obvious that it is hard to understand how James could have remained unmoved by them if he really held the views against which they were directed.[9]

And in the words of V.J. McGill,

Moore does go on to consider very carefully other things that James might have meant. . . . Everywhere he is successful in showing that if James meant what he literally seems to mean, he is saying either truisms, obvious dubieties or absurdities. But nowhere does he manage to explain how a thinker of James' caliber could be guilty of such things.[10]

In other words it is suggested that Moore's critique was so successful that he showed James possibly meant something other than the untenable theory of truth that a straightforward interpretation of his words indicated.

There is, of course, another possible tack: one could argue that while these criticisms make James *look* foolish, he was *not* foolish, therefore there is something wrong with the criticisms. While acknowledging that James's words require a modicum of interpretation, it will indeed be argued in the following pages that all of the specific criticisms developed by Moore, and accepted by subsequent writers over seven and a half decades, were specious.[11]

Moore's paper was long, and its structure relatively complex. He started by distinguishing three broad theses that William James was 'particularly anxious to assert about truth',[12] and the first of these was then analysed into four narrower theses. The points discussed in Moore's paper can be summarized as follows:

(A) James 'is plainly anxious to assert some connection between truth and "verification" or "utility". Our true ideas, he seems to say, are those that "work", in the sense that they are or can be "verified", or are "useful".'[13] Here James wishes to assert, according to Moore,

   (1) 'That we can verify all those of our ideas, which are true.'
   (2) 'That all those among our ideas, which we can verify, are true.'
   (3) 'That all our true ideas are useful.'
   (4) 'That all those of our ideas, which are useful, are true.'[14]

(B) James 'seems to object to the view that truth is something "static" or "immutable". He is anxious to assert that truths are in some sense "mutable".'[15]

(C) James 'asserts that "to an unascertainable extent our truths are man-made products".'[16]

Moore's treatment of these various theses will be examined in turn. But, putting aside for a moment the issue of whether James really did hold them, it should be noted that a prima-facie case can be made that (B) and (C) are quite *compatible* with relativism. For it can be argued that if truth is regarded as being relative to a theoretical frame, when frames change or evolve then so does the truth. (If this argument is regarded as being too naïve for any red-blooded relativist to accept, then, as will be seen, it might be reasonable to regard it as too crude for James to have swallowed as well.) Furthermore, it is reasonable to construe relativists as holding that because truth is relative to theory, then as new theories are constructed, in a sense new truths are being made – truths are, in a manner of speaking, 'man-made'. But to return to Moore.

In opening his discussion of James's first general theme (A) – the relation between truth and verification or utility – Moore failed to appreciate the main point at stake. There are historical factors why Moore can be partially exonerated: James was writing under the influence of C.S. Peirce's pragmatic criterion of meaning published thirty years earlier, and of course this was not widely known in 1908. Most likely, Moore would only have come across James's loose exposition of Peirce earlier in the book *Pragmatism* whose chapter on truth he was dissecting. So when James stated, in lecture VI of this book, that true ideas may copy or agree with reality as most philosophers hold, but it is essential to determine what 'agreement' and 'copying' mean, Moore did not fully appreciate that here James was embarking on an application of the Peircean criterion of meaning to these terms which were too often used in an 'off-hand and irreflective' way.[17] In other words, James was setting out to ask what 'sensible effects' these particular words were intended to indicate, a quest that he made fairly clear:

> Pragmatists . . . begin to quarrel only after the question is raised as to what may precisely be meant by the term 'agreement', and what by the term 'reality', when reality is taken as something for our ideas to agree with.[18]

And a little later,

> Pragmatism, on the other hand, asks its usual question. 'Grant an idea or belief to be true,' it says, 'what concrete difference will its being true make in anyone's actual life? How will the truth be realized? What experiences will be different from those which would obtain if the belief were false?'[19]

Moore completely misinterpreted James's words. He took it that James's only objection to the correspondence theory of truth was that not *all* ideas actually copy reality; James had in fact mentioned this point, but only to raise the general problem of what 'copying' and 'agreement' mean. Moore's mistaken argument is worth quoting:

> And he [James] first briefly considers the theory, that the sense in which our true ideas agree with reality, is that they 'copy' some reality. And he affirms that some of our true ideas really do do this. But he rejects the theory, as a theory of what truth means, on the ground that they do not *all* do so. Plainly, therefore, he implies that no theory of what truth

means will be correct, unless it tells us of some property which belongs to *all* our true ideas without exception.[20]

At the outset of his paper, therefore, Moore was already at cross-purposes with James. He had failed to appreciate the problem James was concerned with: How do we come to *ascribe* truth to an idea, that is, what experiences lead us to recognize that an idea is true – what is truth 'known-as', what is its 'cash-value in experiential terms'?[21] The passages already quoted make it clear that James accepted the correspondence theory as a *definition* of truth, but that he also regarded this as fairly unenlightening. So, his interest was elsewhere; he wanted to establish a *criterion* of truth, to establish a procedure for identifying 'true ideas'. As Richard Rorty recently put it, the pragmatists 'think it will not help to say something true to think about Truth'.[22] Or as Richard Hertz pointed out, James was interested in the 'art of good believing', and Moore misunderstood because his interests lay 'in the art of good defining and logical precision'.[23] It is interesting to note here, too, that Israel Scheffler almost hit upon this interpretation of James, but perhaps because his own predilections were similar to those of Moore, he ended by passing it by. Scheffler wrote that

> The truth of a statement must, of course, be clearly distinguished from its being taken, at a given time, to be true or estimated as true. . . . Clearly, we have, at any given time, ideas or propositions we estimate as true or take to be true.[24]

It is precisely this that James was attempting to elucidate; but throughout, Scheffler persisted in criticizing him from the perspective of non-Jamesian 'Truth'.

The endeavour upon which James was embarking has an interesting series of parallels with Popper's philosophical programme. Indeed, it can be argued that in many respects James was an incipient Popperian (or, alternatively, that Popper unwittingly was a neo-pragmatist).[25] Popper, too, has accepted the correspondence theory (which he regards as having been revitalized by Tarski), and he also acknowledges that it is a mistake to expect that a satisfactory theory of truth (which, unfortunately, he neglected to spell with a capital 'T') would also be a theory of true, well-founded belief.[26] The latter is reached by way of testing and refutation. Popper writes:

So one great advantage of the theory of objective or absolute truth is that it allows us to say – with Xenophanes – that we search for truth, but may not know when we have found it; that we have no criterion of truth, but are nevertheless guided by the idea of truth as a regulative principle.[27]

The main sentiment that James would quarrel with here is the one with which the passage opens; he once wrote that the notion of absolute truth 'runs on all fours with the perfectly wise man' – the problem is that we have to *live* today 'by what truth we can get today'.[28] Popper, in other words, is not wrong but from James's perspective he had the priorities the wrong way around (and so, no doubt, had Moore). And James would have added, of course, that we *have* developed a criterion of truth.

IV

Moore's shortsightedness about James's work was reflected in the way he discussed the four particular sub-theses James advanced about (A), the relation between truth, verification and utility.

(1) In the first place, Moore considered James's thesis that 'we can verify all those of our ideas, which are true'.[29] Moore's procedure, to be repeated throughout his paper, was to refute by producing counter-examples – in this case examples of true ideas which could not be verified. Suppose I have written a letter, he argued, and later some doubt arises as to whether I used a particular word in it. The letter may now be lost, but I hold one idea on the matter in dispute and the person who received the letter holds another.

Can we then always verify which of our ideas is the true one? I think it is very doubtful whether we can *nearly* always.[30]

Similarly, a group of card-players may discuss one of the previous hands in order to determine whether a particular player held a certain card. Different players have different recollections.

Is it always possible to verify which of these ideas is the true one? Either the player did or did not have the seven of diamonds. . . . And it is certain that one or other of these two ideas is true. But can they always verify either of them?[31]

From the point of view of the problem that concerned James – not the one that Moore erroneously supposed to be at issue – these examples are far from being an embarrassment. Moore concentrated on the fact that in his examples one of the two mutually exclusive ideas presented in each case must be true, yet neither could be verified; James would not contest this, but he was concerned with the different issue of how, in practice, truth would be ascribed – what difference would it make to say that one or other idea was true? In Moore's examples, where the possibility of finding evidence to support either of the rival ideas has been ruled out, in practice no idea would have truth ascribed to it as neither could be 'verified'. This, of course, is not to deny that either may be true. It is noteworthy that in neither of his cases did Moore say which idea was true; in other words he, too, did not ascribe truth to any of the ideas in dispute, presumably because his examples deliberately withheld evidence as to which of the ideas was true. It is not James's theory of truth that is made problematical by these examples; what is odd is that Moore, and subsequent commentators, took them to be decisive counter-examples.

(2) On the other hand, Moore's discussion of James's second thesis – 'all those . . . ideas, which we can verify, are true' – was remarkably short. This, Moore stated, was 'certainly true, in its most obvious meaning',[32] and as a result he was not certain that James was 'really anxious' to assert it. Moore immediately turned his attention to James's third and fourth particular theses, and his arguments here, according to V.J. McGill, were 'altogether faultless'.[33]

(3) Moore embarked on his discussion of the thesis that 'all our true ideas are useful' by admitting that one of the preliminary points made by James was 'indisputably true', namely that true ideas sometimes occur when they are not useful. The idea 'twice two are four' is sometimes useful, but on many other occasions it would be 'positively in the way'.[34]

But if a true idea can occur at times when it is not useful – a point James acknowledged – then it is possible that a true idea that occurs just once may occur at a time when it is not useful. In Moore's words:

> But there seems to be an immense number of true ideas, which occur but once and to one person, and never again either to him or to anyone else. I may, for instance, idly count the number of dots on the back of a card, and arrive at a true idea of their number; and yet, perhaps, I may never think of their number again, nor anybody else ever know it. . . . And

237

is it quite certain that all these true ideas are useful? It seems to me perfectly clear, on the contrary, that many of them are not.[35]

There are several lines of reply against this attack. In the first place it can be countered that if, indeed, a completely useless idea occurs to us, then we would not ascribe truth to it – we would have no basis for doing so. Moore argued that nevertheless the idea could be true, but here he was operating with what James identified as the 'intellectualist' conception of truth that was worthless for day-to-day life unless some account could be given as to how such an idea would be *known* to be true. As James derisively put it in an answer to his critics a year or so after Moore had attacked him:

> *Essential* truth, the truth of the intellectualists, the truth with no one thinking it, is like the coat that fits tho' no one has ever tried it on, like the music that no ear has listened to. It is less real, not more real, than the verified article.[36]

No doubt Rorty had passages like this in mind when he wrote that if pragmatists are asked about the nature of Truth, 'They would simply like to change the subject'.[37]

Secondly, it is possible to argue that Moore's idea that there was a particular number of spots on the back of a card was not useless if, in fact, the idea resolved the puzzle about the spots that presumably initiated the process of counting them. If the idea resolved the 'irritation of doubt' as C.S. Peirce called it, then the idea might well have truth ascribed to it, especially if no countervailing evidence were available as to the number of spots. As James put it in a passage that Moore could well have paid more attention to,

> Any idea that helps us to *deal*, whether practically or intellectually, with either the reality or its belongings, that doesn't entangle our progress in frustrations, that *fits*, in fact, and adapts our life to the reality's whole setting, will agree sufficiently to meet the requirement. It will hold true of that reality.[38]

This is instrumentalism, certainly, but it is not particularly pernicious. Clearly James was not holding to the extreme relativistic view that there are multitudes of realities for our ideas to be true of, nor was he holding to the extreme subjectivist position that whatever pleases us is true. Indeed, he was as much a realist as Popper or Moore:

> Truths emerge from facts. . . . The 'facts' themselves mean-while are not *true*. They simply *are*. Truth is the function of the beliefs that start and terminate among them.[39]

(4) Moore embarked on his discussion of what he thought was James's fourth thesis, that every idea, which is at any time useful, is true, with the judgement that 'it seems hardly possible to doubt that this assertion is false'.[40] He then produced what he took to be counter-examples, that is, examples of useful ideas that were false. The following is typical: suppose we are in a state of war, and the enemy get a false idea of our location at a certain time.

> Such a false idea is sometimes given, and it seems to me quite clear that it is sometimes useful. In such a case, no doubt, it may be said that the false idea is useful to the party who have given it, but not useful to those who actually believe in it. And the question whether it is useful on the whole will depend upon the question which side it is desirable should win. But it seems to me unquestionable that the false idea is sometimes useful on the whole.[41]

Popper put forward a similar example in the course of one of his attacks on the pragmatic theory of truth:

> Similarly, if there exists something like the correspondence of theory to the facts, then it is clear that a theory which corresponds to the facts will be as a rule very useful; more useful, *qua* theory, than a theory which does not correspond to the facts. (On the other hand, it may be very useful for a criminal before a court of justice to cling to a theory which does not correspond to the facts; but as it is not *this* kind of usefulness which the pragmatists have in mind, their views raise a question which is very awkward for them: I mean the question, 'Useful for whom?')[42]

These examples can be interpreted in a manner that supports rather than refutes James's position. The clue lies in Popper's 'awkward question'. To stick with Moore's formulation of the counter-example, he did not take enough care in distinguishing the ideas held by the two warring sides, nor in deciding which of these

ideas was useful and which was true. Moore uncritically assumed
there was only one idea involved, namely the false one that 'we are
in position X', and it was useful for us that the enemy believed it,
although of course it was not useful for them. However, an accurate analysis of the situation is somewhat more complicated. In the
first place, there is the idea believed by the enemy that 'we are in
position X'. This idea is false, and it turns out to be far from useful
for those who believe it. But we do not believe it. We believe a
second idea which is true; namely, 'it will be useful for us if the
enemy believe we are in position X when we are elsewhere'. Thus
the force of Moore's counter-example is dissipated: the true idea is
revealed as the one that is useful, and the false idea is shown to be
the one that lacks utility. The same could be shown in Popper's
example.

Moore, however, being satisfied that he had shown James's first
four theses about truth and utility to be untenable, pushed on with
his discussion. He spent several pages investigating other possible
theses that James might have intended to express, and he narrowed
the field down to one:

> Plainly, therefore, Professor James is intending to tell us of a
> property which belongs both to *all* true ideas and *only* to true
> ideas. And this property, he says, is that of 'paying'. But now
> let us suppose that he means by 'paying', not 'paying *once* at
> least', but, according to the alternative he suggests, 'paying in
> the long run' or 'paying for some time'.[43]

Moore's objections to this were firstly that he doubted, but admitted he could not prove, that this property applied *only* to true ideas,
and secondly that 'it is only too obvious' that the property did not
belong to all true ideas, as many do not *have* a 'long run'. The
transient and rather trivial ideas that Moore had in mind here – such
as the number of spots on a playing-card – have already been
discussed; they did not pose a difficulty for James's position. But
there is a deeper point at issue. James used many different examples
and verbal formulations to illuminate his meaning, a style that
many commentators have traced back to his expertise as a teacher
and public speaker where it is an undoubted strength to proceed in
this way. But it is therefore essential that an isolated sentence not be
taken and dissected apart from the many others that James also used
to express the same point. And it is here that Moore can be accused
of being shortsighted. Reading James with his own definition of

'Truth' in mind, Moore consistently overlooked or misread long passages, such as the following, that should have given him quite a different perspective on the problem with which James was attempting to deal:

> True ideas lead us into useful verbal and conceptual quarters as well as directly up to useful sensible termini. They lead to consistency, stability and flowing human intercourse. They lead away from eccentricity and isolation, from foiled and barren thinking. The untrammelled flowing of the leading-process, its general freedom from clash and contradiction, passes for its indirect verification; but all roads lead to Rome, and in the end and eventually, all true processes must lead to the face of directly verifying sensible experiences *somewhere* . . .[44]

It is time to apply a variant of Occam's Law: Quotations must not be multiplied beyond necessity. There have been sufficient to show that James has been much maligned.

V

Moore's misunderstandings also affected his treatment of James's second major thesis (B) that 'truth is mutable'. After some initial skirmishing to settle whether James meant that *all* truth is mutable, in other words whether all ideas which are true at one time are at some other time false, Moore disputed that *any* truths were, for it seemed to him

> that there is a sense in which it is the case with *every* true idea that, if once true, it is always true. That is to say, that every idea, which is true once, *would* be true at any other time at which it were to occur . . .[45]

Moore acknowledged that *reality* is mutable; as he put it, many things in the future 'will be different from what they are now'. On this point he was in agreement with James, but unfortunately James did 'not mean *merely* this, when he says that truth is mutable'.[46] So Moore turned to another possibility.

Perhaps James was thinking of expressions like 'I am in this room'; today it is true, but tomorrow when I am in the country it will not be true.[47] Here, Moore argued, there is a confusion of words or sentences with ideas. The *words* 'I am at a meeting of the

Aristotelian Society' are true now, but not if used tomorrow.[48] But if we concentrate not on the words but on their meaning, then the situation changes. The meaning is that on a given date I was at the Aristotelian Society, and if it was true that I was at the society on that day, then it will always be true that I was there. So an idea 'which is true at one time when it occurs, *would* be true at any time when it were to occur',[49] and in this sense truths are not mutable. Moore concluded:

> Does he [James] hold that this idea that Julius Caesar was murdered in the Senate House, though true now, may, at some future time cease to be true, if it should be more profitable to the lives of future generations to believe that he died in his bed?[50]

This is not only an anti–instrumentalist argument, for it also applies against relativism. Judged relative to theory T_1 it may be true that Caesar was murdered in the Senate, but relative to theory T_2 it may not be true. However, one can hear Moore cry from the Great Beyond (or perhaps from Popper's 'third world'), either Caesar was murdered in the Senate or he wasn't, but he could not both have been murdered and not. Against the relativists he might have a point, but not against James.

For unfortunately all of Moore's arguments against James's second major thesis were irrelevant. James's point was that there are many historical cases, of the sort cited by Moore, where an idea had truth *ascribed* to it on the basis of a certain body of available evidence, only later to have the judgement rescinded – 'the world is flat' will suffice as an example. This idea was once regarded as true because it 'worked' in the sense indicated in the various passages from James's book that were quoted earlier; and with the advancement of knowledge the idea ceased to 'work' in this way. It is incredible that Moore could overlook the whole point of James's position, especially in the light of passages such as the following:

> The 'absolutely' true, meaning what no farther experience will ever alter, is that ideal vanishing-point towards which we imagine that all our temporary truths will some day converge. It runs on all fours with the perfectly wise man, and with the absolutely complete experience; and, if these ideals are ever realized, they will be realized together. Meanwhile we have to live today by what truth we can get today, and be

ready tomorrow to call it falsehood. Ptolemaic astronomy, Euclidean space, Aristotelian logic, scholastic metaphysics, were expedient for centuries, but human experience has boiled over those limits . . .[51]

VI

When he turned to James's third and final major thesis (C), namely that to a degree 'our truths are man-made products', Moore promised that his comments would be brief. He first considered that James was referring to human *beliefs*, rather than truth, and he acknowledged that our forming of true beliefs does depend 'in some way or other upon the previous existence of something in some man's mind'.[52] But James must have meant far more than this when he insisted that 'our truths are man-made'. I may believe that it will rain tomorrow, Moore argued, and this belief may turn out to be true. But, if it is true, have I *made* it true?

> We should say that I had a hand in making it true, if and only if I had a hand in *making the rain fall*.[53]

Similarly, if I have true historical ideas, then James must say I had a hand in causing the French Revolution and so on – a classic argument by *reductio ad absurdum*.

Once again Moore missed the essence of James's position. Of course we, now, do not cause the French Revolution, then. But historians have formulated an idea of the French Revolution in order to cope with a body of evidence; and in the course of their inquiries further facts may emerge which cause them to readjust their idea. Without inquiry, testing, verification, they will not ascribe truth to the new idea. It is in this sense, a sense not discussed by Moore, that truth is man-made. As James picturesquely put it, in another passage that Moore did not appreciate,

> In the realm of truth-processes facts come independently and determine beliefs provisionally. But these beliefs make us act, and as fast as they do so, they bring into sight or into existence new facts which re-determine the beliefs accordingly. . . . The case is like a snowball's growth . . .[54]

Popper was closer to James on this matter than was Moore. There is a sense, Sir Karl acknowledged, in which the third world of objective knowledge 'originates as a product of human activity', but nevertheless is autonomous and 'transcends its makers'.[55] Men and women interact with the third world, add to it, and are affected by it. If James was not a proto-Popperian, perhaps Popper was a neo-Jamesian.

VII

There are some important conclusions to be drawn. In the first place, it would appear that over the years the commentators have been seriously in error. It is not the adherence of William James to an 'obviously untenable' theory of truth that is blameworthy, rather it is the shortsightedness of G.E. Moore in misreading James (to name only the classic culprit). Furthermore, once James is read correctly, a reassessment is called for concerning his relationship to other writers (such as Popper).

Second, the record needs to be set straight concerning the distinction between the pragmatic or instrumentalist theory of the ascription of truth on one hand, and on the other, the relativist theory of the meaning of 'truth' which too often has been confused with it. Somewhere in the midst of the fray here Richard Rorty is shedding some light, but of course his chief aim is not to rescue James but to reach his own tactical objectives. The following passage, for example, while strictly true of James, is apt to give the false impression that the latter is a relativist (the throw-away remark 'if any' is particularly misleading):

> For the pragmatist, true sentences are not true because they correspond to reality, and so there is no need to worry what sort of reality, if any, a given sentence corresponds to – no need to worry about what 'makes' it true.[56]

It would have been better, too, if Rorty had changed the opening of the statement to read: 'sentences are not taken or judged as true'. In battles, however, one cannot afford to cry over spilt milk.

A third, and related, consequence should by now be clear: a Jamesian instrumentalist also can be a realist, and hold to the notion of 'Truth' (and Popperian 'approach to the truth') as a regulative ideal, as an ideal 'towards which we imagine that all our temporary beliefs will some day converge'.[57] This path is not traversable by a relativist.

All this points the way to a final, and somewhat more radical, conclusion. Members of the philosophical community have been remiss in writing of 'instrumentalism' in the singular. Actually there are two varieties – what may be called 'ascriptive instrumentalism' and 'relativistic instrumentalism'. The first of these is a doctrine about how to recognize or ascribe truth, while the second is a doctrine concerning the ontological status of theoretical entities and laws (namely, at most they are intellectual tools). The first, in the form advocated by James, is not relativistic; the second, as held by most instrumentalists, cannot help but be so. And while none of Moore's arguments touch the first, some of them may be damaging to the second. But to establish this would involve rejoining the battle.

NOTES

I am indebted to Brian Lord, Harvey Siegel and Jonas Soltis for helpful comments.

1 Elliot Eisner, *The Educational Imagination* (New York, Macmillan, 1979), 214.
2 Karl Popper, *Conjectures and Refutations* (New York, Harper, 1968), 224–8. It is interesting to note that the diagram Popper includes in chapter 3 (108), is meant as an illustration of instrumentalism, but it also comes close to illustrating relativism (for the view that α causes β is true only in the context of theory ϵ).
3 Cited by Popper, ibid., 4–5.
4 Israel Scheffler, *Four Pragmatists* (New York, Humanities Press, 1974), 110.
5 Ludwig Wittgenstein, *On Certainty*, trans. D. Paul and G.E.M. Anscombe (New York, Harper, 1972), 37, 74.
6 ibid., 52, 54.
7 Richard Rorty, *Philosophy and the Mirror of Nature* (Princeton, NJ, Princeton University Press, 1979), 373.
8 G.E. Moore, 'An autobiography', in P.A. Schilpp (ed.), *The Philosophy of G.E. Moore*, 2nd edn (New York, Open Court, 1952), 27.
9 A.J. Ayer, *The Origins of Pragmatism* (London, Macmillan, 1968), 198.
10 V.J. McGill, 'Some queries concerning Moore's method', in Schilpp, op. cit., 483–514.
11 Not quite all subsequent writers – after this refutation of Moore was first drafted, a paper was discovered that offers a similar interpretation. See Richard A. Hertz, 'James and Moore: two perspectives on truth', *Journal of the History of Philosophy* IX, 1 (January 1971), 213–21.
12 G.E. Moore, 'William James' 'Pragmatism', in his *Philosophical Studies* (London; Routledge & Kegan Paul, 1960), 161; all page numbers in the text refer to the present volume (hereafter cited as WJP).

13 ibid.
14 ibid., 163.
15 ibid., 161.
16 ibid., 161.
17 William James, *Pragmatism: and Four Essays from The Meaning of Truth* (New York, Meridian, 1955), 99; all page numbers in the text refer to the present volume (hereafter cited as *Pragmatism*).
18 ibid.
19 ibid., 100.
20 G.E. Moore, WJP, 162.
21 James, *Pragmatism*, 100.
22 Richard Rorty, 'The fate of philosophy', *The New Republic*, 18 October 1982, 28.
23 Hertz, op. cit., 221.
24 Scheffler, op. cit., 112–13. In places Bertrand Russell reacted similarly.
25 D.C. Phillips, 'Popper and pragmatism: a fantasy', *Educational Theory* 25 (Winter 1975), 83–91.
26 Popper, *Conjectives and Refutations*, 224.
27 ibid., 226.
28 James, *Pragmatism*, 99.
29 Moore, WJP, 163.
30 ibid., 164.
31 ibid., 164.
32 ibid., 168.
33 McGill, op. cit., 485.
34 Moore, WJP, 169–71.
35 ibid., 171.
36 William James, *The Meaning of Truth* (London, Longmans, 1909), 205.
37 Rorty, 'The fate of philosophy', 28.
38 James, *Pragmatism*, 105.
39 ibid., 110.
40 Moore, WJP, 172.
41 ibid.
42 Karl Popper, *Objective Knowledge* (London, Oxford University Press, 1972), 311.
43 Moore, WJP, 173.
44 James, *Pragmatism*, 106.
45 Moore, WJP, 184.
46 ibid., 185.
47 ibid., 186.
48 ibid., 187.
49 ibid., 189.
50 ibid., 190.
51 James, *Pragmatism*, 109.
52 Moore, WJP, 190.
53 ibid., 192.
54 James, *Pragmatism*, 110.
55 Popper, *Objective Knowledge*, 149. (See also 160–3.)

56 Richard Rorty, *Consequences of Pragmatism* (Minneapolis, MN, University of Minnesota Press, 1982), xvi.
57 James, *Pragmatism*, 109.

INDEX

Absolute 10, 27–8, 32, 42, 49–53,
    63–4, 66, 68, 71, 77, 125, 128–9,
    134, 137, 141, 150, 152, 153,
    189, 206; advantages 235–6;
    consequences 78, 128–9;
    hypothesis 206; theory 84–5; use
    130, 146–8; world of 137
abstract/tions 34–7, 48, 219–20;
    ideas 71, 104, 127; principles
    57–8
agree/ment 99, 115, 162; defined
    105–6
Ampère, André-Marie 95
anti-realism 5–6
Archimedes 97
Aristotle 41, 109, 243
assertion theory 223–7
Ayer, A.J. 222–3, 226; *The Origins*
    of Pragmatism 232

Balfour, Arthur James, *The*
    Foundations of Belief 62
beliefs 101, 110, 113, 190–5, 201,
    204, 207–9, 215, 228n, 243;
    consequences 145–7, 152–3
Bergson, Henry 120
Berkeley, George 4, 41, 55–6, 57,
    93, 95, 113, 151
bivalence, thesis 5
Black, Max 22, 223
Bosanquet, Bernard 27
Bradley, F.H. 77, 120, 123;
    Appearance and Reality 32
Browning, Robert 59

Caird, Edward 27, 36, 119
Caird, John 27
categories 91, 92, 94
causal unity 75–6
causality 90
Chesterton, G.K., *Heretics* 21
Clerk-Maxwell, James 99, 107
common sense 93, 94, 107, 151,
    196–7; consolidated stage 95–6;
    as good judgement 88; suspicion
    97–8
concepts 93; defined 58–9; systems
    89
concrete 218–20; consequence 41
correspondence theory 234–5
Curio, Coelius Secundus, *De*
    Amplitudine Regni Coelestis 30

Dalton, John 94
Dante 63
Darwin, Charles 64–5
Democritus 93, 97
design, in nature 49, 64–6, 69, 71
Dewey, John 44, 46, 47, 51, 99,
    113, 114, 120, 212, 213
Diogenes 124
dogmatism 25, 198
Duhem, Pierre 44, 97

Emerson, Ralph Waldo 114
empiricism 23–6, 33, 41, 49, 53,
    73, 120
Eucken, Rudolf 123